THE endtimes
OF human rights

THE endtimes
OF human rights

stephen hopgood

CORNELL UNIVERSITY PRESS   Ithaca and London

First published 2013 by Cornell University Press

Printed in the United States of America

Library of Congress Cataloging-in-Publication Data

Hopgood, Stephen, author.
   The endtimes of human rights / Stephen Hopgood.
      pages cm
   Includes bibliographical references and index.
   ISBN 978-0-8014-5237-6 (cloth : alk. paper)
  1. Human rights—International cooperation. 2. Human
rights—Moral and ethical aspects. 3. Human rights—
Political aspects. I. Title.
   JC571.H65   2013
   323—dc23   2013016127

Cornell University Press strives to use environmentally
responsible suppliers and materials to the fullest extent
possible in the publishing of its books. Such materials
include vegetable-based, low-VOC inks and acid-free papers
that are recycled, totally chlorine-free, or partly composed
of nonwood fibers. For further information, visit our
website at www.cornellpress.cornell.edu.

Cloth printing   10 9 8 7 6 5 4 3 2 1

contents

preface

Writing this book has been on my mind since Mary Robinson visited Dili in East Timor in 1999. Indonesia's brutal occupation had recently ended. Robinson, at the time UN high commissioner for human rights, opened a two-day workshop designed to embed East Timor's pledge to uphold international human rights law. Her speech was titled "Building the Future of East Timor on a Culture of Human Rights." Each of 160 participants received a kit containing all the major human rights documents and a badge that carried the words "Human rights: know them, live them, defend them," written in the local language, Tetun.[1]

For twenty-five years, since 1975, the East Timorese had fought a guerrilla war against the Indonesian military and militias. Civilian deaths from hunger, illness, killings, and disappearances during this period are conservatively estimated at more than one hundred thousand. This was out of a population of under a million. Numerous human rights abuses were committed.[2] Somehow, led by future president Xanana Gusmão, the armed Timorese resistance kept the fight alive as the international community made empty, rhetorical protests. Even the international human rights activists and journalists who highlighted East Timor's cause made little impact.

Gusmão's liberation fighters always seemed to me exemplary human rights defenders. What they knew was that no one else was coming to save them. Through their own tight communal bonds, shoulder-to-shoulder with people on whom they depended and who in turn depended on them, they defeated a threat to their very existence. During this time, the United States continued to train some of Indonesia's top army officers.[3] One of them, former president Suharto's son-in-law

General Prabowo, accused of masterminding systematic human rights abuses in East Timor, is now a leading candidate for the 2014 Indonesian presidential election.[4] More than ten years after Indonesia was driven from the country, there has still been no accounting for the crimes committed under occupation.[5]

The East Timorese knew what human rights were: they had fought and died for them every day. The arrogance of the high commissioner's lecture and those badges still seems to me obscene. All she should have come with was an apology. International human rights had failed East Timor when it mattered. Grotesquely, having resorted to violence to protect their own lives and freedom, East Timor's guerrillas would not be considered true "human rights defenders" at all by international agencies. How could the heart of global human rights advocacy be so cold and so naive in the face of such courage? This book is an attempt to answer that question. To do so is to reject overly idealistic accounts from within the human rights discourse and to ask searching and critical questions of this ubiquitous language of global rules and norms.[6] After all, human rights advocates proselytize in the name of humanity, and that means they claim to speak for me and for you.

In truth there were two forms of human rights at work in East Timor. One is the local and transnational networks of activists who bring publicity to abuses they and their communities face and who try to exert pressure on governments and the United Nations for action, often at tremendous personal cost.[7] This form of activism I'll term *human rights*, with lowercase initials. In combating violence and deprivation, any language is useful that helps to raise awareness, generate transnational activism, put pressure on governments, facilitate legal redress, and attract funds for campaigning, whether it is that of human rights, compassion, solidarity, freedom, brotherhood, sisterhood, justice, religion, grace, charity, kin, ethnicity, nationalism, pity, love, or equality. The endtimes can never come for this form of "human rights" in the same way that nothing can stop people banding together to demand their own freedom or justice in whatever language they prefer. These ethical and political claims are rooted in our shared interest in fair and equal treatment. The call for human rights at this instinctive level is really the demand "No more, stop, enough!"—the name of the report produced by East Timor's truth and reconciliation commission

("Chega!" in Portuguese).[8] Human rights can be used tactically to help prevent torture, disappearances, or extrajudicial executions or to demand economic and social rights to food, water, and health care. It is a flexible and negotiable language. It does not "defend human rights," it defends the person. It is a means, not an end in itself.

None of this is what Mary Robinson meant by human rights. She was talking about *Human Rights*, capitalized. Human Rights is a global structure of laws, courts, norms, and organizations that raise money, write reports, run international campaigns, open local offices, lobby governments, and claim to speak with singular authority in the name of humanity as a whole. Human Rights advocates make their demand that all societies adopt global norms on the basis of a uniquely universal and secular moral authority. Often highly legalized, Human Rights norms are not flexible and negotiable. They are a kind of secular monotheism with aspirations to civilize the world. The East Timorese, heavily Catholic, had rooted their fight as much in everyday Christianity as any abstract secular norm.[9] The arrival of a UN transitional authority now subjected East Timor to the regime of Human Rights norms that had so conspicuously failed it before. Of this global regime, Mary Robinson was the highest of high priests.

This book is about the endtimes of Human Rights. It is an argument, not a history.[10] By making my claims in bold terms, I endeavor to cut through some of the hype with which Human Rights advocates often surround themselves. I will argue, in contrast, that we are on the verge of the imminent decay of the Global Human Rights Regime. Through my previous work with Amnesty International I know only too well how many hardworking, well-meaning people of good faith are active all over the world for human rights.[11] They work, however, within global Human Rights institutions that have permanency, organizational interests, and ambitions that far outweigh the impulse many of us share to stand up for the abused or cheer the end of tyrants. Taking care that this global regime remains true to its core principles requires us to understand just what those principles are: What is it that gives Human Rights its moral authority? This question is harder to answer than you might think. But without an answer, how do Human Rights advocates, who assume unto themselves the right to speak for everyone, mobilize the faithful and legitimate their demands?

Organizations tend to stifle protest, nonhierarchical and even violent disruption often a more effective strategy for provoking change, as the Arab Spring showed, than disciplined and institutionalized resistance which is the stock in trade of global advocacy.[12] The tension between top-down fixed authority and bottom-up (spontaneous, diverse, and multiple) authorities is exactly that between Human Rights and human rights. For all that several influential accounts stress the transnational linkages between these two worlds, I suggest that the global inevitably structures, disciplines, channels, institutionalizes, and eventually colonizes the local reproducing hierarchies of power and influence familiar from the worlds of domestic politics and of interstate relations.[13] This is partly because the transnational space is structured by a political economy that is almost wholly controlled by global Human Rights centers (in western Europe and the United States). But it is also because the singularity of the Human Rights message resists local adaptation on any basis other than a transient and tactical one. What is at issue is who gets to decide global rules and to define legitimate *exceptions* to them. This is the essence of sovereign power—setting, and breaking, the rules.[14] To become the supreme authority—a court of law above all politics, national and international—is the inner logic of Human Rights.

My argument is simple: humanism (the cultural precondition for Human Rights) was a secular replacement for the Christian god. Nineteenth-century middle-class Europeans elevated it into a set of social practices and institutions, most prominently the International Committee of the Red Cross (ICRC). The importance of this transformation cannot be underestimated. It is only as a strategy for coping with what Nietzsche called "the death of god" in the West that we can begin to understand the real social function of humanitarianism and human rights in the twentieth century. The ICRC was, I argue, the first international human rights organization. It was a secular church of the international. The laws it wrote and the humanitarian activism it undertook were grounded by a culture of transcendent moral sentiment with strong Christian components. At the heart of this was the suffering innocent, a secular version of Christ.[15] In other words, bourgeois Europeans responded to the erosion of religious authority by creating authority of their own from the cultural resources that lay scattered around them. And then they globalized it via the infrastructure that the imperial civilizing project bequeathed to them.

This project came crashing to the ground in 1939. The Holocaust and the Second World War destroyed the moral legitimacy and political power, if not the ideological ambition and cultural arrogance, of Europe. It was an existential crisis that involved "the very survival of our Western Christian civilization, if not of mankind," as the international lawyer Josef Kunz wrote at the time.[16] A desperate attempt was made between 1945 and 1949 to create even more ambitious global institutions, particularly in international law, to repair the devastation done to European claims to superior authority. But the center of gravity of world affairs had permanently shifted. Power passed to the United States and the Soviet Union and slowly, over several decades, to liberated former colonies and subaltern states. Attacks on the legacy of the European civilizing project gathered pace. Postcolonialists targeted the murderous arrogance of imperial ideology, while postmodernists attacked the whole basis on which self-righteous Europeans claimed to have discovered definitive answers to questions of truth and freedom. This postwar malaise was the milieu for the creation of the first modern global human rights organization, Amnesty International, formed in London in 1961. It was, I have argued elsewhere, a look back to the past, not a vision of the future.[17] In its secular religiosity it was more like the social rescue project of the ICRC than the herald of a brave new world to come.

What changed, what turned human rights into Human Rights, was American power. From the 1970s onward, a new kind of advocacy emerged that sought to pressure the American state into using its vast resources to coerce, cajole, and induce improved human rights abroad. New organizations, of which by far the most successful has been Human Rights Watch, were the product not of a popular movement but of elite mobilization. The language of human rights soon took root, creating a large constituency of supporters, but these new activists were only in some cases like the solidarity-inspired members of the postwar years. Seismic shifts had taken place in transforming the narrow middle class of old Europe into a wide, transnational class of consumers. The majority adopted human rights as a kind of lifestyle choice, joining and campaigning for human rights as a global language of freedom and justice rather than for any specific cause with which they were personally linked. They were a paying audience as much as an activist base. The *global membership* model Amnesty International had pioneered proved a singular one, and while it persisted it was not replicated.

Despite internal differences between the expansionist liberalism of neoconservatives under Ronald Reagan and the liberal internationalists of Human Rights Watch, human rights were intimately tied to the export of neoliberal democracy using American state power. This "democracy first" approach can be contrasted with Mary Robinson's formulation at her East Timor workshop: "Human rights must be guaranteed because they are the foundations on which democracy, the rule of law and sustainable economic and social development are built."[18] Her formulation is naive, as we will see. It is only as a by-product of American power and money that human rights have been globalized, and for American advocates democracy comes first. For European human rights supporters this is not the case. Amnesty International, for instance, has had no position on the desirability or otherwise of democracy. All regimes are expected to respect human rights before any question of legitimate government can be addressed. That neoconservatives and liberal internationalists in the United States both supported intervention in Libya in 2011 is a sign of the ground they continue to share even under the Obama administration.[19]

The high point of this new world of Human Rights was from 1991 to 2008—the "unipolar moment" of American post–Cold War dominance. An alliance between international advocates and the United States established international criminal tribunals in 1993 for the former Yugoslavia and in 1994 for Rwanda, the momentum of these eventually leading to the creation of an International Criminal Court that began work in 2002. It was followed by a new doctrine of human rights–led humanitarian intervention, the "Responsibility to Protect," which got increasing international attention after 2005. These global Human Rights institutions seemed to mark the beginning of the golden age of international humanism, but in reality decline had already set in.

The old model, secular religiosity, anchored moral authority on detachment from power politics, a detachment that infamously led the ICRC to keep silent about the Holocaust. Amnesty International has always been skeptical about governments and corporate money, seeing its moral mission as the very antithesis of power. But this secular religiosity had very limited capacity to affect world politics in any deep way. Its achievement was to keep open the idea of impartial, neutral space over and above politics and conflict. Yet this virtue was also its weakness in terms of impact, assisting individuals a symbolically powerful but politically ineffectual form of activism against determined opposition. Unsurprisingly, most American advocates were far keener to harness state power to the task. But the alternative, siding with liberal states to reform the world, has I will argue an even more truncated shelf life. Once the alliance was made with money and liberal power, the core of moral authority, acting without self-interest, was gone. What had been seen as moral norms—applicable to all and justified as beyond ideology—were revealed to be social norms that advanced one conception of what constituted a good society. The opportunity to build global normative institutions using state power comes with a caveat, in other words: when the sovereign changes its mind and declares itself and its clients exempt from its own rules, the Global Human Rights Regime is left bereft of moral authority, its claim to universal legitimacy undermined, its compliance with power exposed. It is not credible to name and shame a government with which you consistently align. Human Rights, handmaiden to neoliberal democracy, are unveiled as ideological, opening a legitimacy gap that has allowed their opponents to make increasing inroads against them.

This decline has been accelerated because the United States itself is losing power. It is first among equals in a system where other states have started to assert their sovereignty, declaring their right to make exceptions, whether in terms of the International Criminal Court, torture, suspension of civil liberties, or targeted assassinations. Even if there was a time when the United States might have supported multilateral liberal norms outside the trade arena, it has passed. The rise of China, but also of states like India and Brazil, and the sustained influence of Russia, make the post-2013 world "neo-Westphalian." Sovereignty will be reaffirmed, global markets will be extended, and some forms of transnational culture will grow, but global liberal norms will stagnate and even contract in terms of meaningful impact on the daily lives of ordinary people, the only kind of impact worthy of the name.

Emboldened by the cracking moral authority of Human Rights, religious authorities have also made a comeback. The increasing use by advocates of the language of "dignity" to anchor human rights can be understood as an attempt to hold ground in the face of eroding authority, but resurgent gods have spoken the language of dignity for centuries. In the end, the decline of Europe means the decline of the vision of universal and nonnegotiable global rules authorized in a secular way. In other words, it means the eclipse of *jus cogens*, that is, of laws of humanity which may *never* legitimately be broken. The United States has not been a reliable supporter of such rules, and with its focus moving rapidly to Asia-Pacific, its interest in Europe is waning all the time. The space for norms has narrowed: it was built after 1863 by the European bourgeoisie—carved through sacrifice and courage out of political space—and as the power of that class has dispersed and globalized, so the moral authority they created has fractured.

This is not bad news for the original humanist social practice: unconditional Good Samaritan–style humanitarian assistance. This is much more human rights than Human Rights. Reciprocity was a mechanism that gave states an incentive to treat other nationals according to agreed minimum standards, and that timeless logic works today. In addition, the expertise of relief workers is as useful for states suffering a catastrophe as the hiring of any professional to provide specialist equipment or services you cannot provide for yourself. Once we enter the post-crisis development phase, however, we will see pushback everywhere, except in the most fragile states such as Haiti. If the "humanitarian wing" of the humanist international gets less attention in this book, it is largely because the last three decades have been the era of global Human Rights norms. These have, I argue, colonized international humanitarian law. The ICC, for example, is supposed to be a humanitarian law court but is to all intents and purposes founded on human rights law. The Russian international lawyer and Red Cross delegate Fyodor Martens, whose preamble to the Hague Conventions of 1899 and 1907 is an iconic statement of the underlying moral narrative of humanism, believed that there was but one law running through the history of nations, "the principle of respect for the human person." As early as 1882 he wrote: "It is our conviction that once the human being as such is recognized by the State to be the source of civil and political rights, international life will reach a high degree of development, law and order."[20]

Reduced ambition will help create a more sustainable space for human rights as locally owned and interpreted principles for political action. In the end politics trumps law, and the local trumps the global. Once it was stable, East Timor was overseen until 2002 by a UN transitional government whose administrator was Sergio Vieira de Mello. His next job would be following Mary Robinson as United Nations high commissioner for human rights, until his assassination in 2003 in Baghdad. Just five months before his death, he told delegates at the Commission on Human Rights in Geneva:

> The culture of human rights must be a popular culture if it is to have the strength to withstand the blows that will inevitably come. Human-rights culture must be a popular culture if it is to be able to innovate and to be truly owned at the national and sub-national levels.[21]

De Mello's capacity for striking a deal rather than sticking dogmatically to a prescribed set of norms was one of the things that made him successful as a UN troubleshooter. He had even negotiated with the Khmer Rouge. During his time in East Timor he had learned to speak the local language, and on hearing of his death, President Gusmão released a statement expressing deep sadness:

> Sergio Vieira de Mello endeared himself to the people of East Timor with his common touch, sensitivity, sense of humour and charisma. As a leader he fought tirelessly for democracy, human rights and sustainable justice for the people of Timor-Leste and represents the men and women of the international community who dedicate their lives to the pursuit of peace and the service of humanity.[22]

In his complicated legacy, de Mello represented Human Rights but understood them as human rights. To work they had to belong to the people. He combined the pragmatic search for a political solution with a commitment to the *idea* of global norms. What mattered was reaching a workable compromise which real people would actually endorse. Complexity in his own life nurtured perhaps a sympathy within him for the complicated reality of any and all human endeavor. As Human Rights lose their force in the neo-Westphalian world of declining American power, so local interpretations of what rights are and which rights might be sustainable will be essential if human rights are to flourish. To achieve this, democratizing Human Rights (that is, transforming it into human rights) is an essential first step.[23] We return to de Mello later. Before that we begin by considering how this global regime of liberal norms came about in the first place.

1 MORAL AUTHORITY IN A GODLESS WORLD

We are living through the endtimes of the civilizing mission. The ineffectual International Criminal Court and its disastrous first prosecutor, Luis Moreno-Ocampo, along with the failure in Syria of the "Responsibility to Protect," are the latest pieces of evidence not of transient misfortunes but fatal structural defects in international humanism. Whether it is the increase in deadly attacks on aid workers, the torture and "disappearing" of al-Qaeda suspects by American officials, the flouting of international law by states such as Sri Lanka and Sudan, or the shambles of the Khmer Rouge tribunal in Phnom Penh, the prospect of one world under secular human rights law is receding.[1] What seemed like a dawn is in fact a sunset. The foundations of universal liberal norms and global governance are crumbling, creating a vacancy where sovereignty and religion now make dramatic inroads in the post–Cold War world.[2]

Universal humanist norms once served a very specific historical purpose: to inspire a sense of the secular sacred among the new middle classes of a rapidly modernizing Europe. This secular religiosity enhanced and extended the social order nineteenth-century Europeans had created and idealized. It was an antidote to a troubling *contradiction*, the coexistence of progress with intensifying violence, vast social and economic inequality, and fears of "the disenchantment of the world."[3] Not only has that historical purpose become defunct, but the institutions that were created to perform it now function as self-perpetuating global structures of intermittent power that mask their lack of democratic authority and systematic ineffectiveness. The best they may occasionally do, and it is often a lot even if wholly inadequate to the task, is provide relief in situations of great distress. Much of what remains is a mixture of false hope and unaccountable intervention. They survive as parts of a grand narrative that gives an ideological alibi to a global system whose governance structures sustain persistent unfairness and blatant injustice.

Responding to a widening crisis of authority after 1848, nineteenth-century middle-class Europeans sought to resurrect a voice of *definitive moral authority*, a new Tower of Babel, this time in secular form. This tower was embedded in an enhanced sensibility, even sentimentality, about human suffering and fears for the future of the bourgeois social order.[4] Its walls were made of law written to protect the individual from harm. The International Criminal Court (ICC) and the Responsibility to Protect (R2P) bring the tower to near completion, with only the utopia of universal jurisdiction to go. When the ICC opened in 2003, its home city, The Hague, was described as "the judicial capital of the world."[5] The Coalition of ICC supporters (the CICC) wants the court's new building to symbolize "the will of an epoch translated into space."[6] Preeminent R2P advocate Gareth Evans subtitled his recent book *Ending Mass Atrocity Once and for All*.[7] And the deputy director of Human Rights Watch and former UN humanitarian chief Jan Egeland believes we can be "the generation that can end the suffering."[8] For true believers in humanism's promise we are on the cusp of a hard-won future of realized justice. They are willfully mistaken, but why?

First, the vast superstructure of international human rights law and organization is no longer "fit for purpose." Indeed, once one strips away its self-justifications—that it is legitimated by unmet needs, that is a product of natural justice codified in positive law—we see it is and was always a partial, ideological answer to the question of how to handle the crisis of authority brought on by modernity. How different would the world really look without the multibillion-dollar humanitarian, human rights, and international justice regimes? How much less chronic suffering would there really be? The shallow roots of Human Rights institutions in practical political situations are the revelation of this underlying reality, exacerbated by increasingly rapid and radical change to which the one-size-fits-all universalism of global Human Rights is an outmoded response. Integral to this obsolescence is the decline of Europe, the institutional echo of its ideological ascendancy finally failing having far outlasted its imperial political power. The cataclysmic blow of the Holocaust was followed in the 1970s by the ascendancy of a more democratized and political conception of human rights under American leadership, which condemned European "secular religiosity" to marginal status. The result, by the 1990s, was Human Rights, a last moment of brightness before decline set in.

Second, the deep norms that sustain this superstructure are under attack as never before by conservative nationalist and religious forces. Few advocates see the need to argue explicitly that global norms must be secular, universal, and nonnegotiable—that they apply to everyone, cannot be authorized by a god, and cannot be traded away. But this is a claim, one that confident modern Europeans took for granted, and not a fact. Humanist moral authority remains always in play because in representing all equally it represents no one directly. Even if it privileges middle-class interests, it cannot be named as such, for to acknowledge its ideological roots would destroy its self-understanding and legitimacy. Add to this the role of spoilers, who actively seek conflict, and the difficulties of speaking with "one voice" across huge cultural and geographical distances, and the picture is even bleaker. The universal, secular, and categorical basis of global norms undermines their local political effectiveness. For example, in relation to survivors and witnessing, what is seen is often less important than who sees it. The politics of authority is critical in areas that challenge humanism's core norms, such as everyday violence or family, gender, and sexual norms, where the impact of global human rights in the face of competing local authorities is virtually nil.

Third, a shift in the distribution of power globally, away from a unipolar American-led system toward a more multipolar world, has revealed just how much Human Rights institutions rely on liberal state power and its reinforcement by the middle classes who staff and finance humanist organizations. International nongovernmental organizations (INGOs) and Human Rights advocates gain political traction internationally only when they serve the functional requirements of powerful states. The NATO-led intervention in Libya in 2011 and NATO's impotence in Syria in 2013 are a good illustration. NATO is the battering ram. And as power has shifted, so states large and small, particularly in Asia, feel empowered to reject human rights norms. The outlier here is the United States, a spoiler when it comes to global norms and so the key legitimizer of a shift toward sovereignty and reciprocity-based international law.

In this sense, talk of "the West" is misplaced. In terms of attachment to sovereignty, self-determination, and national exceptionalism, the United States finds itself more like China and less like Europe.

The Human Rights Imperium

> The speed with which human rights has penetrated every corner of the globe is astounding. Compared to human rights, no other system of universal values has spread so far so fast. . . . In what amounts to an historical blink of the eye, the idea of human rights has become the lingua franca of international morality.[9]

In recent accounts with titles like *Humanity's Law* and *The Justice Cascade* prominent scholars agree: we are living in an era of unprecedented normative progress.[10] In 1992, heralding this development, UN Secretary-General Boutros Boutros-Ghali declared that "the time of absolute and exclusive sovereignty has passed," and the subsequent expansion of human rights discourse would appear to bear him out.[11] Some date the roots of change to 1776 and 1789, most to 1945, a few to the 1970s. All agree, however, that by the 1990s Human Rights had achieved ascendancy.

During these years the United Nations High Commission for Human Rights was established by a 1993 World Conference on Human Rights in Vienna. It stated in Article 1 of its concluding declaration: "The universal nature of these rights and freedoms is beyond question." This was followed by the remarkable story of the arrest of General Augusto Pinochet, former Chilean head of state, in London in 1998 under a warrant issued by Spanish judge Baltasar Garzón. Garzón charged Pinochet with multiple counts of torture committed in Chile, citing the principle of universal jurisdiction to demand the general be extradited to Spain. The British House of Lords enhanced the case's impact by ruling that some international crimes were too terrible to be covered by head-of-state immunity.[12] Pinochet was controversially released and returned to Chile in 2000 on health grounds, but the precedent had been set; in 2009, for example, then Israeli opposition leader Tzipi Livni canceled a visit to Britain after a warrant was issued for her arrest on war crimes charges.[13]

International justice has been the vanguard of this transformation. Nominally born out of developments in international humanitarian law and domestic mechanisms of transitional justice, these institutional innovations have been heavily influenced by the idea of human rights.[14] The United Nations Security Council created international criminal tribunals for Bosnia (1993) and Rwanda (1994) after mass atrocities in both countries. It also referred the situations in Darfur (2005) and Libya (2011) to the ICC. A Special Court for Sierra Leone (SCSL), as well as tribunals for Lebanon and Cambodia were established, and since 2002 the ICC has been a standing, permanent court in The Hague to try individuals accused of genocide, crimes against humanity, and war crimes (and eventually, its supporters hope, aggressive war). Now, ten years after its founding, it has had its first successful prosecution, that of the Congolese militia leader Thomas Lubanga Dyilo on charges of recruiting, enlisting, and using child soldiers. In May 2012 former Liberian president Charles Taylor was also convicted by the SCSL (sitting in The Hague) of aiding and abetting war crimes and crimes against humanity in Sierra Leone and sentenced, pending appeal, to fifty years in prison. Overall, it is estimated that by 2015 the major international criminal courts will have cost nearly $6.3 billion. The largest burden was initially carried by the United States, but as the ICC comes to take up a bigger percentage of tribunal spending, the Europeans will soon provide 60 percent of all funds for the courts.[15]

While the Rome Statute of 1998 establishing the ICC is a state treaty, a 2005 International Committee of the Red Cross study on international humanitarian law concluded that most provisions of the Geneva Conventions were also customary international law, meaning they apply even if a state has not ratified the conventions (more than 190 states already have).[16] Finally, in 2011, the principle of the Responsibility to Protect was, its advocates argued, fully recognized in two Security Council resolutions that authorized military action in Libya. This doctrine, the successor to humanitarian intervention in the 1990s, emerged out of post-Kosovo concern that NATO's bombing campaign against Serbia had been illegal. R2P was intended to resolve this dilemma, putting pressure on states to protect their own citizens and legitimating the international community to step in if states failed. Critical to these developments has been the idea of *crimes against humanity*. Nominally part of international humanitarian law—and codified in the Rome Statute—the charge of crimes against humanity is set to be the *jus cogens* (natural law) for our age. In the ICC and R2P, in other words, global human rights are embedded as the fundamental normative principle by which the behavior of all political entities—states, non-state armed actors, communities, and individuals—is to be judged.

The foremost lobbyist for international criminal justice, and first president of the International Criminal Tribunal for former Yugoslavia (ICTY), Antonio Cassese, claimed that the first international war crimes prosecution since Nuremberg in 1945 (of Bosnian Serb torturer Duško Tadić), with which he was intimately involved, was the moment when Human Rights finally triumphed over state power in principle. For Cassese, Tadić's trial shifted the world community from a "reciprocity-based bundle of legal relations, geared to the 'private' pursuit of self-interest, and ultimately blind to collective needs, to a community hinging on a core of fundamental values, strengthened by the emergence of community obligations and community rights and the gradual shaping of public interests."[17]

This transformation comprised a space of impartial judgment over and above sovereignty legitimated by the "interests of humanity" *and* the specific content of those judgments. It tied primary and secondary rules together. Primary rules are norms and obligations of behavior (e.g., against torture, war crimes, or crimes against humanity); secondary rules specify which primary rules are valid so that "the fact of their violation [can be] conclusively determined."[18] Recognition as an authority on secondary rules confers the ultimate power to adjudicate primary rules, that is, *to validate the law.* This is the humanist utopia: to speak in the name of Human Rights is to put the neutral, objective, and universal ahead of the partial and subjective. It is to become *The Authority.* If we imagine Karl Popper's "open society" as a place of tolerance for all ideologies except those that threaten tolerance itself, humanists like Cassese aspire to enlarge and defend that archetypally liberal space.[19]

The true achievement of humanists has been to embed their authority claims in tangible, concrete institutions like the ICRC and the ICC. It is political strategy 101: *turn your ideology into facts on the ground.* Make laws, set up courts, prosecute people; build the power of law through political action. Selling Babel to skeptical states and nations for more than a century meant persuading people to believe the authority of secular norms was as infinite and absolute as that of the Christian god had once been. But this claim to wield superior authority is "never more than an act of social magic that works."[20] Trust, in reality neither natural nor transcendent, must be *constructed*. As a result, it remains always and permanently contested.

Humanist social magic has successfully rendered "humanity" objective enough that crimes can be committed against it and subjective enough that it can defend itself with massive violence (R2P) and pursue retribution against its enemies (ICC). The original "constitutional moment" was the Geneva Convention (1864) born out of the traumatic wounds of the battle of Solferino in 1859. Advocates have been striving for more than a century since to use moments of extreme suffering to ground the architecture of law, seeking always to establish their preeminent authority. This means fusing the secular word of god (natural law) with positive law, that is, law to which states have explicitly agreed, and customary law.[21] Being based on agreement, positive law is always in principle open to revision, reservation, and derogation, but it remains an essential first line of defense for natural law. Customary law—the residue of state practice over time—is the fallback position, although it is notoriously difficult to codify. When effectively embedded, this natural-customary-positive combination becomes *jus cogens*—law that can never be legitimately broken.

For legal scholar Stephen Gardbaum "there is undoubtedly something inherently constitutional in the very nature and subject matter of human rights law." He adds that "a small, but critical core of the most important human rights law has achieved *jus cogens* and, thus, higher law status as binding treaty makers and probably also trumping conflicting custom (if such a conflict is a conceptual possibility), although there is less consensus about how . . . norms achieve this status, which may prevent the list from being added to."[22] Another prominent advocate of the humanist international, Theodor Meron, echoing the legendary humanist international lawyer Louis Henkin, concurs that *jus cogens* norms reflect a "new law of fundamental values adopted by the international system" that "would not derive from or depend on State practice or on law made purposefully by the consent of States."[23]

Thus we have the aspiration: Human Rights as a constitutional moment for humanity, a "basic norm" (to use Hans Kelsen's phrase) or "unmoved mover" (to use that of Aristotle and later Aquinas) back beyond which we need not go. Once this is established, we cease to ask "why?" questions and start to ask "how?" This is the essence of the Human Rights project: place "why" questions out of bounds. And that mean politics, constructing and institutionalizing superior power. In what follows I argue this has been a deliberate process, intended to create universal, secular law, what Ruti Teitel calls the "humanity law framework," an amalgam of international humanitarian law, human rights law, and international criminal justice united by its claim to represent a "normative order that is grounded in the protection of humanity."[24] It is a vision of global law that transcends the authority of states and peoples.

The Origins of Secular Humanism

There are two broad accounts, not mutually exclusive, of the origins of human rights as legacies of the Renaissance, the Reformation, and the Enlightenment—the pillars of "European civilization." The *idealist* account stresses unfolding ideas about dignity, freedom, and justice, often going back to Grotius via the French and American Revolutions and Thomas Paine's *The Rights of Man*. These ideas coalesced in the decades around the Lisbon earthquake of 1755 and the publication of Rousseau's *The Social Contract* in 1762. By 1769, Voltaire could write of torture, for example, that no civilized nation could tolerate such "atrocious old customs" any longer.[25] The high point of this movement would come with the campaign to end the slave trade.

Underlying these progressive ideas was a vast *social* transformation: accelerating industrialization, the rapid integration of world markets, and the expansion of the European (and American) bourgeoisie. European international trade in the years 1830–1870 grew at an astonishing 16.1 percent a year; the 1830–1913 annual average was 6.8 percent (Switzerland's exports were the fastest growing).[26] Global price gaps narrowed (in 1869 both the Suez Canal and the Union Pacific Railroad were completed), and capital export from Europe to the rest of the world increased prodigiously. Migration from Europe to the United States reached a million people a year by 1900. Industrial innovation in science and technology also fed into weapons; for example, during the American Civil War the use of conical, hollow bullets, which shattered bones rather than broke them, greatly increased suffering in combat.

Labor, too, organized: in 1864 the International Workingmen's Association (the First International) was formed in London, with an international congress held in Geneva in 1866. Karl Marx, author in 1848 with Friedrich Engels of *The Communist Manifesto*, and in 1867 of *Capital*, was elected to its General Council. In 1859 Marx had outlined an interpretation of history that argued, "The mode of production of material life conditions the general process of social, political and intellectual life."[27] That is, law and human rights were bourgeois ideology.[28] The Paris Commune in 1871 was the first, brief, example of the working class taking power in a major European city.

Wealth and power, suffering and resistance: this reflected a dilemma for the new middle classes. How could the contradictions within scientific and industrial progress be reconciled while sustaining public order and avoiding social revolution? The answer was through Victorian moralism and missionary work—that is, via forms of secular and religious evangelism at home and abroad.[29] These had a twofold function: spread civilization overseas using European imperial power as a vector, and energize professionals (doctors, lawyers, soldiers) and businessmen (industrialists, bankers) to intervene domestically; but also consolidate a sense of confidence, piety, responsibility, and purpose among the new bourgeoisie. A compassionate sensibility emerged that was romantic, heavy with pathos and notions of love and family, and marked by a vicarious openness to suffering. This was a "revolution in moral sentiments."[30] The three branches of the humanist tree we now call humanitarianism, human rights, and international justice all grew from this fertile soil.

The ICRC museum in Geneva, while careful to date "the concern for human life" cross-culturally back to Leviticus, Confucius, and Muhammad, asserts that nineteenth-century Europe saw "a more general awareness of a notion going beyond mere charity."[31] At its core was the image of a heroic bourgeoisie symbolized in concrete individuals whose remarkable personal exploits in the face of suffering represented and inspired the progressive ideology of an entire class. Critical in these accounts was the idea of sacrifice: of pioneers doing against the odds what circumstances did not force them to do. Florence Nightingale was a forerunner of the man who gave his name to pure humanism, Henri Dunant. In *A Memory of Solferino*, his memoir of the 1859 battle whose aftermath he witnessed, Dunant brilliantly captures the aura of bourgeois dread:

A son idolized by his parents, brought up and cherished for years by a loving mother who trembled with alarm over his slightest ailment; a brilliant officer, beloved by his family, with a wife and children at home; a young soldier who had left sweetheart or mother, sisters or old father, to go to war; all lie stretched in the mud and dust, drenched in their own blood! The handsome manly face is beyond recognition, for sword or shot has done its disfiguring work. The wounded man agonizes, dies, and his dear body, blackened, swollen and hideous, will soon be thrown just as it is into a half-dug grave, with only a few shovelfuls of lime and earth over it! The birds of prey will have no pity for those hands and feet when they protrude, as the wet earth dries, from the mound of dirt that is his tomb. Later someone will perhaps come back, throw on some more earth, set up a wooden cross over his resting place—and that will be all![32]

Dunant's description calls to mind the phrase in *The Communist Manifesto* where Marx and Engels describe the proletariat as the gravediggers of the bourgeoisie. Indeed, Dunant was at Solferino trying to save his own floundering colonial investments in Algeria by appealing to Emperor Napoleon III.[33] It is clear from this account that for Dunant the middle class, his class, was humanism's natural constituency. These were cultural Christians, overwhelmingly Protestant and pious, their social lives organized around conventional patriarchal family relations, as his vivid imagery conveys; and while outside both state and church hierarchies, this was a socially reformist, status quo–oriented audience. Later Dunant writes about the power of the "public" including all classes, but his real message is to his own kind, the newly ascendant bourgeoisie. He evokes a sense of lost innocence and disenchantment, the contradictions of modernity exposed in a hideous death on the battlefield.

Rather than the rather arid notion of "witnessing" we have today, which means little more than observing and recording, Dunant understood himself as part of the "Christian witness" to suffering and to the grace of god. He was "bearing witness" in this more profound, dual way, revealing a kind of *moral knowing*, the apprehension of an absolute truth, that he and his audience were all implicated in suffering by virtue of being god's children. His last sentence, in the passage above, also expresses a deeper fear: the simple, Protestant cross is an inadequate afterthought. Modernity was too much for the post-Reformation Christian church. Nietzsche would soon articulate this idea by announcing god's death and asking what secular "festivals of atonement" would need to be invented in god's stead.[34]

Humanitarianism was precisely such a festival. The humanitarian hero, a modern-day version of the Good Samaritan, was mirrored by the suffering individual who slowly replaced Christ as the raw material for the culture and aesthetic of protection. This innocent victim formed a new sacred object, the *totem*, "the visible body of the god" of secular religiosity.[35] This totem fused a desire to hang on to transcendent authority in the face of revolutionary social change with a sense of individuals *as individuals* (not as bearers of social identities like "Christian" or "European").[36] The importance of innocence, a Christian legacy, remained—the young and women, as Dunant invoked them, the most marked by moral purity and thus most amenable to being sacralized.[37] In the embrace between heroes and innocents, the European bourgeoisie found a way of going on despite the cracks opened up by modernity's shadow side. The bourgeoisie retained their unique sense of historical destiny, saving their own souls through the act of saving others. In the assumption of the superiority of European civilization, humanists were men and women of their time. They had privileged insight they believed was denied to all less "civilized" (that is, "backward" and "barbarous") societies, cultures, religions, and races; and this provided legitimation, as far as they were concerned, for their assumption of a responsibility to manage the lives of others.

The years of expansion, from the 1860s to 1920s, saw the self-confidence of middle-class and professional Europeans lead them with their growing expertise into every niche of the social world. They bolstered an increasingly secularized position of superiority in their own minds by fusing two great callings, the search for truth and the search for freedom, both of which they felt they had acquired. In doing so they felt they had transcended belonging, identity, particularity, the messy business of everyday local life. This detachment was claimed as a guarantee of *impartiality*, their lack of ties making them "socially dead" and thus credible witnesses and trusted authorities.[38] Their estrangement from social necessity grounded a claim to rule, the idea being that strangers

would judge matters fairly, like Adam Smith's internalized "ideal spectator," who arbitrated appropriate action not through passion or sentiment
but from "reason, principle, conscience, the inhabitant of the breast, the
man within, the great judge and arbiter of our conduct."[39] To be a stranger
was to have moral authority.[40] In this way what were culturally specific
norms about how to live were elevated into moral norms (applicable to all
regardless of context). This was "social magic" at work.

These European strangers exported "a normative order and the rule
of law, which [would] in turn safeguard conditions of social peace and
individual security poorly defended in pre-civilized settings."[41] The
moral power of suffering innocents was used to ground the logic and
authority of law beginning with the Geneva Convention. Before long,
this infrastructure absorbed the sacred aura of suffering itself. Laws
and courts, trials and judgments, were (and are) defended as if victims
themselves are under direct attack. International law, the preserve of a
phalanx of high-minded European jurists after the 1870s, benefited most
from this form of moral armament, even though it was close to disintegration after 1939 when the whole idea of European civilization neared
collapse.[42] Indeed, the Second World War and the Holocaust gave irresistible impetus to institutional innovation. The shock of a world destroyed
saw advocates redouble their efforts to restore the authority of humanist institutions via the Genocide Convention, the Universal Declaration
of Human Rights (UDHR), Nuremberg, and the idea of crimes against
humanity as justiciable international law, and the Geneva Conventions
of 1949.

Human Rights Endtimes

Isn't the decline of Human Rights the last thing we should expect in the
era of the ICC? Not if we get beyond blind faith and look harder. Contemporary developments give us plenty of clues to the shift that is under way.
Things paradoxically began to change at the moment in the 1970s when
human rights seemed to have struck gold: at last Americans became
involved in a systematic way with the global human rights regime which,
newly empowered, was transformed into Human Rights. The cost of this
was a move away from the "secular religiosity" I have been outlining

toward a more political, openly pro-democratic form of advocacy and an embrace of the logic of money as power that made explicit what had been implicit within international humanism: Human Rights and liberal capitalism were allies, not enemies. There was no contradiction. This would be made manifest in the transformation from a producer-driven to a consumer-driven "market for suffering."

International human rights are not in reality embedded to anything like the degree required for us to speak of them as global norms. To disguise this fact, the double meaning of "norm" is routinely deployed by advocates. "Norm" can describe both what is desirable and what is accepted practice. The gap between the two is the territory of "lawfare," where, to cite Jack Goldsmith, a Pentagon lawyer under President George W. Bush and now a Harvard law professor, the president's lawyers "are in constant battle—with the media, NGOs, and terrorists in federal court—for their favored understandings of the law, and in these battles they interpret and employ law strategically to further their aims."[43] The prohibition against torture is supposed to be desirable *and* accepted practice (the British House of Lords thought so in their *Pinochet* decision): *jus cogens* (natural law), customary law (accepted practice), and treaty law (a signed convention) all reinforce each other. And yet the United States, Western, liberal-democratic, and culturally Christian, tortured or disappeared many of its alleged enemies on the back of some creative legal analysis.[44] Even under the Obama administration, Guantanamo Bay has not been closed, Khalid Sheikh Mohammed has not been tried (he has been in custody for ten years), and the number of drone strikes has increased. The White House even undertook a fifty-page interpretation of domestic, constitutional, and international law to justify the assassination by a drone strike of US citizen Anwar al-Awlaki in Yemen in 2011.[45] Law was used to *defend* an executive decision, in other words, not to decide if it should take place at all.

Claims that the ICC and R2P enjoy universal support among western governments and publics are merely theoretical. Such claims are really natural law—that is, laws of humanity—and as such, and despite being disguised behind customary and treaty law, are deeply contested. The main civil society support group for the ICC, the Coalition for the International Criminal Court, has been leading a global ratification campaign for the Rome Statute that as of January 16, 2013, had seen 139 states having signed and 121 ratified (Guatemala the latest to join).[46] Its target of the month in March 2013 was Algeria followed by Cameroon and Ukraine in May. Of the 193 states in the international system, this is a ratification rate of nearly 63 percent and a signing rate of 72 percent. Is this a norm?[47] Not every accession is of equal value. When the nonjoiners include the United States, China, India, Indonesia, and Russia (the world's most populous countries, including three out of five Security Council permanent members) even a rate of 95 percent would hardly constitute a norm. Resistance on the part of these major powers is not transient or instrumental but, in the case of the United States and China, based on deep-seated objections. The same is true with the anti–death penalty campaign. Or with Russia's objections to R2P. The relative success of the ICTY is the exception that proves the rule. And it is a court *in Europe* for *Europeans*, the continent of the Holocaust. Despite rhetoric to the contrary, the evidence that international criminal justice has a deterrent effect is also negligible.[48]

There is now more pushback than ever before. It comes not just from states in the international system that feel empowered to defy the international community (Syria, Uzbekistan, Sri Lanka, Cambodia, Israel, Sudan) but also from newly confident major powers: China, Russia, Brazil, and India. There is both a rise in conservative religious observance worldwide and a growing confidence particularly within Christian churches about challenging the secular, universal, and uncompromising nature of the global humanist regime. The challenge is acute on questions of gender and sexuality. It is precisely in local spaces that religion and nonliberal (not necessarily illiberal) norms retain significant legitimacy. Under empire, these spaces were targeted for conversion. If Human Rights advocates entertained similar hopes, they are being dashed. A disconnect is opening up between global humanism with its law, courts, fund-raising, and campaigns on the one hand, and local lived realities on the other. It is a disconnect between Human Rights and human rights, and Human Rights are a tough sale for moral spectators to close because they are strangers who do not themselves need what they are selling. They work on the rights of others because their own rights are secure. The time when international humanism was about self-denial, sacrifice, and an aversion to power are long gone. Extremely high salaries are now paid to attract the very best human rights and humanitarian advocates, particularly in human rights work where lawyers and journalists have good exit options into the private sector. Prior government service is no longer a problem either.

To take one of many examples: In January 2012 Suzanne Nossel was appointed executive director of Amnesty International's US section (AIUSA). She had previously worked for the State Department, the *Wall Street Journal*, and management consultants McKinsey and Co. This was, to put it mildly, a cultural shift. She lasted barely a year, leaving in January 2013 after controversial positions she espoused—including that NATO was defending women's rights in Afghanistan (in a billboard campaign titled "NATO: Keep the Progress Going!")—provoked outraged calls for her resignation.[49] The insight this clash of cultures gives us into how human rights became Human Rights in the 1970s will become clear. Human rights language is now familiar in many complex settings where global laws and precedents, as well as rights-related transnational funding streams, play a role in furthering local causes. But in the world of "human rights," advocates do not aspire to hegemony, and rights are malleable and frequently integrated into more syncretic belief systems (including religion). Human rights are one political language alongside other authorities, norms, and beliefs. What brought down dictatorships in the Middle East and North Africa was people power, not the humanist international.

Religious movements often have millions of adherents and provide both spiritual and material support. They also have a wide array of mechanisms to induce norm-following (schools, family, and community pressures) against which abstract human rights norms are weak. In daily "lifeworlds" long-term reciprocity-style relations are key.[50] You help out today and someone will help you if you need it tomorrow, next week, next year. The hierarchy of Human Rights mitigates against this peer reinforcement. Strangers who stay cease to be strangers, swapping one form of moral authority (of not-belonging) for another, more political form (belonging). But only not-belonging can underwrite universal, secular, and categorical norms. And the fiction of not belonging to a social class was the ultimate conceit of Christian and secular European civilizers. Its collapse after 1945 and its overhaul in the 1970s by American democratic pragmatism sped the Human Rights project along but left its unique legitimation exposed and foundering.

For a while American power obscured these tattered foundations. Now, however, not only is the world moving rapidly from a briefly unipolar system to one of bipolarity or even multipolarity, but American exceptionalism has shaken the foundations of the humanist legacy. Europe, the continent from which universal secular humanism was exported, has lost its capacity not just to make international norms effective but, much more important, to defend the idea that those norms must be universal, secular, and nonnegotiable. This is a long way from the Hague Conventions of 1899 and 1907 when Europe was ascendant. The Martens Clause of the Hague Conventions stands as a definitive statement of the law of humanity:

> Until a more complete code of the laws of war is issued, the High Contracting Parties think it right to declare that in cases not included in the Regulations adopted by them, populations and belligerents remain under the protection and empire of the principles of international law, as they result from the usages established between civilized nations, from the laws of humanity and the requirements of the public conscience.

The world in which this claim to moral authority carries the day is vanishing fast.

Ambivalence and Irrelevance: The United States and Europe

The construction of the United States Holocaust Memorial Museum (USHMM) was a difficult political and design process with many sensitive issues to be resolved.[51] The principal architect, James Ingo Freed, a Jewish child refugee from Germany in the 1930s, understood—after visits to Holocaust sites in Europe—that visitors to the Washington, DC, museum also had to "leave" the Mall in Washington and travel back in time to Europe in the 1930s and 1940s. He was careful to observe for his final design how the death camps were built; he would use steel, brick, and glass in ways that disoriented the visitor immediately and echoed the architecture and construction of the Holocaust.[52] The Hall of Witnesses where one stands after entering the USHMM could easily be a German or East European railway station, embarking Jews for Auschwitz, or a concentration camp. Even at its nadir, in other words, European civilization occupied center stage, producing villains on an epic scale to rival heroes of the European past.

For four centuries Europeans dominated the telling of world history, controlling the story of their heroic role in spreading progress through Christianity and liberalism. Despite the catastrophe of 1939–1945, and with significant American help, the Europeans survived. Through the European Community and NATO, Germany was reintegrated and collective dispute resolution embedded. The unity stimulated by the threat of Soviet invasion consolidated this community and kept the United States heavily involved in European affairs. The empires had to go, of course: they were too expensive; resistance was immense after 1945, particularly in post–Japanese invasion Asia; and the American way of doing things—control through economic conditionality and military coercion, not occupation—was the only game in town, as the Suez Crisis demonstrated in 1956.

With paltry political and military power in the Cold War world, European self-importance sustained itself through a series of institutions. Most visible was the United Nations, successor to the League of Nations; permanent Security Council seats for France and Britain on the cusp of their steep decline was a real coup. Allied to progressive sentiment in the United States, exemplified by Eleanor Roosevelt, the president's widow and chairwoman of the committee that drew up the UDHR, there was a scramble to institutionalize universal norms while the opportunity existed. A huge lobbying effort resulted in the Genocide Convention in 1948.[53] And from 1945 and Nuremberg onward, the Allies cooperated in a series of war-crimes trials in Germany and Japan that established vital precedents and jurisprudence for international criminal justice. The charges at Nuremberg were drawn up by the Allies largely on the basis that the crimes committed by the Nazis were against international customary law as contained, for example, in the Martens Clause.[54]

Closely allied to each other through these years by historical experience, strategic dangers, diaspora and class links, finance, trade, and political culture, the United States and Europe were natural allies in the cause of universal law and institutions. At least on the surface. Underneath, however, the United States—with unrivaled economic and military power, coastlines on the Atlantic and the Pacific, its own constitutional tradition that for many Americans was superior to international law, a sense of its own manifest destiny, and a Cold War to fight—has not been a reliable ally. There were decades of Senate resistance to the Genocide Convention, the refusal to ratify the Children's Rights Convention, the revocation in 2001 of President Clinton's assent to the Rome Statute that established the ICC, and the explicit use of torture and extraordinary rendition during the global war on terror, to name only the most high-profile of many acts of noncompliance with international norms.

Even the language of human rights, used freely in American foreign policy, is rarely heard domestically, as if the legal rights Americans enjoy are not grounded in their human rights. Reservations about the ICC went as deep as the Bush administration signing into law in 2002 the American Service-Members' Protection Act designed to "protect United States military personnel and other elected and appointed officials of the United States government against criminal prosecution by an international criminal court to which the United States is not party." This was nicknamed the Hague Invasion Act. It is a massive repudiation of the idea of customary international law. In essence, and acknowledging the many differences of opinion within American society, the United States has shown minimal need or interest in driving international human rights law as a multilateral institutional framework that might constrain America's own power. When Barack Obama said he felt more at home in Asia than Europe, he was the advance party for a seismic shift.

This aversion to institutionalism internationally, except in trade liberalization, assumes much greater importance now the focus of world politics is moving rapidly to Asia. It is only twenty-five years since the end of the Cold War, and it has taken that long for the realities of shifting power and influence to unwind. The rise of China and its power to pursue an independent foreign policy in relation to international norms complements the role of the United States and Russia, all with a strong discourse of national distinctiveness. In terms of R2P, India, Brazil, Russia, and China have all strongly condemned the "neocolonial" nature of the claims made by R2P advocates. Both Brazil and India have made the point that domestic commitment to rights and democracy is very different from accepting the authority of the Global Human Rights Regime to dictate domestic priorities.

In countries as diverse as China, Iran, India, Zimbabwe, Afghanistan, Algeria, Sudan, Brazil, South Africa, Kenya, Nigeria, Rwanda, and Vietnam, invoking European colonialism still has political resonance. In Central Asia and East Europe there is deep resistance to the demands of human rights activists (witness widespread antihomosexual sentiment in Ukraine in 2012). The Europeans have used "international" law in these societies before, when they were colonies or supplicants, in support of economic and political goals. All these societies have a multiplicity of social, legal, and moral norms, long-established cultures, religious and linguistic and ethnic diversity, different and complex historical experiences, and divergent interests and problems. Why do we assume that they should all obediently march in the direction of universal, secular, categorical norms? And why should they recognize the ultimate authority of the Human Rights empire? What if they argue it is ideology masquerading as truth? What if they ask "by what legitimacy do you claim a right to rule"?[55] R2P is not a norm, and the ICC is rejected by the great powers. This European imperial conceit about its uniquely privileged role in civilization is just that, a conceit.

Containing China has become pivotal to American foreign policy. The 2012 Obama Defense Strategic Review made clear that Asia was the United States' primary concern. Getting more involved with ASEAN and APEC, basing troops in Australia, agreeing to share nuclear material with India—such moves are all about China. American decline is overstated, but the United States is increasingly first among equals, with less and less capacity to make its will felt without a disproportionate investment of resources. China, India, Russia, Brazil, South Africa—collectively the BRICS—will radically change the alliance dynamics within global politics and institutions. The BRICS are not necessarily against international law as such, but this regime with rules they did not write will be more about sovereignty as prerogative than as responsibility. In such a system reciprocity will reassume its historical importance as the key mechanism for making norms effective at the expense of customary law. Skepticism about "European" courts, shared by the United States, will take hold. Syria from 2011 onward has been a test case for this new dispensation. Only pressure from China and the United States could feasibly make a difference to President Vladimir Putin's calculation that his interests are best served by protecting Syria from R2P intervention.

Neo-Westphalia

In the endtimes, multipolarity will mean gridlock over norms at the global level, with sovereigns and religious authorities increasingly able to block progress in civil liberties and gender and sexual orientation. In the June 2012 Rio+20 Conference on Sustainable Development, for example, a coalition of religious and national groups removed language on reproductive rights from the final outcome document despite the efforts of the UN, states such as Norway and Iceland, and organizations like Human Rights Watch. In doing so they reversed twenty years of work to embed the phrase "reproductive rights" in UN discourse.[56] Without deployment of serious American diplomatic resources, little happens. Europe, devoid of moral and political capital, is no substitute. Increasingly, only issues of security, natural resources, and trade will excite multilateral engagement. These are the concerns of great-power foreign policy. Law for a flat system—reciprocity law—will increasingly replace that for a hierarchy: Global Human Rights. The implications for the United Nations are profound: more of the Security Council, more Permanent Five, less Human Rights in New York, and less of a role for UN operational agencies spreading global secular norms.

Finding it harder and harder to get traction, international human rights and humanitarian organizations will turn increasingly to self-promotion. They will be concerned more than ever with themselves. Money pressure will exacerbate this trend because, given the difficulties inherent in proving the impact of global human rights, it is the symbolic value of rights that will need to be monetized. We will see the substitution of the appearance of moral power for the reality of waning influence. It will be all circuses. The ICC is a portent of this: monumental ambitions and paltry tangible results. Global Human Rights institutions will be less and less able to persuade skeptics, generating an increasingly insular, self-sustaining dialogue in which the Potemkin village of the ICC and R2P must never be openly doubted. Blind faith will increase, but the gap with reality will also grow. The faithful will dwindle in number. Religion, renewed nationalism, and new forms of transnational solidarity will emerge, reducing Human Rights to human rights, a language no longer necessarily universal, secular, or categorical. The end of traditional wars will only exacerbate this shift, as diverse forms of political, urban, and personal violence continue in areas where Human Rights have no impact at all.

The one area of the world in which Europeans will continue to have influence is sub-Saharan Africa, because it is the one continent where Europe's weakened influence is less easily resisted by internally fractured African states tied by proximity, language, and other institutional links into post-imperial networks of power. The French intervention in Mali in January 2013 is a perfect example. Africa will remain a laboratory for European moral spectatorship, although given Europe's relative global decline, self-reliance and church support will likely be the future for the poor and the suffering south of the Sahara. Only the region's role as a treasury of natural resources and a potential security threat will keep it in the spotlight.

This may all seem like downside, but there is a potential upside. Religious, nationalist, ethnic and family structures, located much closer to people and integrated within their everyday needs and identities, their "lifeworld," hold more promise for creating sustainable reciprocity-based and socially reinforced norms that reduce suffering, even if they fail to deliver on the promise of global liberal norms. Certainly after decades of violence and war in the Democratic Republic of the Congo, for example, or persistent global poverty and widening inequality, there might just be another way that is crowded out by humanist norms. Perhaps the answer is in more international funding and expertise in areas like public health, disease, communication, and mediation—the Médecins Sans Frontières approach—which is more conducive to longer-lasting and effective change than are the often-symbolic efforts of large-scale global institutions. Moreover, acute crisis will always open a space for very practical but time-limited relief work in logistics, search and rescue, medicine, disease control, and food and shelter. Much international activism that funnels resources like information into indigenous networks may also continue to be effective, as long as it is anchored in the expressed desires of communities of solidarity, in women's rights and LGBT networks for example. This entails an end to the dependency culture that sees local groups as clients of the money, access, and influence of the Human Rights Imperium. Finally, there may also be some meager virtue in a system where the hypocrisies of power are more brutally exposed. In Chinese and Russian indifference to the suffering of Syrians lies a kind of cruel truth: ultimately even Western powers have propagated or tolerated mass violence to get what they want. The rejection of R2P by the Russians is a blow in favor of transparency and reality.

What people do not need is another universal church. Once Human Rights becomes human rights again, a globally unowned and unownable claim of human moral equality as the anchor of fair treatment and nothing more, other alliances can grow. Human rights can be a kind of "popular front," to use the language of international socialism, where diversity of motivations and outlook is prized in the furtherance of concrete improvements in everyday lives on all measures: nutrition and health, disease, security, education. What happens after that is a syncretic, political, ground-up process of mobilization. It could even lead us toward more genuinely transnational social communities based on a shared economy rather than identity or ideology. The churches may be a model for this form of activism. It may not prevent mass atrocities, but the alternative has failed in that endeavor as well.

The remaining chapters of this book are organized as follows: Chapter 2 looks at the early history of the humanist international, beginning with the foundations of the ICRC as the first "secular church." Chapter 3 examines what we'll call the "metanarrative of moral authority" and shows how it operates within international humanist politics, highlighting the crucial importance of the Holocaust both as event and as representation. The final part of this chapter looks at the ways in which the metanarrative is challenged and defended. This examination continues in chapter 4 with the aesthetic of atrocity, analyzing how its claim to be progressive is actually underwritten by an inherent conservatism. The assertion of transcendent authority in the face of the postmodern challenge is at the root of this attempt to hold to the past against the tide of history.

Chapter 5 analyses the shift from moral to political authority in the 1970s and the trend, accelerated since, toward marketing atrocity. Critical here is the move from a secular-theocratic to a democratic legitimation for human rights under the influence of American pragmatism. Chapter 6 argues that since 1991, with the new dawn of international courts and trials, a kind of human rights constitutionalism has taken hold that is colonizing humanitarian law in the name of justice. This is the era of Human

Rights. Despite the apparent triumph of the ICC and R2P, I'll argue that these are not sustainable long-term institutions.

The final two chapters argue for the "endtimes." Chapter 7 looks at the renewed importance of religion and nationalism and at the enduring reality of American exceptionalism. These forms of mobilization tap into deep normative structures and increasingly make inroads against secular humanism at the global level (Sri Lanka and Cambodia are cases in point, as is resistance to rights norms about gender and sexuality in the name of tradition and religion). In chapter 8, I argue that the shift to multipolarity represents an epochal movement away from impartial moral authority back to a world of diverse normative forms in which the only effective international law is based on the reciprocal interests of states. The key state here is the United States, whose religious fervor and nationalist ethos have remained undimmed despite decades of talk about "the West." The ICC and R2P are the last stand of a European imperial vision of one world united around impartial, neutral, and apolitical norms. The view from nowhere, always an aspiration, is soon to be a relic of a bygone era we can visit only in museums.

THE CHURCH OF HUMAN RIGHTS

To say the pioneers of organized humanism were bourgeois is to say something obvious yet important about the social order underlying liberal democracy. Without it we cannot understand human rights, humanitarianism, and international justice today; these social practices are the modern professionalized descendants of humanism and play a similar function in our era to that humanists and their new cultural sensibility played in the political life of nineteenth-century Europe.[1] This rising class was precisely in the middle. Having wrested power from a fading nobility, many of whose members became enthusiastically engaged in "nonpolitical" humanitarian work (a sign of humanitarianism's conservatism in itself), they then protected their gains from proletarian agitation fueled by rapid industrialization and urbanization. Indeed, they saw their social (let alone racial and religious) inferiors as needing all manner of moral improvement, which it was their duty to provide. "The liberal bourgeois was never a revolutionary for long," as Carl Schmitt pithily put it.[2] Zealous bourgeois reformism was as much about political consolidation as material progress—the insecurity brought by the promises and dangers of modernity had to be managed and controlled.

Existing cultural resources were not adequate for this purpose, the pace of change in science and medicine, communications, and weaponry, let alone art and culture, far too much for Christianity to integrate. Protestantism, particularly Calvinism, had already taken a large step in the direction of weakening the institutional power of the established church hierarchy through its emphasis on individual conscience.[3] By the 1850s the ongoing effect had been to undermine the monopoly authority of Christianity (even as diverse everyday ways of being Christian persisted). What would fill the void? Faith in secular humanism was the answer, and the International Committee of the Red Cross (ICRC) in Geneva was its first international church. That Switzerland would be its home was entirely appropriate; landlocked, neutral, federal, and pious, the mountain state thrived on its strategic position, particularly in finance, a pivotal but liminal country at once in but not of imperial European great-power politics.

The first major cause to arouse the fledgling middle class in Europe was the abolition of slavery.[4] The antislavery campaign was half of the old world, half of the new. Abolitionism was driven by nonconformists, particularly Quakers, and liberal Protestants, many of whom were sympathetic to modernity (e.g., to science and rights) but who still hoped to redeem Christianity from the *sin* of slavery.[5] The Christian god in one form or another remained their ultimate moral reference point.[6] But there were marked differences with humanism. First, the vanguard of antislavery was solidly in the major slave-trading states, Britain, followed by France and the United States, whereas organized humanitarianism was a more continental European phenomenon.

Second, various incarnations of organized antislavery (in 1787, 1823, 1839) were single-issue societies fighting on principle for revolutionary change in a fundamental norm. The ICRC made its case as the provider of a humane service on the battlefield and stressed how it was to the benefit of armies that their own wounded were cared for and repatriated and all at someone else's expense.[7] It spoke from within the prevailing discourse without an explicit moral critique of war. Third, the humanitarian movement was more completely a product of the "bourgeois public sphere" and its sense of itself as a distinct class with a distinct sensibility; despite the number of nobles and royals subsequently involved in national Red Cross societies, those who built the global organization were thoroughly bourgeois.[8] Fourth, while the inspiration and cultural milieu of the ICRC founders was pure Swiss Protestantism (Geneva was the city of Calvin, after all), the organization they established and the practices it spread were about redeeming civilized society and the lives of its members, not about saving the church. The language of suffering in modern warfare was a language of inhumanity, not of sin.

As a result, the ICRC was constituted as secular from the beginning. Secular in this sense means nondiscriminatory, that is, *neither legitimated by nor privileging in principle any social or personal aspect of identity, faith, or belief.* There still were, still are, numerous advocates and activists for human rights and humanitarian work who possess strong religious motivations. Many of the ICRC's earliest members emphasized their faith, and their background assumptions about "Christian civilization" were inseparable from it. But this was neither necessary nor defining for the ICRC as a whole. In all the voluminous documentation about the ICRC as an organization, the Christian god rarely features, except when personal motivations are being described. The ICRC was also self-consciously "international" at a time when, as word and concept, "international" was far from commonplace. Divergence between the private identities of members and the seemingly identity-less public organization they founded made this a very different kind of church. Organizations of this sort—universal, secular, and categorical—embody the moral spectator in institutional form, furthering the needs and interests not of those who belong but of those who do not.

The displacement of Christ's sacrifice in favor of human suffering was the first step in the sacralization of humanity, the new *totem*, that would define humanism in the twentieth century.[9] Durkheim saw this, noting that "the human being is becoming the pivot of social conscience among European peoples and has acquired an incomparable value. It is society that has consecrated him."[10] The egalitarian aspirations of Protestantism were critical for this shift. Catholicism, the global hierarchical church with the crucified Christ at its core, could not have substituted the human person for the son of god. Increasingly it would be secular wounds that anchored the moral force of the newly emerging law of humanity, making the ICRC the prototype for a century of international humanist NGOs. The professional practices we call "humanitarianism," "human rights," and "international justice" began to evolve in more distinct form for the first time in the years after 1918, but all were rooted in the same sentimental nineteenth-century bourgeois Protestant culture of human suffering. For all of them the mission was (and is) *to protect the innocent* (and by extension the *idea of innocence*).[11] This innocence was a quality, of existential goodness, purity, and blamelessness, that existed within *individuals*. It was a kind of secularized *soul*.

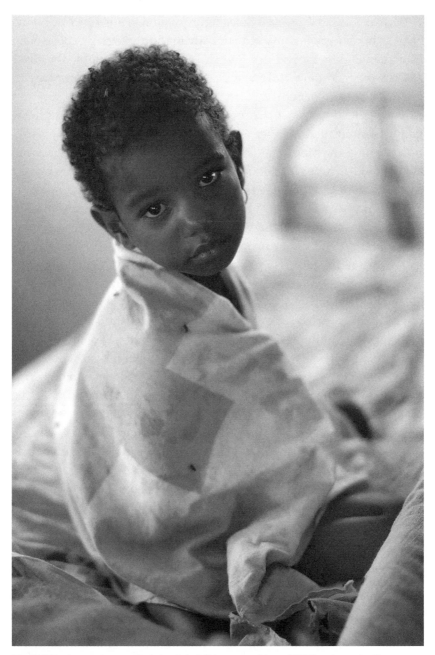

Fig. 1. "War's most innocent victim." A child wrapped in an ICRC sack at a feeding center in Ethiopia, 1986. © Steve Raymer / National Geographic Stock.

That an idealized and sacralized figure of human innocence lies at the heart of humanism is conveyed perfectly in the photograph above of an Ethiopian child wrapped in a Red Cross sack, which adorns the cover of François Bugnion's 1161-page *The International Committee of the Red Cross and the Protection of War Victims*.[12]

Former ICRC president Cornelio Sommaruga eulogizes this photograph as encapsulating "a sense of poignancy without which any reflection on the alleviation of suffering would be incomplete." He goes on: "How could anyone remain unmoved by the gaze of the child wrapped in a sack marked with the red cross, a look that expresses a seriousness beyond his years, an appeal to which no one can remain insensitive, a dignity that distress only serves to reinforce?"[13] This was 1999, 140 years after Solferino, and yet the mixture of pathos, entreaty, and sentimentality remains nearly identical.

But this interpretation of the picture is thoroughly idealized. It is about what *we* see, not about the child. Perhaps the photo was partially staged, the Red Cross sack rearranged across the child's shoulders, his body moved slightly to let the light fall more effectively on his face. We have no idea what he was really feeling (curiosity, boredom, irritation?). He is never named, and we do not find out what happened to him. Was his family standing beside the bed, out of the shot? The photo implies he is alone, "orphaned," but is he? There are several more pictures of suffering children, and of the mother and child, in the original *National Geographic* article in which the child in the Red Cross sack was featured. Was this shot not selected from a contact sheet by the picture editors and then by the ICRC (and then for the cover of this book) because of something *we* project onto the child that is part of *our* moral imaginary? The picture has undeniable aesthetic appeal: it is a beautiful, compelling, romantic encapsulation of the "humanitarian imperative," the pitiful child without any obvious marks of violence and suffering. We are in a sensory world somewhere between art and the sublime.

It is this "cultural emotion" and its aesthetic representation that grounds European-style humanism, whatever contradictions and lacunae exist in the profane world of political practice. Honoring the secularized Christ child, a learned cultural response dating back to the 1800s, *is* (or has been until now) the secret of global humanism. In *Reimagining Child Soldiers*, Mark Drumbl critiques the pervasive image of young combatants as "faultless passive victims" that dominates "the international legal imagination."[14] But the use of such totemic images in a binary narrative of good versus evil is *exactly* their function. International justice is about real victims only in a secondary sense. It is now almost entirely about *itself*. Collapse begins at this paradoxical point: the reiteration of a metanarrative of heroism and innocence ceases to be essential to sustain global normative structures at the moment its use becomes ubiquitous. But the loss of the metanarrative's connection to an underlying social purpose or functional reality, beginning in the 1970s, marks the beginning of the *endtimes*.

Around this child with his beseeching eyes, moral ideas like "dignity" and "human rights" coalesce, circulate, and grow. Such existential innocence is claimed for all children, is assumed or hypothesized in women (particularly but not only as mothers), and is considered inherent in categories like "civilian," "wounded," "imprisoned," and "tortured."[15] All these are hors de combat. Such innocence is heavy with a sense of being demasculinized, of being incapable of violence or resistance, of being unable to bear responsibility. Associated notions of broken family relations (defenseless child, nurturer-mother, protector-father) are never far away. Echoing Dunant, protecting innocence is a symbolic palliative (and distraction) from modernity's dark side and a powerful alibi when the destruction, violence, and cruelty seem unending. It is an anesthetic against the facts, not for those few who directly confront the wounds—they unavoidably absorb the sins of complicity for us all—but for the dispersed global middle class that are Dunant's heirs in the television and social media age. This aesthetic of innocence obscures the contradictions between progress and devastation, wealth and poverty, freedom and servitude, security and crimes against humanity. And as with any church, the moral power of the wounds of victims and survivors has seeped into the structures—the ICRC, the red cross emblem, the Geneva Convention, the idea of neutrality, the Hague Conventions, R2P and the ICC—that were established to protect the *totem*. These laws and norms are now defended with the same intensity of purpose as the idealized innocent child him or herself. As Drumbl writes, referring to the *Lubanga* case at the ICC: "Nuance stands at cross-purposes with the prosecutorial imperative to convict."[16]

The Origins of the ICRC

The men who founded the ICRC in 1863 are shown in the image below.

> All five men belonged to Geneva's oldest, most prosperous fami-
> lies, active over many generations in the law, medicine, the army,
> and politics, and three of them—Dufour, Moynier, and Appia—
> were rich enough not to have to work. All were Protestant and prac-
> tising Christians and shared Dunant's feelings about the ethics of
> war, "the moral sense of the importance of human life, the humane
> desire to lighten a little the torments" of the wounded.[17]

All were also socially engaged. Moynier, for example, was involved with
as many as forty charitable societies (many to "improve the lot of the
working class"),[18] while Appia had published a treatise on the treatment
of war wounds. Moynier would be president of the ICRC from 1864 until
his death in 1910, when his aging nephew, Gustave Ador, succeeded him
(until 1928). As late as 1914, says Moorehead, "members continued to
be selected from a tight-knit, interrelated group of people, prosperous
Genevans from the city's oldest families. There were no women and no
Catholics among them."[19] Members were often blood relatives through
successive generations. The first woman appointed as one of the ICRC's
twenty or so committee members (a year before the first Catholic) was
Marguerite Frick-Cramer (who served 1918–1946), and she was related
to seven other committee members.[20] The contrast between this narrow
Geneva-based elite and the wider Red Cross movement would come to
a head in the 1920s when the ICRC clashed with several national Red
Cross societies, especially the American Red Cross, which had twenty-
eight million members in 1918.[21] And yet the ICRC survived, largely
intact, its brand of Genevan "enlightened conservatism" persisting into
the 1970s and beyond.[22]

Humanist ideology's social base in the nineteenth century was
composed of members of this widening bourgeois class, increasingly
conscious of themselves *as a class* after decades of reading about and dis-
cussing "social affairs" together.[23] Non-patronage-based professions like
law and medicine had been particularly important as avenues for middle-
class advance in Europe, making lawyers and doctors increasingly

Fig. 2. The Committee of Five who founded the Red Cross in 1863: Louis Appia, Guillaume-Henri Dufour, Henry Dunant, Théodore Maunoir, and Gustave Moynier. © ICRC.

influential in the years after 1859. These men—and they were overwhelmingly men—sought not to rule directly but rather, as a public of concerned private citizens, to hold the state to account.[24] The logic of science and the law were powerful allies in this process.[25] Their *lifeworld*, the "always already familiar" they shared, gave them "unproblematic, common, background convictions that [they] assumed to be guaranteed."[26] Far from being a problem, the ICRC viewed this as a positive thing. "Because it was a compact group of homogeneous social structure, educated in the same schools and nourished by the same traditions, it was able to judge and to act with force and cohesion," argues André Durand.[27] The social inequality inherent in being a wealthy Genevan citizen was a stark contrast with the moral equality of all as *"human beings pure and simple"* that legitimated moral expansionism under the label "humanity."[28] This was definitely not politics. Redistribution of power and resources was not an option, one reason why a happy alliance was forged in European capitals like Berlin and St. Petersburg between humanitarians and the aristocracy (Queen

Augusta of Prussia even wore her Red Cross armband in public).[29] Any notion of social solidarity was a self-comforting myth.

As prideful Europeans these bourgeois felt, like most members of their class, a Christian duty to globalize their own civilization, whether through missionary work or secular zeal. Lady-of-the-lamp Florence Nightingale and Nietzsche's madman with his lantern warning god was dead exemplified the sense of obligation to *enlighten* others, to bring light into the darkness. Moynier, for example, had an ongoing interest in bringing Christian civilization to the Congo via Belgian colonial power.[30] He was clear that the Red Cross could be successfully transplanted only to places where Westernization had occurred, for alternative civilizations (let alone "savages or barbarians") lacked the necessary moral standards to show pity for the wounded and respect for the red cross (the totemic symbol).[31] The assumption of superiority on the basis of class, race, and religion held by the Genevans and entirely commonplace throughout the bourgeoisie in Europe was a prerequisite for moral advance.[32] Dunant, lest we forget, was at Solferino to advance his own imperial project in Algeria. Such were the ICRC's social roots. "It is impossible not to see [in it] a product of Christian civilization," admitted Moynier.[33]

And yet this self-confidence was vulnerable. Marx and Engels had perfectly captured modernity's revolutionary nature when they wrote in 1848: "All that is solid melts into air. All that is holy is profaned."[34] Enlightenment hubris was at its height in the century after 1750, during which, as Thomas Haskell puts it, the "European man felt so sure that merely by daring to use his own reason he might make himself master of both nature and fate."[35] He adds: "The supreme sense of individual and collective potency that prevailed in these decades made all existing institutional constraints seem malleable and contributed powerfully to the creation of a situation in which slavery could be challenged and other humanitarian reforms set in motion."[36] As the century wore on, however, the sense of imminent danger and threat accelerated. The American Civil War of 1861–1865 and the Franco-Prussian War of 1870–1871 were a frightening portent of the "total wars" to come.[37] And rapid industrial growth fueled urbanization on an unparalleled scale. In 1800, 12 percent of Europe's population lived in sizable cities. By 1900 the figure was 30 percent, an unprecedented shift that gave rise to a wide array of new social problems and responses.[38]

By 1906 the old moral certainties were gone. For Durkheim: "From this it results that morality appears to us less as a code of duties, a defined discipline, than as an attracting ideal, half glimpsed at. The incentive to a moral life is not so much a feeling of deference to an uncontested imperative, but rather a sort of aspiration towards an elevated but vague objective."[39] The secular church grew in this ambiguity. A shared sense of "aura" or "effervescence" emerged from secular efforts to ameliorate death and suffering, and this formed the basis for the new church. Trauma invested its structures with moral power through the "extraordinary contagiousness of the sacred."[40] And Dunant, the visionary, provided the spark. His capacity to invoke the totem was remarkable. Here he describes a squadron of cavalry,

> which gallops by, crushing dead and dying beneath its horses' hoofs. One poor wounded man has his jaw carried away; another his head shattered; a third, who could have been saved, has his chest beaten in. Oaths and shrieks of rage, groans of anguish and despair, mingle with the whinnying of horses. Here come the artillery, following the cavalry, and going at full gallop. The guns crash over the dead and wounded, strewn pell-mell on the ground. Brains spurt under the wheels, limbs are broken and torn, bodies mutilated past recognition—the soil is literally puddled with blood, and the plain littered with human remains.

The dread is all too real. This cataclysmic imagery recalls the four horsemen of the apocalypse—conquest, war, famine, and death—heralds of the Last Judgment. Dunant fused the social and personal in an extremely powerful way, implicating all readers in what was happening around them. By individualizing their suffering, Dunant gave the wounded men a sliver of anonymous identity. Usually the dead were simply tipped into unmarked mass graves. By the 1914–1918 war, the fate of individual soldiers would be far better known, owing in no small part to the ICRC's efforts collating lists of the wounded and the dead.

Dunant had been seriously involved in evangelism and faith revivalism since his youth. *A Memory* was a best-selling testimony of this Christian witness.[41] His version from later in life of his awakening has a strong born-again dimension:

> In writing *A Memory of Solferino*, I was, as it were, lifted out of my-self, compelled by some high power and compelled by the breath of God. . . . In this state of pent-up emotion which filled my heart, I was aware of an intuition, vague but profound, that my work was an instrument of His Will; it seemed to me that I had to accomplish it as a sacred duty and that it was destined to have fruits of infi-nite consequence for mankind. This conviction drove me on and I had the sensation of being urged by a force beyond myself . . . the power certainly came from above for in truth I had no thought for myself. This recollection had to be set down; I cannot explain it in any other way.[42]

This account is the heart of humanitarianism's creation myth, "Dunan-tist" now a sanctified synonym for purity of motivation, despite what a careful reading of his text reveals about his class and gender assump-tions, particularly his idealization of aristocratic women and their noble virtues.[43] Origin stories like this are important for two reasons. First, the moment of illumination, of seeing the light (as the prophet Daniel did in his apocalyptic visions), facilitates a rhetorical clean break with history, its cultural resources freed up for a new project. Suffering and sacrifice purify what has gone before. Second, the inspirational story of divine rev-elation enables a complex message about new forms of social action to be simplified into one person's awakening—into, that is, the metanarrative of innocent suffering and heroic rescue. Converts could follow Dunant's example without worrying unduly about theology.

These sacred myths institutionalized the new church as they had with Dunant's most distinguished predecessor, Florence Nightingale, whose "self-sacrifice" he called "sublime" and "heroic and holy" in *A Memory*.[44] The reality of Dunant's life, that he was soon penniless and outcast as a bankrupt and spent nearly thirty years in obscurity before an encounter with a journalist led to a decade of fame and a share in the first Nobel Peace Prize in 1901, is irrelevant. Beatification requires objectification, the taking of a point in time, like the still photograph of the Ethiopian child, that can be frozen and venerated. The resulting gap between myth and reality is nicely illustrated in the story of Dunant's appearance at the Universal Exhibition in Paris in 1867. Homeless and disgraced, he was hungry and sleeping in railway station waiting rooms while his bust—crowned with laurel leaves—had a place of honor at the exhibition, alongside a large display of Red Cross medical equipment.[45] He had served his purpose, his actual self, inspired but unreliable, now surplus to requirements. In a world with a failing god, the idealized Dunant was an early secular martyr.

The more utilitarian Moynier, not Dunant, built the new church, with firm organization, not soaring rhetoric, and he was adamant that the ICRC was not faith based.[46] Moynier detested "philanthropical dilettantes and humanitarian dreamers" and came to despise Dunant.[47] Unveiling a bust of Moynier in Geneva in 1989, then-ICRC president Sommaruga said of him: "He was not a man of lofty imagination or original insight, but one who was able to recognize the value of certain incipient ideas and strive with uncommon perseverance to give them life."[48] Moynier had even written a book about Saint Paul, builder of the Christian church, before becoming ICRC president. Cultural Christianity fused with medicine and law to create a new form of secular religiosity visible in symbols like the red cross and the Geneva Convention that for a century partly compensated for the loss of religious authority under modernity. Rather than reason versus faith, what developed was more like *the faith of reason*. For a century until the 1960s, this sacredness in action was at the very heart of human rights and humanitarian work.

Neutrality and the Red Cross

Summary minutes of the first discussions of the "committee of five" in 1863 were reprinted in the *International Review of the Red Cross* in 1963.[49] Written by Dunant, as secretary, the text confirms how practical the conversations were, with little rhetoric or grandiloquence. No one asked about foundational authority or legitimacy. The founders were charged by the Public Welfare Society of Geneva (which Moynier chaired) to act on the call for a relief society to be set up in peacetime. They immediately voted to be a "Permanent International Committee" (outstripping the Welfare Society's mandate). At their first meeting on February 17, 1863, Dunant outlined the basis of what would in 1864 become the Geneva Convention by reiterating his hope that "the civilized powers would subscribe to an inviolable, international principle that would be guaranteed

and consecrated in a kind of concordat between Governments" to safeguard those devoting themselves to relief work.[50] Note the word *consecrated*. Dunant saw the need for a convention at the heart of which would
be a norm, "some sacred, international and formally recognized principle," that provided the necessary protection for medical personnel in battle. That sacred principle, given moral power by totemic suffering, was
neutrality.[51] Dunant quickly and unilaterally advocated neutrality for the
wounded and for ambulances, hospitals, relief services, and the medical
corps, an idea initially opposed by Moynier.[52]

The ICRC's secular-sacred institutions had a head start gaining traction in Europe because of their association with Christianity. With a nod
to religious sanctuary, Dunant called neutrality "the truce of god."[53] Created in 1863, the red cross is an iconic secular sacred symbol. But recognition is an ambiguous good. Militaries, firms, and health-care providers
have traded on its symbolic power whether knowingly or not.[54] During
the Franco-Prussian War it was used and abused (including as a targeting
device for German artillery).[55] In 2008 one of the Colombian commandos
who freed presidential candidate Ingrid Betancourt and other hostages
from the guerrilla group FARC used a Red Cross vest (allegedly in error)
as part of an operation to trick kidnappers into thinking the soldiers were
aid workers.[56] Making the red cross sacred has been a costly signal to
produce, but it remains an easy one to fake, even if its illegitimate use is
considered a war crime under the Geneva Convention.

According to François Bugnion,

> There is every reason to believe that the October 1863 Conference
> did not have the slightest intention of conferring any religious sig-
> nificance whatsoever on the distinctive sign for medical services,
> and was not in the least conscious that any religious significance
> could be attached to the emblem, since the very aim of the founders
> of the Red Cross was to set up an institution which would transcend
> national and religious frontiers.[57]

The ICRC did not need to confer religious significance on the red cross
because it already possessed it. Appia wanted a symbol "the mere
sight of which" would stir the spirit of common humanity, and the
cross, the pivotal Protestant icon, was an obvious answer.[58] Choosing

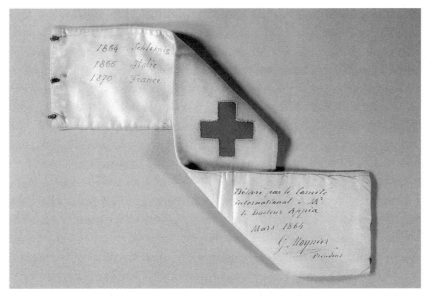

Fig. 3. The original red cross armband first worn by Dr. Louis Appia in Schleswig in 1864, signed by Gustave Moynier. © ICRC / Thierry Gassmann, 1996.

the cross, oversight or not, linked the ICRC into its natural Christian community, providing continuity between the church and the secular future, thus reassuring potential supporters that the organization's unstated values were those of Christian civilization. If it proved politically awkward, its underlying effect was precisely to further the European moral power of which Christianity remained a vital component. This had serious negative consequences, with allegations that Turk soldiers fighting Serbs in the Balkans in 1876 actually targeted and mutilated those wearing a Christian symbol of holy war.[59] The Ottoman Empire unilaterally informed the ICRC that it would use the red crescent to protect its own forces.[60]

The power of the symbol was clear by 1884 when the International Committee renamed itself "of the Red Cross" and not, as it had been, "for the Assistance to Sick and Wounded Soldiers." In other words, the sacred totem (innocent suffering) was now fully substitutable by its symbolic representation.[61] Henceforth the ICRC would be as much about protecting the sacred symbol as the victims of war. Like a modern brand, this symbol could now migrate to people and things at great distances, hugely leveraging the moral power of the original suffering. It is for this reason, after the red crescent fait accompli, that the ICRC has tried so hard to prevent proliferation. The introduction of a "Red Crystal" in 2005, in the third additional protocol to the Geneva Conventions, was to avoid problems with Red Cross societies who had their own national symbols (in particular the red Star of David in Israel), which couldn't be used internationally, the Geneva Convention until then recognizing only the red cross and red crescent. The Israeli Red Cross (Magen David Adom) joined the international movement in 2006 using the red Star of David inside the red crystal at the international level.[62] The fact that a seemingly meaningless symbol (a crystal) can be given moral significance because the ICRC anoints it is a further sign of secular sacred power. Even association with other humanist logos like that of the UN has been met with skepticism by the ICRC, concerned not to pollute the purity of the cross.[63]

On the surface this purity has a functional rationale: to protect various categories of people and installations in armed conflict.[64] In the case of deliberate unsanctioned use (rather than abuse) of the red cross symbol, the position is that "misuse in 'good faith' in armed conflict also has grave and easily imagined consequences, for it blurs the lines between those entitled by international humanitarian law to signify their protection by displaying the emblem, and those who are not entitled to do so."[65] International humanitarian law (IHL) is cited here as a primary authority, but this has the relationship the wrong way round. Rolle and Lafontaine argue: "It is important to bear in mind that international humanitarian law—and not the emblem itself—grants protection to the persons or objects displaying the emblem. Yet the emblem is the visible manifestation of such protection, which explains why the present article refers to its 'protective value.' "[66] This is an excellent example of social magic at work: in truth the totem empowered the symbol, which gave moral authority to the law. And now the law is held to be the source of primary authority. This encapsulates the process of constructing moral authority in order to replace an ailing god with human law.

There is a paradox in vigorously policing the red cross symbol. The more the ICRC curtails good-faith usage, the more valuable misuse becomes.[67] Because the red cross symbol is so easy to replicate, it is the integrity of the sacred thing rather than its functional effect that is really the issue. Dilution could *reduce* the prospect of misuse because the symbol is less trusted, but that in turn allows its symbolic power to wane. It needs to be used sparingly and with ceremony, the plain red cross, the tangible totem, restricted by the Geneva Convention to the battlefield (and proximity to raw suffering). There are decades of agonized analysis about using the cross, to which was added a further and exhaustive "Emblem Study" submitted to the ICRC's Council of Delegates in 2009.[68] We can see the sacred quality of the cross clearly in discussions about associating it with commercial activities to raise funds by national Red Cross societies, even the use by these societies themselves tightly regulated by the ICRC. Invoking the Geneva Convention, the ICRC polices a distinction between "protective" and "indicative" use (the indicative use—branding and identity—powerful only because of the protective use). Sacred objects are cordoned off and hemmed in by prohibitions, and even a cursory glance at the ICRC's huge discourse and rule book about emblem use shows we are in a realm beyond the functional. The ICRC controls use of the church's most powerful symbol.

The red cross was a stroke of genius as far as secular iconography was concerned. It was tied from the start to a second concept, *neutrality*—the use of moral authority to cordon off a sanctuary within political space. Neutralization was, in 1864, at the core of the diplomatic conference established to create the Geneva Convention and central to many of its articles. The point was made explicitly that wearing the red cross on an armband was a sign of neutrality.[69]

The ICRC's victim was an archetype, to be "regarded merely as a suffering human being" without country, affiliation, or politics, said Moynier.[70] These claims to be impartial and neutral but not religious were pioneering in a secular idiom (religious organizations like the Quakers had made similar claims to be politically neutral). Although ideas about neutrality in warfare and in soldiers' field manuals were familiar by 1863, as Bugnion points out, the ICRC founders made a decisive contribution by their commitment to permanent organization on an international basis in a range of practical ways.[71] This was Adam Smith's moral spectator made real—what, to paraphrase Georg Jellinek, we might call the "normative power of the factual."[72] Before long the ICRC's imperative was as much a matter of protecting what gave the church itself value: the totem vested in the cross, neutrality, and the Geneva Convention. In 1898 Moynier described the committee's "main function" as "to safeguard the fundamental interests of the Red Cross" even if this put it in opposition to national Red Cross societies (in this case the Spanish Red Cross).[73] In the dispute over the Red Cross movement's future after 1919, the ICRC would make it clear it was the guardian of the fundamental principles of the Red Cross, a mission Gustave Ador equated to "safeguarding the principles of humanity."[74] This self-appointed role as "custodians of the sacred fire" particularly incensed the huge American Red Cross led by J. P. Morgan banker Henry P. Davison who was closely aligned with US president Woodrow Wilson.[75] But the ICRC prevailed. It maintained its structural estrangement from political life, its all-Swiss membership defended as a means to that end, making it a trusted intermediary and keeper of secrets, as Georg Simmel predicted.[76] One of those secrets would be the Holocaust.

Globalizing Humanism

Gustave Moynier was a central figure in the group of international lawyers who, in 1873, set up the Institut de Droit international (IDI), a permanent institution to further the "scientific" study of international law as "the legal conscience of the civilized world."[77] This gathering too was deeply bourgeois, its members searching for the law's source by examining their own consciences, confident—in the way that only the self-authorizing modern bourgeois could be—that their own views represented objective truths (most IDI members were active Protestants).[78] Examining their own consciences would lead them to stress moral character as a critical variable, with their own moral characters, unsurprisingly, as the ideal.[79]

Disappointed that conscience backed by public opinion had not enforced the Geneva Convention during the Franco-Prussian War, the real public proving to be bellicose and belligerent, Moynier pressed for an independent international court of arbitration, established by treaty, that would force compliance with the convention and mount prosecutions for crimes against it.[80] Moynier's idea was an international court that would try *individuals*, not states, for in his humanist naiveté he was skeptical civilized states would commit unlawful acts.[81] This was a major step in the direction of an international criminal court for war crimes.

Other public lawyers objected to the idea, but a critical mass supported the fallback proposal of a standing council of international jurists, "without Pope or infallibility," to promote international law and provide expert commentary on the laws of war. This was the Institut de Droit international.[82] Allied to the Geneva Convention (amended in 1906) and the Hague Treaties of 1899 and 1907, this structure was the foundation of modern international humanitarian, human rights, and justice law. The canonical statement referring to the "laws of humanity" in the 1899 Hague Convention preamble by IDI member and Russian Red Cross delegate Fyodor Martens encapsulated this new regime. His claim in 1879 that "protection of the individual is the ultimate purpose of the State and goal of international relations" is as clear an assertion of human rights as one could hope for.[83]

After fifty tumultuous years it would be the First World War that finally established the ICRC as a permanent global moral authority. While governments during the war questioned the ICRC's activities and the validity of some of its demands, few challenged the ICRC's right to criticize state practice.[84] For its guardianship of the Geneva Convention and its Prisoners of War Agency it was awarded the Nobel Peace Prize in 1917. In addition, Article 25 of the League of Nations Covenant formally committed the League to "encourage and promote" national Red Cross societies to improve health, prevent disease, and contribute to "the mitigation of suffering."[85] The Red Cross even escaped Bolshevik opprobrium toward the "league of bourgeois robbers" that had rejected it for membership and received Lenin's assent to continue working in the Soviet Union (despite its prior aristocratic associations).[86]

In this moment of unprecedented institutional innovation, the League of Nations towered above everything else. The international finally had its epiphany, its "constitutional moment." Ideas about limits to sovereignty like rights, democracy, and the customs of war had been plentiful previously, but here, come at last, was tangible and permanent institutional reality: buildings, bureaucracy, authority, money, law. Political capital now flowed within this new forum for managing global order, the first truly international organization authorized explicitly by the idea of humanity, not the Christian god nor the divine right of kings and emperors nor imperial notions of manifest destiny. The League was a "permanent, transnational, institutional, and secular regime for understanding and addressing the root causes of suffering."[87] As such it was the fountainhead for ambitious global governance structures that the ICRC and the Red Cross pioneered. It gave rise to collective security and efforts at disarmament, financial regulation, and a Permanent Court of International Justice; to UNESCO, the ILO, and the WHO (a direct descendant of Red Cross work); to a system for institutionalizing the responsibility of civilizing colonial peoples and to committees on opium eradication and women and child trafficking. All would now revolve around the secular papacy at Geneva, enthroned in its purpose-built palace, chosen rather than the more martial Paris because of its "spiritual orientation" (Carl Schmitt would later quote the writer Paul Guggenheim to the effect that the city of Calvin, Rousseau, and the "International Red Cross" was a city "whose spiritual fate was so closely tied to the world of the Anglo-Saxon democracies"[88]). The League was, in the words of its first chronicler, "a more or less direct and successful attempt to begin building a world society."[89]

At the core of this new humanitarian cathedral was the idea of *protection*. The League took on the role of protector for the complex of "civilized values" imperiled both by liberal humanism's troubled relations with alternative belief systems (communism, Islam) and its internal contradictions (war, disease, poverty, refugees). That complex was anchored, as I have argued, on a gendered idea of existential innocence, an idea that today is more often termed "dignity." After 1920, child welfare, prostitution, and the trafficking of women and children was immediately a concern.[90] Much work was done on reintegrating orphans and on reconstructing fractured family relations. In sum, the League was a new institutional form for protecting civilization. As missionary activity went into decline, the League took up the torch, advocates moving effortlessly from their religious idiom into that of welfare and development precisely because at the roots of this secular shift was cultural Christianity centered on the innocent child.

British prime minister David Lloyd George saw the League as a bulwark against the atheistic Bolsheviks, prevailing with President Wilson against those like Winston Churchill and French prime minister Georges Clemenceau who wanted to invade Russia. Lloyd George described the League as an "effective guardian of international right and international liberty throughout the world."[91] South African prime minister Jan Smuts called it a "great caravan of humanity."[92] Underlying this humanist enthusiasm was, nevertheless, a determination to maintain the structures of power that were integral to the European imperial project. Mark Mazower's verdict: the League was an "eminently Victorian institution" designed to carry out a "global civilizing mission through the use of international law."[93] Alfred Zimmern, an early international relations theorist and a significant influence on the League of Nations, could not see this. He advocated a multinational commission to look "at the problem from the point of view of the world as a whole," without comprehending that it was just another version of the same bourgeois-Christian civilizing project made "legitimate" because it was promoted by an international organization (although one still dominated by Europeans).[94] The reality can be seen in the League's dealings with the Ottoman Empire and in the racist attitudes—by no means unique—of League of Nations commissioner Karen Jeppe toward Islam and the Turks in her work to rescue Armenian women and children enslaved by Ottoman officers and soldiers.[95]

These were fledgling days for advocates of protection, prevention, and prosecution. Too little was known, too few experts existed, and too many vested interests were involved to mobilize major intervention. The most serious efforts at prosecution were led by Lloyd George and Clemenceau, who wanted the German kaiser, in exile in the Netherlands, tried as a war criminal.[96] The British also went some way toward prosecuting the Turks for the mass killing of Armenians, and it was in relation to this charge that the phrase "crimes against humanity" was first used.[97] The essence of modernity, that human beings, not god, were responsible for their own progress and suffering, meant responsibility and blame became part of the lexicon of humanitarian politics. The innocent and the hero were joined by the perpetrator. Carl Schmitt attributed this critical departure to Articles 228–230 of the Treaty of Versailles, which ordered defeated states to hand over their nationals *as individuals* for trial.[98] This was a portent of things to come. The call for an international criminal court first made by Moynier was now taken up by others. In the 1920s it was made by René Cassin—a major figure in the drafting of the Universal Declaration of Human Rights in 1948—as it was in the 1930s by the prominent international legal scholar Hersch Lauterpacht.[99]

While the League lost its political battle to preserve a peaceful global order, its early efforts at "global governance" were more long-lasting. What was initially a bewildering mix of organizations, movements, and cultures formed itself slowly into a more orderly set of professional disciplines, with the League at its core. Within humanism, the split between humanitarianism, human rights, and international justice began to embed itself in more formal legal and institutional identities. During and after the war, the ICRC and Red Cross societies led the way in extending protection. Attention to suffering in civil wars (e.g., in Russia)[100] and to the persecution of political prisoners added to the efforts the ICRC had made to visit prisoners and mediate civilian suffering during the war.[101] The ICRC's work on internees, hostages, and deportees was as much about civilians as prisoners.[102]

What we would now call "human rights" was integral to these efforts, the work Amnesty International began in 1961 little different from the ICRC's work on political prisoners except for the peacetime/wartime distinction, which broke down anyway in civil conflict. The ICRC had in reality done prisoner work since 1870, concerned even then with "the protection of man against the absolute power of an enemy."[103] This move into civil forms of armed conflict was accompanied by an emphasis not just on wounded combatants but on the humane treatment of all victims. Policy for this followed, rather than preceded, action, and by 1938 the ICRC explicitly mentioned its assistance for "political prisoners," a core human rights concern. In Hungary in 1919, the ICRC's work had been mainly about political prisoners and civilians.[104] Although language about civilians did not make it into 1949's four Geneva Conventions, common Article 3 did open a space for human rights work on political prisoners in civil wars in terms, for example, of fair trials and humane treatment.[105] It also forbade "outrages upon personal dignity." These protections were extended to international war in 1977's Additional Protocol 1, Article 75.[106]

By 1919, the ICRC was increasingly empowered as the self-appointed guardian of the Geneva and Hague regimes and was able to function as a moral fountainhead for emerging humanist institutions. The founding of the Save the Children Fund International Union illustrates this. The Save the Children Fund, founded in 1919 by British sisters Eglantyne Jebb and Dorothy Buxton, raised money to feed children in Europe without discrimination as to nationality (including German and Austrian children, therefore).[107] Jebb was fully aware of the "fund-raising potential in starving children."[108] The "neutrality" in which she believed, based, said Jebb, on our status as human beings first and national citizens second, allied her closely with the ICRC, and she traveled immediately to Geneva to set up the International Union with ICRC support.[109] Gustave Ador was on the board, and ICRC delegate George Werner chaired the union's executive committee, Jebb recognizing the ICRC as the supreme coordinating authority for child relief work.[110] To extend "our duties to all the children of the world," Jebb then wrote a Declaration of the Rights of the Child to provide a more solid basis for her demands. This was read out by Ador from the transmitter of the Eiffel Tower in 1923 and then endorsed by the League of Nations.[111] Although in content this declaration was as much about welfare as rights, it provided a formalized international "constitution" for child protection and was the first rights charter of its kind endorsed by the world's first international organization.

After 1919, the lifeworld of nineteenth-century bourgeois European Christians became the basis for an international governance system that was considered universal, secular, and absolute. The reach of this system was to be total. "The rationalism of the Enlightenment rejected the exception in every form," as Carl Schmitt put it.[112] The space for non-state social action widened with the decline and then collapse of the European empires. The fledgling legal regimes of Geneva and The Hague, of crimes against humanity and of human rights, would become after 1945 three separate streams of legal and judicial activity (1945, Nuremberg; 1948, UDHR and the Genocide Convention; and 1949, the amended Geneva Conventions). Different law meant different legal cases and precedents that over time created more specialized lawyers, until these institutions of the law had taken on an independent life of their own. A generation of post-1945 international jurisprudential advocates oversaw this system, seeking to advance international humanitarian, human rights, and justice law on all fronts until, after 1989, their moment arrived to reintegrate.

This humanist regime's moral power had come from suffering, from Dunant and from Jebb "saving the soul of the world."[113] At its root were bourgeois cultural archetypes: victim, hero, good, evil. The law was the totem institutionalized. Globalizing this law after 1920 meant creating a "metanarrative," an account that anchored law in the deep moral truth of innocent suffering. Only with this metanarrative could resources be mobilized and pity give way to retribution. To make the metanarrative effective it also had to be *authentic*. Courts, conventions, rights declarations, agencies, and the accumulated narrative and visual material that tells the human rights story are all symbols of immutable authenticity set out *against* history. They speak to the timeless, the infinite and absolute. The pivotal event in this metanarrative is the Holocaust.

3   THE HOLOCAUST METANARRATIVE

Until the Holocaust, international humanism's attention had been on dying, not killing. Pity and compassion meant not apportioning blame. Wounds were detached from their causes, just as victims were detached from the reasons for their persecution. This was the theory, at least. In reality, Red Cross societies had become thoroughly nationalized as auxiliaries of their own militaries by the time of the First World War.[1] The ICRC, by contrast, absorbed the lesson of detachment so well it was incapable of dealing with the moral challenge of Nazism and the extermination of the Jews and remained silent to protect its own (and Swiss) neutrality.[2] Punishment for inflicting suffering had always been an option, as Moynier's abortive plan for an international criminal court showed. And as casualties became "victims," by definition unjustly attacked, perpetrators entered the picture. Like victims, perpetrators were treated as individuals by the law, reinforcing the idea of a humanity beneath identity by deemphasizing the political and cultural context of killing.

The ICRC's Holocaust failure was symptomatic of a deeper collapse in Enlightenment ideals and bourgeois self-confidence.[3] Fears of modernity's dark side had been fully realized, undermining any European claims to be the vanguard of civilization.[4] None of the developments associated with humanism, whether law, humanitarian practice, rights, criminal justice, or international organization, had prevented the deliberate murder of six million Jews and millions of others right in the heart of Europe. The Prussian state that had been so prominent a supporter of the ICRC was part of a Nazi empire that had committed unparalleled crimes. Something more radical was needed to repair the gaping wound in Europe's moral fabric. Whereas previously Dunant's form of witnessing implicated us all in suffering, a legacy of the Christian idea of original sin, the Holocaust was a crime of such magnitude, a crime that exploded "the limits of the law," that it could not be integrated within humanist ideology.[5] The racist nature of the Holocaust, during which civilized Europeans had deliberately murdered millions of Jews, unveiled in brutal fashion the race prejudice deep in European culture. The Holocaust had to be *externalized* as a breakdown in modernity, not *conceded* as one of modernity's potential inner contradictions.[6] The answer was to portray the Nazis as *beyond* civilization—that is, as evil.

Unsurprisingly, humanists, products of imperial Europe, faced intensifying resistance as the empires imploded. Postcolonial writers and leaders urged political and ideological liberation from the metanarrative of Europe-led moral progress, while postmodern authors argued there was in reality no "ultimate meaning," no singular hidden secret to find in ethical, scientific, and cultural life.[7] They sought to undermine the authority of secular monotheism, the European "Author-God" who insisted history had one meaning only.[8] This critique contained the seeds of a transition from the classic secular religious conception of humanism to a new foundation that emerged in the 1970s under American tutelage. Human rights advocates, prevented from capitalizing on the Holocaust for thirty years by the Cold War, would then reverse engineer their argument for enduring progress by claiming that Auschwitz and Nuremberg had been the start of a steady, final climb toward global justice.

Recent historical scholarship on human rights and its origins has proved this triumphalist metanarrative to be of doubtful accuracy by pointing out anomalies, contingencies, manipulations, and contradictions.[9] And yet despite such persuasive critiques, the metanarrative persists. Empirical refutation is not an effective way to challenge moral beliefs anchored in deep culture. Doubt strengthens the resolution of advocates by triggering emotional and cognitive defenses. The humanist international model is built on keeping alive *the indivisible truth* present in the eyes of the innocent child and embedded in the law. What is being protected is faith in transcendental humanism along with the power of those who claim to be its privileged interpreters.

Auschwitz and Nuremberg

Investigations into war crimes and crimes against humanity committed by Turkey and Germany after 1914 had produced two institutional innovations: first, the phrase itself, "crimes against humanity," gave the Martens Clause's "laws of humanity" more potential to mobilize political power; and second, the move to hold individuals accountable *as individuals* began to erode protection for acts undertaken in the name of the state.[10] Failure in the interwar years to embed international organization or justice as a constraint on state violence weighed on those who sought to build a new peace in 1945. The true importance of Nuremberg's International Military Tribunal, in particular, was understood by men like chief Allied counsel and Supreme Court justice Robert Jackson, who called it "an exercise in the reconstitution of the law, an act staged not simply to punish extreme crimes but to demonstrate visibly the power of the law to submit the most horrific outrages to its sober ministrations . . . the trial was to serve as a spectacle of legality, making visible both the crimes of the Germans and the sweeping neutral authority of the law."[11]

The years 1945–1949 would be the last time Europe held such a central place in the design of world order. It was a last moment to embed the humanist dream before the empires were gone. Institutionalizing universal, secular, and categorical norms had various elements: first, the tribunals at Nuremberg and Tokyo (1945 and 1946); second, the Genocide Convention and the Universal Declaration of Human Rights (1948); and third, the revised Geneva Conventions of 1949. For both Nuremberg and the Geneva Conventions, the Martens Clause formed an essential precedent and component.[12] The United Nations, legitimated by the idea of universal and secular norms but based in the United States, would only assume a leading role much later on.

Nuremberg and the Holocaust, exemplified by Auschwitz, have become seminal representations of mass atrocity and justice, of the wound and the law. Kerwin Lee Klein argues that a central aspect of memory politics is the relationship between memory as "the return of the repressed" and memory as "the belated response to the great trauma of modernity, the *Shoah*."[13] These two ways of seeing memory can be fitted together, memory functioning as both a form of re-enchantment against postmodernism, emphasizing the ineffable or unsayable or some other mystery-laden absolute, and a way for the traumatized to make their suffering palpable.[14]

For us, in 2013, Auschwitz and Nuremberg have indelible cultural markers. For Auschwitz, overcrowded railway wagons, the "Arbeit Macht Frei" sign, selection ramps, lines of doomed Jewish victims and the "gate of death" at Auschwitz-Birkenau, piles of suitcases, shoes, and hair, striped uniforms and barbed wire, all set against the backdrop of wooden huts arranged in rows on the barren, wintry landscape of occupied Poland. Nuremberg, meanwhile, is known mostly through a photograph of the two rows of defendants, with Hermann Goering at the front and first in the row next to Rudolf Hess, most wearing translation headsets, the courtroom before them packed with lawyers, desks, and piles of paper, behind them a phalanx of white-hatted military policemen standing at ease.

The images are iconic now, but the Holocaust was slow to embed itself in public culture. Aryeh Neier, cofounder of Human Rights Watch and a child émigré from Germany in the 1930s, recalls:

Today the bookshelves of my apartment in New York City are laden with books about the Holocaust—diaries, memoirs, biographies, histories, polemics and a few novels—but they include only a handful of works published in the 1940s and 1950s. Though I was not aware of the absence at the time, in retrospect I find it bizarre and now believe that it contributed to a somewhat distorted political consciousness in which I failed until much later to appreciate the nature and extent of evil in the twentieth century.[15]

In fact there was general indifference throughout these decades to the Holocaust and its survivors.[16] Even in Israel the integration of survivors took second place to nation building and the independence wars. It was the trial of Adolf Eichmann in 1961 that elevated the status of survivors to that of a bridge between the European past and Israel.[17] Before Eichmann's trial, *The Diary of Anne Frank* (as a book in English in 1952, a play in 1955, and a movie in 1959) had been the most influential source for raising Holocaust awareness.

Fig. 4. The Gate of Death at Auschwitz-Birkenau through which as many as a million Jews passed to be murdered in underground gas chambers. © Michael Zacharz, 2006, Creative Commons.

It was precisely how *little* attention had been given at Nuremberg to the suffering of the Jews as the main targets of Nazi extermination policies that led Israeli prime minister David Ben-Gurion to "orchestrate" Eichmann's 1961 trial.[18] Israeli attorney general Gideon Hausner, who led the prosecution, characterized the trial as in part an antidote to Nuremberg. It would allow the Jews who had suffered to at last be heard, privileging testimony over documentation in order to "reach the hearts of men" and let survivors tell their story.[19] Deborah Lipstadt argues it was the constant use of the term "Holocaust" by Israeli translators and American journalists during the trial, rather than *Shoah*, or "catastrophe" in Hebrew, that introduced it into the public lexicon (giving a significant boost to the sacralizing process by encompassing this long and complex genocide under a single, unforgettable name).[20] Before then, says Peter Novick, the Holocaust was seen as "history." It had not yet "attained the transcendent status as the bearer of eternal truths or lessons that could be derived from contemplating it."[21] The Eichmann trial separated out "the Holocaust" as something distinct from the rest of Nazi barbarism.[22]

Fig. 5. The Nuremberg International Military Tribunal Courtroom, 1945. Hermann Goering is in the bottom left corner of the dock. © United States Holocaust Memorial Museum.

The killing of six million Jews became the holocaust and then The Holocaust. Anything that comes into contact with suffering on this scale absorbs some of its "extraordinary contagiousness," augmenting the event's sanctity by reinforcing the "extreme strictness of the prohibitions" that protect it from pollution by the profane.[23] The moral authority of survivors is the ultimate example of this sacred power: as the Holocaust became an increasingly resonant feature of American public culture, from the 1970s onward, so it was available for political deployment by human rights advocates in the United States and elsewhere.[24] Khmer Rouge atrocities in Cambodia, widely covered in the international media, soon provided a contemporary example of genocide, with gruesome pictures and commentary to match. In 1979 Médecins Sans Frontières (MSF) demanded action to help starving Cambodians by comparing indifference to famine with silence about Auschwitz.[25] Indeed, Holocaust memory was a vital formative influence on the "third-worldists" and "sans-frontiérists" in postwar France; the latter changed the direction of humanitarian action with the founding in 1971 of MSF with its closer association between human rights and humanitarianism.[26] Auschwitz was made a UNESCO World Heritage Site in 1979.[27]

With the end of the Cold War, the cultural power of the Holocaust and Nuremberg could be used to aid in the globalization of international criminal law. Richard Goldstone, a pivotal figure in this development, argues that "the most permanent, important and unique feature of the Holocaust is that it gave birth to the international human rights movement and the recognition of an international jurisdiction for the prosecution of war criminals."[28] This is a classic retrofitting of the meta-narrative. He goes on:

> If future perpetrators of genocide, crimes against humanity, and serious war crimes are brought to justice and appropriately punished then the millions of innocent victims who perished in the Holocaust will not have died in vain. Their memory will remain alive and they will be remembered when future war criminals are brought to justice. And, it is certainly not too much to hope that efficient justice will also serve to deter war crimes in the future and so protect the untold numbers of potential victims.[29]

David Scheffer, US ambassador-at-large for war crimes in the 1990s, titles his memoir's first chapter "An Echo of Nuremberg," while on page one of the preface to his book *Humanity: A Moral History of the Twentieth Century*, Jonathan Glover begins with Nazi crimes and Auschwitz.[30] The ex-president of Médecins Sans Frontières, James Orbinski, writes at length about the impact that television pictures of the Holocaust, and meeting survivors, had on him as a young man.[31] Geoffrey Robertson, meanwhile, calls Nuremberg "a colossus in the development of international human rights law":

> The spontaneous drama of the courtroom provided the defining moment of de-Nazification on the afternoon when the prosecutor showed newsreels of Auschwitz and Belsen, and the defendants, spotlit for security in the dock, averted their eyes in horror from the ghastly screen images of the emaciated inmates of their concentration camps. Some sobbed, others sweated, or put their heads in their

hands; they sat in stunned silence until the court rose, their individual and collective guilt and shame brought home to them for ever and beyond reasonable doubt.[32]

Robertson's speculative imputation of "shame" reinforces the metanarrative through the idea that, confronted with their crimes, even Nazis realized they were wrong.[33] At other moments a gloating Goering got the better of the prosecution and particularly Justice Jackson, even taunting the Supreme Court justice at one point that his questions were too broad and inconclusive.[34] When the defendants watched the film *The Nazi Plan*, which included footage of Nazi rallies, they had an altogether more enthusiastic reaction.[35]

Johannes Morsink goes even further than Goldstone and Robertson. For the drafters of the Universal Declaration of Human Rights (UDHR), he says, their experience of the Second World War was "the epistemic foundation of the rights in question."[36] It is moral repulsion, not Enlightenment truths, that lie behind the UDHR, he says, its justification to be found in "shared abhorrence of what the Nazis did to their victims." He adds: "To see the truths of the Declaration, we need to listen to those who tell the story of the Holocaust."[37] Samuel Moyn argues, in contrast, "There was no widespread Holocaust consciousness in the postwar era, so human rights could not have been a response to it."[38] The supreme charge the defendants at Nuremberg faced was waging aggressive war.[39] G. Daniel Cohen takes a position between Morsink and Moyn, arguing that the postwar human rights regime was "loosely Holocaust-centric," becoming the first "*international* site of Holocaust remembrance."[40]

A Task Force for International Cooperation on Holocaust Education, Remembrance, and Research established in 1998 through the efforts of former Swedish prime minister Göran Persson publicized what has become known as the Stockholm Declaration, whose first (of eight) principles is

The Holocaust (Shoah) fundamentally challenged the foundations of civilization. The unprecedented character of the Holocaust will always hold universal meaning. After half a century, it remains an event close enough in time that survivors can still bear witness to the horrors that engulfed the Jewish people. The terrible suffering of the many millions of other victims of the Nazis has left an indelible scar across Europe as well.[41]

This statement could have been written in 1948 not 1998, right down to the remarkable phrase "foundations of civilization," a calling card for European dreams of old. Building on this declaration, UN Secretary-General Kofi Annan explicitly tied the Holocaust to the UDHR (rather than "civilization") in a speech at the first-ever UN Conference on Anti-Semitism in 2004.[42] The UN General Assembly then passed a 2005 resolution designating January 27 (the day Auschwitz was liberated) as an international day of commemoration of the victims of the Holocaust, encouraging member governments to set up national education programs and requiring the secretary-general to establish a United Nations Holocaust outreach program.[43] This resolution, timed to coincide with the sixtieth anniversary of the liberation of the camps and the defeat of the Nazis, drew explicit links between the Holocaust, the UDHR, and the Genocide Convention.

The political effect of deeper international institutionalization added to the moral pressure on decision makers to invoke the Genocide Convention and intervene in places like Sudan. A large and influential "Save Darfur" coalition in the United States lobbied hard to get the conflict in Darfur recognized as genocide.[44] When Secretary of State Colin Powell did so in 2004 (after the first ever "genocide emergency" alert issued by the United States Holocaust Memorial Museum), it pushed the conflict higher in American foreign policy priorities.[45] Once a regime is accused of genocide, and its leaders by association with the Nazis are labeled "evil," there is no room for compromise. The whole conflict takes place in a kind of sacred space where moral absolutes clash, a place "without history and without politics."[46] In 2010 chief ICC prosecutor Ocampo successfully applied for the charge of genocide against Sudan president Omar al-Bashir, despite the fact that an investigation by Antonio Cassese in Sudan in 2004 for Secretary-General Annan had found the government had *not* pursued a policy of genocide ("intent" was the issue—allegations of crimes against humanity that Cassese's report did substantiate having no such threshold).[47] In 2013 the Save Darfur website in its primer on Darfur still refers to genocide committed by the Sudanese government and the *janjaweed*.[48]

From the 1970s onward, the Holocaust has been part of a critique of totalitarian regimes in the United States that legitimated an expansionist American foreign policy in favor of liberal democracy. Given the role the Holocaust has played in American culture since that time, the fact that the engagement of US policymakers with R2P has also been through the frame of genocide is unsurprising (even given Senate ambivalence).[49] If genocide is the crime of crimes at the global level it is also, in terms of the resonance that Jewish survivors and Israel continue to have in American public life, a crime whose imagery is typically drawn from the example of the Holocaust. In 2007 a Genocide Prevention Task Force cosponsored by the USHMM was set up in Washington, DC, chaired by former secretary of state Madeleine Albright and former secretary of defense William Cohen. In its 2008 report, *Preventing Genocide*, the task force touches immediately on key elements of the sacred metanarrative by dedicating the report to "the millions of innocent children, women, and men who have suffered and died from mass atrocities and genocide," by using the phrase "never again," as well as explicitly honoring "the memory of past victims of genocide" by preventing future ones.[50] It begins with a nuanced account of the relationship between the sacred and the profane:

> Some we see; others remain invisible to us. Some have names and faces; others we do not know. We speak of the victims of genocide and mass atrocities, their numbers too staggering to count. . . . Individual lives—disrupted, damaged, and lost forever—are never far from our minds as we write this report. By its nature, a blueprint for U.S. policymakers must be concrete to be credible. Inevitably, it must confront the challenges of bureaucracies and budgets, policies and political will. But we must never lose sight of the evil inherent in the subject matter and the human beings who suffer as a result of that evil.[51]

The report identifies "genocide and mass atrocities" as a threat to American values and interests as well as "a direct assault on universal human values, including, most fundamentally, the right to life."[52] In August 2011 the report's core recommendation for better coordination within the US government to prevent atrocities was met as President Obama created an Atrocities Prevention Board to encourage interagency cooperation.[53] This board, chaired by Samantha Power, the president's top human rights ad-viser and author of *A Problem from Hell*, was formally launched on April 23, 2012, at the USHMM, with the aim of making "never again" a reality, said Mr. Obama.[54] Vice President Joe Biden had in February 2011 linked the task force, R2P in Libya, "never again" and the Holocaust at a speech at the USHMM in honor of recently deceased congressman Tom Lantos, a Holocaust survivor.[55] Secretary of State Hillary Clinton and UN Ambas-sador Susan Rice, along with the longtime humanitarian intervention ad-vocate Samantha Power, applied significant pressure on President Obama to intervene in Libya in 2011 in the name of human rights.

The Sacred Metanarrative

"Auschwitz stands for the Holocaust and the Holocaust for the evil of a century," argues Timothy Snyder.[56] For Didier Fassin and Richard Rech-tman, "the memory of the Holocaust is clearly the starting point for the contemporary manifestation of collective trauma in the public arena."[57] This trauma is a "testament to the unspeakable," the hope of survivors and their advocates that "giving form to the memory would . . . leave a kind of moral trace in the collective consciousness that should prevent humanity from repeating its horrific mistake."[58] Trauma was raw mate-rial for the metanarrative, the journey from savagery to civilization that UDHR co-drafter, committed Christian, and Heidegger student Charles Malik called the "modernizing of the world."[59] This metanarrative is

> All persons have inalienable rights as individuals by virtue of their mere existence as humans; they have always had those rights; all legitimate moral claims must recognize those rights; denial of those rights is a crime that must be prevented or punished; not punishing the perpetrators of such crimes will lead to future atrocities like the Holocaust. This truth must be defended.

The metanarrative's main function is to strengthen the faith of advo-cates and mobilize support for a global legal, judicial, and policing infrastructure. The religious language of evil has become as much a part of the complex of "secular sacredness" as innocent suffering. Evil, too, combats "disenchantment" by connecting us to the life beyond. The virulent attack on Hannah Arendt for portraying Adolf Eichmann as a bureaucratic functionary lacking moral imagination rather than as a monster, and for drawing attention to the ways Jewish councils negotiated with the Nazis, can be explained by this sense that the crimes of the Holocaust are diminished if the cruelty, as well as the suffering, are reduced in stature.[60] The use of religious imagery associated with evil is ubiquitous in humanist culture (*Shake Hands with the Devil, A Problem from Hell, All the Missing Souls, Deliver Us from Evil, Hope in Hell*).[61] It was part of Arendt's concern to characterize the Nazis as criminals, not as part of a world-shattering transcendent struggle between archetypes, whence her book's infamous subtitle, *The Banality of Evil*.

Creating the metanarrative is no longer a question of facts. There is incontrovertible evidence of the systematic killing by Nazi Germany of up to six million Jews, a million of whom were gassed at Auschwitz, while millions more were killed at other extermination camps and in the "bloodlands" between the Nazis and the Soviets.[62] There is a vast trove of empirical material verifying this reality. But facts still belong to the profane human world. They must be transferred to the sacred world through reification, placed beyond question and interpretation, at once historicized *and* de-historicized. In this way the horror and cruelty they contain can be "sacralized" and the metanarrative reinforced. As with the red cross, once Auschwitz was reified as "Auschwitz" it could be used to increase political leverage and close off contestation. The claim for the Holocaust's "uniqueness," that it is an atrocity without parallel, is reification in action.[63]

Now institutionalized in major museums such as Yad Vashem in Jerusalem, the USHMM, the Berlin Holocaust Memorial to the Murdered Jews of Europe, the Imperial War Museum in London, as well as at Auschwitz and other camps, and widely embedded in elite and popular culture, the Holocaust is retold through a vast array of testimonies, stories, photographs, documentaries, movies, art and writings, camp exhibits and artifacts. As Levy and Sznaider put it: "At the beginning of the third millennium, memories of the Holocaust facilitate the formation of transnational memory cultures, which in turn have the potential to become the cultural foundation for human-rights politics."[64] The Holocaust was again invoked in Bosnia in 1992 as pictures of Bosnian Muslims were broadcast and became critical in generating demands for international criminal trials for Bosnian Serbs.[65] Nobel Prize–winning Holocaust survivor Elie Wiesel publicly called on President Clinton to act in Bosnia at the opening ceremony for the USHMM in 1993.[66] This move toward international justice was an early product of the post–Cold War "peace dividend" that left the United States as sole superpower.

The word "atrocities" in the name of President Obama's prevention board (rather than "crimes against humanity") shows some desire, argues Scott Straus, to move beyond genocide as the sole international crime needing American attention.[67] Genocide creates a deep but rare moral obligation for a state like the United States. Crimes against humanity, in contrast, are more encompassing and cover many acts alleged to have been committed by states considered legitimate, including the United States (the dropping of atomic bombs on Japan, for example). For exactly this reason, crimes against humanity are a more effective legal category for humanists to use against states.[68] They cover more crimes, attach to all persons in peace and war, and do not require either intent or discrimination on the basis of identity.

There is an enduring tension, suppressed by the metanarrative, between crimes against humanity and genocide, and within the category genocide a further tension around the question of whether the Holocaust is an atrocity without equal. Advocates who stress the Holocaust's uniqueness lay the blame for it on anti-Semitism. But the Holocaust's vital importance for humanism means the claim that it is an example of uniquely Jewish suffering needs reworking to give it political utility as an example of what anyone can suffer.[69] The Holocaust has to be a crime *against humanity*, and it was treated this way at first even by Jewish advocates.[70] The Genocide Convention, largely the achievement of Raphael Lemkin, spoke directly to the experience of Jews during the Second World War (his mother died in Auschwitz).[71] But he soon found himself at odds with the framers of the UDHR. They felt his Genocide Convention was the past, harking back to the League of Nations project of protecting minorities though international law; individual human rights and moral exhortation were the future, the US-dominated United Nations much less hospitable to international law than the League had been.[72]

The emphasis on the Holocaust as a uniquely terrible atrocity remains. The Imperial War Museum in London has a large and permanent

Holocaust exhibition, a separate crimes against humanity film lasting thirty minutes, and no genocide exhibition. The USHMM is a Holocaust, not genocide, museum. It pays only minimal attention to Bosnia and Rwanda and is belatedly opening a Cambodia exhibit. The museum's design is intentionally all about the Holocaust, its look deliberately that of Europe in the 1940s. What happened in Rwanda has no dedicated museum in a Western capital city; and why would it? Why not a major memorial in London to genocide in Bosnia, the first European genocide after the Holocaust and the one that reinvigorated international justice mechanisms? Or to the Khmer Rouge killings, the nearest to the Holocaust in organizational ambition and scale?

Just as the Nuremberg trials have received more attention than those in Tokyo, so European assumptions of self-importance made of the Balkans a larger international political issue than Rwanda. In drawing attention to what seemed to be extermination camps in Bosnia, the connection was regularly made to the idea of Europe as the continent that had pledged "never again."[73] This link to Europe's past was even more pronounced after the massacre at Srebrenica, which yielded charges of genocide against Ratko Mladić and Radovan Karadžić. Both the BBC and the *New York Times* described it is as the worst crime in Europe since the Second World War.[74] At the opening of a Srebrenica memorial in 2003, former president Bill Clinton told mourners that Srebrenica was "the beginning of the end of genocide in Europe" because it provided the evidence he needed to press for NATO to bomb the Bosnian Serbs.[75] Holocaust imagery and moral power were also deployed to encourage NATO to intervene in Kosovo in 1999, Ellie Wiesel again urging President Clinton to act. The USHMM's "Committee on Conscience" condemned what was happening in Kosovo, calling Serb attacks on Kosovar Albanians "barbaric and genocidal," and commended NATO for intervening.[76]

This is the Judeo-Christian European story. As the crucible of world politics increasingly moves from Europe toward Asia, the "memory of the world" that Auschwitz represents will seem increasingly parochial, more about Europe's relentless persecution of the Jews than about humanity as a whole. The black-and-white Holocaust in central and eastern Europe is a long way from the Technicolor genocides of Cambodia and Rwanda. In India and China people may legitimately ask: Why is this *my* history?

Were law and norms not what European imperial states used to justify their rule over us?

The Holocaust destroyed the idea that a "civilized conscience" could prevent atrocity or that European modernity was inherently progressive, but even so the efforts made to counter it with human rights law kept Europe front and center. Even now the way we commemorate and idealize atrocity is heavily conditioned by the idea that Europe's memory is the world's. Why is the "Memory of the World Register" at Paris-based UNESCO? Would UNESCO be established in Paris if it was set up today? If not, why is the ICC in The Hague and the United Nations High Commission for Human Rights and the Human Rights Council in Geneva? The answer is presumably a better one than inertia. It must be a variant of: These are the global capitals of justice and peace, existing in space that is neutral and moral, not geographical and social (that is, not European and not middle class). They are in "ICRC space." But does *geopolitical location* really not matter? Only if culture no longer matters. It is humanism's aim, as the ideology of modernity, to transcend culture in the name of the secular, universal, and categorical. So why in global memory culture are the world's non-European atrocities not accorded the same grim status as the mass killings by and in Europe?

Asia has its own legacy of mass atrocity, its own ongoing controversies and conflicts, its own history of war and vast suffering still very much alive in the politics of memory about Western imperialism (including the United States in Indochina), Japanese militarism, Chinese revolutionary transformation, the partition of India, anti-Communism in Indonesia, the killing of Bengalis in Bangladesh in 1971, and the Khmer Rouge. For humanists, the uniqueness of the Holocaust makes sense when the Atlantic is the focus of attention but not when the focus switches to the Indian Ocean and the Pacific. It may suit Asian states to bury aspects of this past for political reasons, but that simply confirms how atrocity culture is European at its core. To take one obvious example, deaths during the famine caused by China's Great Leap Forward between 1958 and 1962 have been estimated at between thirty-six million and forty-five million people, all starved, beaten, or worked to death. In the West, as in China, there is near silence about this largest of all twentieth-century atrocities.[77]

Contesting the Sacred

The human rights crusade takes up where Christianity left off, according to Makau Mutua.[78] He argues: "I know that many in the human rights movement mistakenly claim to have seen a glimpse of eternity, and think of the human rights corpus as a summit of human civilization, a sort of an end to human history. This view is so self-righteous and lacking in humility that it of necessity must invite probing critiques from scholars of all stripes."[79] Far from rethinking the basis of its own authority faced with this sort of rebuke, the humanist international has tended to thrive on its sense of transcendent purpose. In the most famous example, the ICRC did not speak out publicly about the Holocaust, in order to protect its "aura of moral leadership."[80]

Whether or not public or private pressure on the Nazis would have made a difference, the ICRC saw saving itself as necessary, independently of the fate of Europe's Jews. Max Huber, the ICRC's deeply religious president, felt that in a world that no longer respected Christian liberal values, it was more, not less, important the ICRC held on to its "capital of moral trust."[81] In the *International Journal of the Red Cross* of August 1943, the ICRC stressed the importance it attached in its *own* operations to deeds, not words, before calling on all parties to respect "man's natural right to be treated according to the law," a canonical statement of the metanarrative. ICRC member Jacques Chenevière explained the logic of "moral trust" in 1946: "Experience proved that public protests by the ICRC not supported by observations of its own were fruitless, doing more harm than good. In the absence of hard proof they were taken by the accused country as evidence of *a priori* bias, and put at once in jeopardy the other activities the Red Cross was duty bound under the Conventions to carry out."[82] This was reinforced by the claim that "the ICRC has a task on which its very existence depends: everything else, practical issues, are purely accessory. This task is to fight for respect of the Conventions."[83]

Indeed, the ICRC worried that getting involved might be outside the scope of the Geneva Conventions and would amount to only a moral (rather than legal) call to respect the human rights of all civilians. It also agonized over whether intervening specifically on behalf of Jews was discriminatory toward other victims. But the decision not to do more for the Jews, taken at a meeting in Geneva in October 1942, also included a significant intervention by the president of the Swiss Confederation and ICRC member Philippe Etter, determined to avoid exposing Switzerland to potential German attack.[84] More evidence has since come to light of Swiss complicity in the German war effort and in profiteering from the Holocaust, as well as of efforts to prevent Jewish immigration into Switzerland.[85]

By resolving on inaction, the secular church defended itself from contamination. The ICRC's postwar mea culpa is an easy-to-make apology, but it is no guarantee that it would not do the same again.[86] In reality, in 1942 the ICRC did not know who would win the war and still envisaged a role for itself in *any* postwar world, even a Nazi-dominated one. Several people did speak out at the October 1942 meeting for public denunciation and more robust private lobbying of the Nazis. Some argued the ICRC should risk extinction rather than abandon "the very moral and spiritual values on which it had been founded," to quote the most outspoken advocate of denunciation, Marguerite Frick-Cramer.[87] Jean-Claude Favez claims that "the importance the ICRC attached to its credibility took it paradoxically down a road that led to a loss of credibility and therefore of authority within the Red Cross movement and in the wider world."[88] But this is a short-term view. In the end the secular church, and the metanarrative, were saved because neutrality was put ahead of speaking out.

Advocates hold fiercely to the faith that they are doing the secular god's work by globalizing humanism even in the face of stern resistance. Some critics have noted the humanist international's tendency to displace political action, while others have questioned its effectiveness. But the most damaging attack, striking at humanism's core, is to its accountability and moral authority.[89] Advocates who argue they are accountable to their beneficiaries are reiterating the metanarrative, because beneficiaries lack any meaningful way of sanctioning international agencies. A more feasible answer recognizes accountability to law, donors, and public opinion. But this too is fraught: the relationship with donors is heavily conditioned by donor priorities, while for humanist INGOs public opinion is as much shaped as shaping, something in evidence in the funding models (children and mothers in need) that are ubiquitous on the home pages of humanist organizations. And what of the law? Underlying this response is an implicit claim that natural law (that is, morality) is the real justification for action. If we changed the law to make waterboarding legal, humanists would not stop campaigning against it, neither would they see abuses not yet codified into crimes as permissible. The law is secondary to the project of globalizing secular moral authority. It is a symptom and not a cause.

To disguise their lack of accountability, or to put it another way, the fact that the authority humanists claim goes no deeper than their own ideological convictions, advocates and activists embed the metanarrative on every front: condemnations, courts and trials, reports, campaigns, museums, visual images, movies, buildings. They create tangible evidence for Thomas Jefferson's iconic version of the metanarrative in the American Declaration of Independence (1776): "We hold these truths to be self-evident." In other words, human rights are *self-authenticating*. As such they disallow principled challenge. For humanist pioneers, it was enough that they searched their own consciences for the sources of deeper law, "looking inwards, into one's own normative intuitions, whose authority lay in their being those of a person educated in the Western canon."[90] This move silences those critical of the supreme authority of rights. After all, look who is arrayed against you:

> As Grotius, Kelsen, Lauterpacht, Henkin, Franck, and others indicate, there is much about international law that transcends the material, positive acts such as consent. International law's claim to be law is based ultimately on belief. It contains peremptory norms, *jus cogens* principles, that cannot be altered by positive acts, including the norms against genocide, apartheid, extra-judicial killing, slavery, and torture.[91]

But challenges there are. Anthropologist Mark Goodale's analysis of the UDHR asks why "liberal (or neoliberal) legal and political theory should continue to prove so foundational when this political choice is no longer necessary."[92] For Sonia Harris-Short: "If the international law of human rights is to work it needs to be rebuilt from the bottom up—this time with its foundations firmly rooted in all of the world's cultures."[93] These are "human rights" objections and ignore the *political* importance for "Human Rights" of the metanarrative and the moral power that invigorates it. Human Rights are legitimated by the idea of objectivity, not representativeness. As Pierre Schlag argues, this "enables legal think-ers to treat the law as an *authoritative* source that exists independently of the beliefs of the legal (or the wider) community."[94] Too many people are too invested in the metanarrative for it to be abandoned so easily. Judith Shklar noted in 1964 that legalism's analysts have also been "zealous par-tisans and promoters, anxious to secure their moral empire."[95]

The Geneva-based International Council on Human Rights Policy (ICHRP) tries a different tactic: decenter the metanarrative. Accordingly, it accepts that "human rights lie within, rather than outside, the universe of normative systems and culture."[96] This forces the following admission:

> The area of family law is most likely to be governed by plural legal orders, because controlling family and intimate relationships is central to the preservation of collective cultural identity. The report raises the question as to why it has come to be largely accepted, even in human rights circles, that family law may be culturally particular rather than subject to universal norms.

They answer their own question by rejecting the superior moral au-thority of human rights. Most family law involves deep-seated cultural norms about gender, marriage, childhood, sexuality, often with a reli-gious and traditional dimension, which are widely supported by com-munities across the gender divide. The ICHRP report goes on: "Human rights analysis suggests that the right to manifestation or expression of religion or other beliefs is trumped by the right to freedom from gender discrimination." *Suggests*? The technical language of "human rights anal-ysis" obscures the fact that individual human rights norms *must* trump "cultural" norms in these cases or they have no moral power.

Geoffrey Robertson is not so pusillanimous:

> We are beginning to call a savage a savage, where he or she is black or white. We are becoming less respectful of old men with beards, be they mullahs or rabbis or patriarchs, who ordain cruelty in the name of religion. There is less mealy-mouthedness about intoler-able behaviour and fewer attempts to suggest that traditional prac-tices are "culturally relative" or that authoritarian governments are reflecting "communitarian values."[97]

This statement presumes an audience who agree with him. We do not send words out into the void. What makes this any more than Robertson's opinion are the background norms established over a century and a half that normalize the universal, secular, and categorical. Against this is raised the specter of "cultural relativism" that poses a stark either/or choice: Robertson's way or mass atrocity. As Europe recedes, the naturalness of this binary choice fades and Robertson's claim to superior moral authority will be increasingly either contested or ignored.

The metanarrative is critiqued on the grounds that we live now in a postmodern world where there are other truths supported by other authorities, a world in which "the eternal becomes contingent," as José Alves puts it. He asks: "Facing such conditions, how can one still uphold the validity of the Universal Declaration of Human Rights, grounded on the rational and humanistic foundations of the Enlightenment, with inputs from its liberal and socialist currents?"[98] Jean-François Lyotard agrees: Why, he asks, would any culture have a reason to "hand over the authority for its narratives to some incomprehensible subject of narration"?[99]

Alan Rosenbaum, in *Is the Holocaust Unique?* gives a sense of what is at stake here in a stinging rebuke to the attack on the idea of a metanarrative:

> Postmodern criticism seems to aspire, through a strategy of deconstructing relevant contexts, texts, and narratives, to dismantle and eradicate faith in a basic belief in universally valid standards of truth, fact, reason, objectivity, and valuation. Given these standards, it is difficult enough to bring reasonable people to agreement about the character or nature of certain events. However, in the absence of universal standards, what remains regarding inquiry is an absurd epistemological nihilism, which results in either a vacuous or chaotic democracy of perspectives where no one claim or viewpoint (e.g., or "truth" or "story") is better or worse than any other claim.[100]

Some historians of the Holocaust have even linked postmodernism with Holocaust denial, claiming that to allow for interpretation in the meaning of the brute facts of systematic mass murder of the Jews opens the door to doubt about those facts themselves.[101] Rosenbaum equates what he sees as the refusal to view the Holocaust as "radical [and] unspeakable evil" with a moral nihilism that privileges power and interest as the determinant of truth.[102]

But acknowledging the ambiguities of authority is not to endorse moral relativism. Social norms rely on people's faith in them, and when that faith is shaken, no amount of wishful thinking can resurrect it. Rosenbaum adds: "We may expect realistically that, over time and with sufficient debate, common sense, a good will, competence, and honesty, it is possible to formulate defensible truth-claims and perspectives."[103] But his appeal to reason and rational discourse is presented in precisely the terms that critics deride. Phrases like "common sense" and "good will" beg the question. There are already defensible truth-claims, and humanists do a heroic job of defending them. The simple message—human suffering is bad and must be prevented, look at this picture of a Holocaust survivor or starving child—must be constantly reiterated. In other words, the answer to Rosenbaum is political, not epistemological. He and millions of others have built the cultural memory of Auschwitz and Nuremberg to ground the metanarrative in deep sentiment, fearful of the chasm opened by the death of transcendent and universal moral authority.

Critiques of the "disembodied" killing of 1991's Gulf War, with its footage from cameras mounted on cruise missiles, must be contrasted, Bruce Robbins argues, with calls for air strikes against Bosnian Serbs surrounding Sarajevo on the grounds that bombing the train tracks to Auschwitz might have saved lives.[104] He links this to taking an "aerial view," as did his father as a B-17 bomber pilot during the war against the Nazis. For Robbins, "the supposed universalists are no longer to be found manning the same old ramparts," allowing, he hopes, for the rescue of terms like "cosmopolitanism" and "internationalism" from the "rationalist universality with which each has been entangled since Kant."[105] Robbins believes the metanarrative has been tempered.

As Geoffrey Robertson's demand that we "call a savage a savage" shows, however, universalists are manning precisely those same ramparts in the field of global criminal justice. If anything, the critique was more present in the late 1940s as UNESCO and the Commission on Human Rights worked on declarations of human rights that sought to create a wider consensus, albeit one heavily influenced by Europe and the United States. "As Europe prepares to leave World War Two behind," says Tony Judt, "the recovered memory of Europe's dead Jews has become the very definition and guarantee of the continent's restored humanity."[106] Can this atrocity memory still be universalized? Can the past be forgotten *and* the political power of the memory remain, especially as survivors, carriers of raw moral authority, die? How can the transcendent that creates moral authority be kept alive? One answer, to which we now turn, is global atrocity culture.

4 THE MORAL ARCHITECTURE OF SUFFERING

In a 2011 documentary, *Sri Lanka's Killing Fields*, a young photojournalist and UN staffer, Benjamin Dix, ordered to depart from Kilinochi, films the hands of Tamils desperately pressed through the narrow gap in the gate of the UN compound. The hands recall those of Auschwitz-bound prisoners on trains pleading for air and water. Dix's camera lingers on one face.

He recalls: "There was one girl at the end who . . . she, her face was . . . she wasn't shouting or chanting she was just still but she had just real sadness in her face. I mean I was quite emotional at that point as well and her face just really captured this. . . . 'Have compassion, stay and watch.' "[1]

The documentary ends with a frozen picture of the girl's face, the voice-over saying, "The survivors are now looking to the international community for justice. Will they be failed again?" The film is a harrowing look, via mobile phone and handheld camera footage, at the Sri Lankan army's bombardment of the "no-fire zones" in the north where hundreds of thousands of Tamils were herded, at the aftermath of artillery attacks and bombings of hospitals, at executions as they happened and the naked bodies of raped and murdered Tamil women being piled up on trucks or filmed as trophies. Dix infers what the girl was thinking, but we never discover her name or what happened to her as the army allegedly set about committing mass murder.[2] The still photograph of her face and penetrating eyes is the innocent archetype personified, the humanist foundation stone.

The power of this totem is perfectly witnessed by David Scheffer, former US ambassador-at-large for war crimes: "I got used to mass graves

Fig. 6. A Tamil girl stares into the UN compound in Kilinochi, Sri Lanka, in 2008 as international staffers prepare to leave their posts as ordered by the UN. © Dixie 2008.

being exhumed, to the sallow faces of the decomposing victims, to the grievously wounded victims populating the filthy wards of buildings that were called hospitals. But I never adjusted to the agony of children. Those who survived would gaze at me searching for answers and relief that I could not provide. I saw so much misery for so many years that my memories remain consumed by human suffering."[3] Or deputy director of Human Rights Watch and former UN humanitarian chief Jan Egeland on Darfur: "One has to have a heart of stone not to be outraged by these accounts of armed men abusing defenseless women and children. 'How can you allow this to happen with total impunity?' we ask ministers in Khartoum and governors in Darfur again and again."[4] Or the ICRC's François Bugnion: "Who could ever forget little Aishah, lying frail in her hospital cot, always alone and yet always smiling to mask her pain? I had walked past her more than a dozen times before I realized with shock and infinite sadness that both her legs had been severed by shrapnel."[5] These are protestations of faith. Scheffer mentions the suffering of children and the Holocaust in his first few pages. He is declaring his membership in the humanist church.

Perhaps the ideal-typical example comes from Samantha Power's *A Problem from Hell.* She grounds her whole Pulitzer Prize–winning narrative in the story of nine-year-old Sidbela Zimic, killed by a Bosnian Serb artillery shell fired into a playground in Sarajevo. Power witnesses the aftermath, finding Sidbela's sister standing next to a "shallow pool of crimson on the playground" where "one blue slipper, two red slippers, and a jump rope with ice-cream-cone handles had been cast down." Power goes on: "On June 25, 1995, minutes after Sidbela kissed her mother on the cheek and flashed a triumphant smile, a Serb shell crashed into the playground where she, eleven-year-old Amina Pajevic, twelve-year-old Liljana Janjic and five-year-old Maja Skoric were jumping rope. All were killed, raising the number of children slaughtered in Bosnian territory during the war from 16,767 to 16,771."[6]

Invoking the child as totem serves to ground action, action that obscures, I have argued, the contradictions integral to modernity (between their want and our plenty, their suffering and our security). Research on the frequency of particular images of women and children as representations of Nazi atrocity, for example, shows that "the suffering of mothers, their death and the death of their children, act as a powerful reminder of a type of human evil that the Holocaust has come to represent in the collective imagination."[7] But the suffering child also embodies the central figure of liberal humanism: The *natural* individual. Innocence is a proxy for naturalness (guilelessness, blamelessness). This "universal essence," or "species existence," identifies a human being as "without differentiation or distinction in his nakedness and simplicity, united with all others in an empty nature deprived of substantive characteristic."[8] In this way both compassion and justice can be anchored on the child. Nothing is more authentic.

Historian of humanitarianism Bertrand Taithe traces the use by Christians of orphans as both a fund-raising technique and a site for conversion, complete with a letter and photo for Christmas, back as far as French Catholic missionaries in Algeria in 1869.[9] Vulnerable children and mothers are ubiquitous on aid agency websites. The ICRC museum in Geneva has an exhibit whose walls are covered in photographs of orphaned children from the Rwandan genocide. Indeed, the ICRC has used "the device of childhood thanks to its universality" in its films since the 1920s: "The abandoned child, the starving child and the war orphan stood out as representatives of universal hardship and became the silent spokesperson of humanitarian organizations."[10] The *silent* spokesperson, the existential human who just *is*.

The front covers of books on humanitarianism often feature either children, often black, or the red cross, and sometimes both. Sometimes they also feature the author as part of the narrative of heroic sacrifice: Orbinski's *An Imperfect Offering* (child and author), Bertschinger's *Moving Mountains* (child, author, and red cross), Chouliaraki's *The Spectatorship of Suffering* (children, red cross), Burnett's *Where Soldiers Fear to Tread* (child soldier), Egeland's *A Billion Lives* (children and author), Cain et al.'s *Emergency Sex* (red cross on UN vehicle), Brysk's *Global Good Samaritans* (baby, UN peacekeeper).[11] These covers give us the metanarrative before we've even opened the book.[12]

In her analysis of images of children in the Holocaust, Marianne Hirsch notes the importance of the innocence and vulnerability of children in Western culture. She argues: "Less individualized, less marked by the particularities of identity . . . children invite multiple projects and identifications."[13] As either the object of protection or the site of projection, the child "screens out context, specificity, responsibility, agency."[14] The child or female archetype, as passive and innocent victim, and as natural human, can then be used to underwrite political demands for action. Anne Frank is in many ways the perfect example. She remains frozen as a child on the verge of womanhood, existentially innocent, the details of her death from illness in Bergen-Belsen, after the death march from Auschwitz, vague. She is perfectly cut out for a kind of mysticism, a silent witness whose diary is her testimony. The Anne Frank House in Amsterdam attracts up to a million visitors a year, the modern well-lit lobby giving way via a set of shiny metal steps to a floor of small, rectangular red bricks that, along with the gloomy, intimate interior, transports the visitor back into Europe's bloody past.

When I visited in 2011, Anne Frank's diary, with its iconic red-and-white check pattern, had been temporarily replaced with a copy. We were told by a notice that we were not looking at the real diary. This is interesting in itself; as it was housed in a glass box, none of us could possibly have known without being informed that it was not the original, but the museum felt it necessary to tell us. The facsimile lacked the authenticity of having been touched by Anne herself, the original diary a sacred relic carrying her presence like a "magic trace" through the intervening decades.[15]

Suffering and Authenticity

Relics of suffering can be extremely powerful. In a dispute over whether human hair shaved from Jews transported to Auschwitz in the 1940s should be exhibited in the United States Holocaust Memorial Museum in Washington, DC, in 1993, preeminent Holocaust scholar Raul Hilberg, many of whose extended family were murdered in the camps, discovered that "one of the problematic 'rules' of Holocaust speech is that any survivor, no matter how inarticulate, is superior to the greatest Holocaust historian who did not share in the experience."[16] Part of the USHMM's mission was to "diminish the distance between the killing fields and the serene atmosphere of the Washington Mall."[17]

Yet some items, and particularly human hair, could not be displayed out of context and still retain the augmented meaning derived from the *unspeakable* atrocity that had made them sacred. Transportation transformed the hair in unpredictable ways. Ardent critics of the plan said the hair should never have crossed the Atlantic—it should be seen only in Auschwitz, where it *belonged*, its "inherent sacredness" at once contaminating and being defiled by "the antiseptic atmosphere of the Nation's capital."[18] Deborah Lipstadt, a consultant during these discussions, tells the same story. The two female survivors who objected most strongly managed to negate a 9–4 vote in favor of using the hair by giving voice to their feelings. One described it as a "violation of feminine identity"; the other said: "That could have been my mother's hair. She never gave you permission to display it. . . . It could have been *my* hair."[19] As Lipstadt says, "The conversation soon ended. There was no vote, but all those present knew the decision had been made."[20]

Survivors make powerful witnesses because they are victims who lived. Lawrence Langer suggests some survivors never step outside "durational time" (that is, they are forever in the moment of atrocity even as the decades pass). A survivor, he says, may be unable to "generalize his or her personal suffering and move beyond the role of victim."[21] These survivors are the most powerful transmission mechanisms. They embody suffering directly because they were present when the everyday world fractured; they carry the physical and mental scars. This "witnessing" is more powerful than reports from those—journalists, aid workers, rights advocates—who were in but not of the atrocity, watching and recording from the sidelines. The more interference between us and the totem, the less direct our exposure. But facts do not speak for themselves. The credibility of witnesses, as our interpreters and translators, is as important as what is said. An audience can rarely independently verify what it is told. Recall the comments about the ICRC: "Public protests by the ICRC not supported by observations of its own were fruitless, doing more harm than good."[22] Amnesty's reasoning about doing its own research was identical. The ICRC and Amnesty were trusted because they had *been there*, like Dunant, as witnesses, *and* because they had the markers of detachment, of the moral spectator who is not directly involved and thus can be trusted to be impartial.

There are two senses of witnessing at work here. One concerns the moral truth in atrocity and the other the facts of atrocity itself. Dunant used a mixture of both, combining graphic description with his role as a Christian witness. Dunant's language is vivid and sensational in contrast to modern human rights reporting, which, sober and disciplined, is intended to convey, by the absence of rhetoric and evaluation, something close to the narratorless moral truth that the reader herself would have observed had she been there.[23] It is a kind of silent witnessing.

Do graphic depictions of atrocity that provoke horror, righteous indignation, and even rage also facilitate emotional connection? A silent ICRC documentary from 1921 made in the Volga region by Fridtjof Nansen showed in detail the dismaying effects of famine, with piles of emaciated bodies, including shrunken dead children, laid out to be filmed.[24] The modern ICRC description of the Volga footage, titled "Famine in Russia," says:

The cameraman was a mere witness. Snatches of the violence, which was ubiquitous not staged, were recorded on camera [the film shows dead emaciated children]. Within days, still photographs taken from the film were published in most European daily newspapers. . . . Millions of people were fed for months owing to the international relief campaign. . . . From then on the force of images would play a decisive role in the success of mobilizations for humanitarian causes.[25]

These images of corpses are brutal, the dead en masse without the consolation of a last moment of human recognition; there is no redemption for them or us, just death. Their collective fate—the lack of a singular face, an individual story, with which we can engage—makes the witness vital. But if we are looking at what the inanimate camera recorded, without any voice-over from a human witness, is it harder to feel the connection that transfers sacred energy from the atrocity to us?[26] Is all-too-real horror somehow not *the real diary* marked by the mystical essence of Anne Frank? Even Primo Levi, survivor of Auschwitz and a prolific writer on the camps, was wary of claiming the full authority of "witness," because for him those who did not survive were the only "complete witnesses."[27]

Didier Fassin and Richard Rechtman analyze in detail "the political uses of trauma."[28] They chart the emergence of the clinical diagnosis of post-traumatic stress disorder (PTSD) and the political implications that flowed from it. From the 1980s onward, "authority to speak in the name of victims [was] now measured by the speaker's personal proximity to the traumatic event." The words of victims came to have a certain "clinical authority" as testimony.[29] In their examples, survivors petitioned the state for redress, the political authority of psychiatrists who diagnosed PTSD enhanced by their role as survivors' representatives. Humanists are not representatives in quite this way; they are not lawyers or experts for *specific victims* but rather for a class of "victims." Evidence for them is a means, not an end; the crime is ultimately a crime not against individuals but against humanity and humanity's law.

Survivors have *personal* and *identity-specific* reasons for speaking out or visiting atrocity sites and memorial museums. They are self-witnesses. But the vast majority of visitors are not survivors, have no shared identity with sufferers, and have *individual* rather than personal reasons for visiting. Because it is not their identity that brought them to the camp or museum, their visit cannot be *personal*, giving it different political implications. They can lobby for retribution or reparation *on behalf of* others but not in their own name. This is the position in which all humanists who are not survivors find themselves. They can only invoke the totem second hand.

Memorial museums and visits to Auschwitz, Srebrenica, Tuol Sleng, Ntarama Church, and Villa Grimaldi have even been called "dark tourism."[30] Janet Jacobs draws attention to the similarities between some Auschwitz exhibits and the obsession of nineteenth-century Europeans with the anatomically grotesque, the deformed, the criminal, the inferior, the racialized "Other."[31] For all nonsurvivors without a personal stake, there is some element of vicariousness, some sense of association with the transcendent as an antidote to *disenchantment*. Some desire to experience the sacred in the midst of modern life with its unremitting technological rationalism. In 1918, Weber observed two forms of withdrawal as responses to disenchantment, and one of them was into the "transcendental realm of mystic life."[32]

By repetition and through the conferring of a certain sacredness to what happened at Auschwitz, the mystical dimension of the Holocaust is accentuated. The most high-profile supporter of this view has been the Holocaust survivor Elie Wiesel. An outspoken proponent of the idea that authenticity is damaged by articulation, Wiesel quotes a nineteenth-century Hasidic teacher: "The unuttered cry is the loudest." Says Wiesel: "The truth of Auschwitz remains hidden in its ashes. Only those who lived it in their flesh and in their minds can possibly transform their experience into knowledge. Others, despite their best intentions, can never do so."[33] He adds: "The Holocaust [is] the ultimate event, the ultimate mystery, never to be comprehended or transmitted."[34]

Giorgio Agamben accepts there is a uniqueness about the Holocaust but asks: "But why unsayable? Why confer on extermination the prestige of the mystical?"[35] James Young is also concerned that the veneration of historical objects in the camps, and the consecration of Holocaust sites, will displace the memory work necessary to understand what happened and why. He fears we will accept the narrative as told not by the artifacts themselves but by their curators.[36] That we will, in effect, hear only the metanarrative. But for a humanism without its own survivors, sacralization is essential to give the law moral authority. The unsayable mysticism, the silent knowing, has political utility by grounding the metanarrative in a felt emotional connection that transcends right and wrong, judgment, context. Not having directly suffered, humanists must manufacture moral capital for themselves, expropriating events, objects, testimony, stories, and images to tell their own version of history and validate their own aspirations to rule in the name of justice.[37] It is moral capital that the ICRC has accumulated, and nothing is more valuable in creating it than the photograph of a human face.

Staring out at us, the faces of the dead and disappeared are the most ubiquitous feature of museums of suffering and atrocity. In the USHMM, says Linenthal, they are "shattering in their power."[38] Walter Benjamin, referring to nineteenth-century European bourgeois culture, says: "It is no accident that the portrait was the focal point of early photography. The cult of remembrance of loved ones, absent or dead, offers a last refuge for the cult value of the picture. For the last time the aura emanates from the early photographs in the fleeting expression of a human face. This is what constitutes their melancholy, incomparable beauty."[39] As he points out: "The presence of the original is the prerequisite to the concept of authenticity."[40] This authenticity is jeopardized by reproduction, "exhibition value" overtaking "cult value."[41]

A literal example was the display at the Museum of Modern Art in New York in 1997 of twenty-two photographs from Tuol Sleng (S-21 prison) taken by the resident photographer before the accused Khmer Rouge cadres in the photo were tortured and killed.[42] Roland Barthes describes the transcendent individual moment in looking at photographs as the *punctuum*: a wound, a poignant bruise, a prick or sting.[43] Many of those who looked at the Tuol Sleng exhibit felt the same; the recorded visitor comments show that some recognized the sacred and mystical in the photographs.[44] Human rights films often use "stilled action" to achieve this effect; for example, showing the silent tears of parents looking at still-photographs of ageless children they have lost.

Black-and-white photographs add to this timelessness; lacking the vividness and life (and modernity) of color, they look back to a lost past. In Cambodia, Tuol Sleng has room after room (these were previously torture cells) of black-and-white photographs of the faces of mostly young people. Their names and stories remain largely untold and certainly didn't feature in the MoMA exhibition.[45] The posters of the disappeared in Argentina have become iconic within the discourse of justice led by the Mothers of the Plaza de Mayo. The poignancy of these photographs of disappeared youths comes not from what *they* know is about to happen (as at Tuol Sleng) but from what *we* know is about to happen to them (that they are about to disappear forever). These responses may seem like Barthes's *punctuum*, but are they in reality what he calls the *studium*, what we recognize because we, who did not directly suffer or lose someone we loved, have been trained to see it this way?[46]

Is this fetishism of the still photograph dated in a digital world? One of the difficulties for modern advocates is precisely that younger generations have a more diverse, multi-vocal *studium*, a more heterogeneous training (if it is a training at all). Getting the sacred into fast-paced, high-quality screen content is increasingly hard. The reason the mini-series *Holocaust* or the films *Schindler's List* or *The Pianist* or *The Boy in Striped Pajamas* (or the scenes of concentration camps and ghettos in the movie series *X-Men*) may prove an effective introduction to the Holocaust is that they make an impression in the art and entertainment forms with which younger generations are familiar. This was true by the 1970s when *Holocaust* was such a huge success in the United States and Germany.[47] The 1984 film *The Killing Fields*, about Cambodia, had a similar impact. For Rwanda and Bosnia things were different because there was so much contemporaneous news footage.

Moving images ought to aid advocacy because narration works against reflection and in favor of action, and the full array of film techniques (music, editing, lighting, sound) can be used to manipulate viewer sentiment. Violence in particular is movement, not stasis, and the effects of bullets, machetes, knives, clubs, fists, even poison gas can rarely be captured in one frame.[48] This is Barthes reflecting on what spectators must invest in a photograph: "Do I add to the images in movies? I don't think so; I don't have time: in front of the screen, I am not free to shut my eyes; otherwise, opening them again, I would not discover the same image; I am constrained to a continuous voracity; a host of other qualities, but not *pensiveness*; whence the interest, for me, of the photogram."[49]

Human rights films and festivals aim to nurture the shared "effervescence" Durkheim understood as essential to religious feeling. Motion pictures want to lift us out of reverie; the camera insists we pass over private grief and *do something*. For George Baker the photograph is always "torn between" narrative and stasis, its apparent suitability for "petrification" confounded by the ways in which still photos are incorporated into sequences and series.[50] And while movies are better able to manipulate us—to tell us what we *ought* to feel and do—we also retain a greater degree of control over their meaning because the director's management of our sensibilities breaks the witnessing spell. In not explicitly asking for or expecting action, photographs may actually transmit the magic trace more effectively. As a compromise, the most poignant parts of a film will sometimes be shown in slow motion, anticipating the coming transcendent moment, halfway *between* the sacred and the profane. Here, identifiably still images move rapidly enough to allow for recognition but not reflection. Direct eye-contact is unavailable except as the right of the survivor.

The appearance of authenticity is vital in dramatizations. Except for one brief scene of a small girl in a red coat, Steven Spielberg's *Schindler's List* was shot entirely in black and white to enhance the movie's sense of being authentic. It ended with footage of elderly survivors from Schindler's factory placing rocks on Oskar Schindler's gravestone. And part of the movie's legacy is the Survivors of the Shoah Visual History Foundation, an archive of testimony from tens of thousands of survivors for dissemination to schools.[51]

The film that best encapsulates this secular sacred, holding together the tension between narrative and transcendence, is *Shoah*, Claude Lanzmann's nine-hour film of the Holocaust told through the testimony of survivors, perpetrators, and witnesses.[52] Lanzmann did not see himself as making a film about the past. "Making a history was not what I wanted to do. I wanted to construct something more powerful than that," he writes in the opening credits.[53] For Lanzmann, trying to find out "why" was an "obscenity," the "abyss" between explanation and the brute facts of the act of atrocity, like gassing children, was too great to be bridged.[54] He talks about "blind seeing," not witnessing as in bearing witness, but as in watching and simply "knowing" the truth and horror without trying to comprehend it. He wanted to portray the totem in sustained narrative form. Fassin and Rechtman describe this as "the attractive idea that something of the human resists all forms of moral destruction."[55] A living legacy, in other words, symbolic life after physical death.

Fig. 7. The Peace Palace in The Hague built by the Carnegie Foundation in 1913 and now home to the International Court of Justice. © The Carnegie Foundation.

The Architecture of Humanism

The moral trace is personal and intimate. Yet moral power has also built palaces on a grand scale. The first examples of humanity's purportedly post-imperial architecture take us back to old Europe: the Peace Palace in The Hague and the Palais des Nations in Geneva.

The Peace Palace was built by the Carnegie Foundation in 1913 to house the Permanent Court of Arbitration, an innovation of the 1899 Hague Convention. From 1922 onward it also housed the Permanent International Court of Justice, a League of Nations court comprising international judges who would adjudicate between states.[56] Its initial design was even more baroque than the final "neo-Renaissance" version. Inside and out, the palace was European to its core, an example of monumental architecture designed to embody an idea—world peace—that in 1913 and 1922 was still assumed to be the business of European states, despite the move to a body of judges with some degree of permanent authority and jurisdiction.[57] The Peace Palace had been the outcome of a fraught design competition in which modernists and traditionalists did battle. This would pale beside the politics of the design competition for

Fig. 8. The Palais des Nations in Geneva, brief and ill-fated home of the League of Nations. The Human Rights Council meets in a building at the rear of the Palais. © Yann Forget—Licence CC-BY-SA.

the Palais des Nations, which was conceived and built in full knowledge of the horrors of the 1914–1918 war.

At the center of the Palais des Nations design debacle was the figure of arch-modernist Le Corbusier (Charles-Edouard Jeanneret). He and his second cousin Pierre Jeanneret were initially awarded the prize in 1927 for a building that would, as they saw it, usher in a new modern age to replace monumental "academic" structures like the Peace Palace. Le Corbusier's vision, termed the "international style," prized space, regularity, freedom from ornamentation, and functionality (he famously called a house "a machine for living in").[58] International style used new materials like steel, glass, and concrete; it emerged in the 1920s at a time when finance and service industries were adding office blocks to the urban landscape. Le Corbusier's modern design for the Palais des Nations split the nine-man committee (all Europeans) and led to his disqualification on a technicality about the ink used for his drawings.[59] The Palais, not completed until 1936, was eventually built on more traditional lines.

The Peace Palace and the Palais des Nations are monuments to European civilizational hubris, overwhelming in their reference to a past during which Europe's religion, wars, and imperial expansion dominated world history. They lacked any engagement with cultural diversity, alternative architectural or aesthetic traditions, modernity, or with the people of the world in whose name the future was going to be managed in Geneva and The Hague.

In the pages of the American journal *Architectural Review* in 1948, major architects like Bauhaus founder Walter Gropius and urban critic Lewis Mumford agreed that classical motifs and the neoclassical style (exemplified by the Palais) were dead; that was the architecture of despots, undemocratic and inegalitarian, the "frozen music" of an extinct European past.[60] Materials, technology, engineering, and functional design, meeting the needs of the economy rather than producing art or enacting theory, would be vital to new democratic forms of architecture. Their views reflected American humanism's pragmatic problem-solving ethos. Some feared this meant no distinction between the architecture of capitalism and that of the public sphere, that in the end buildings would merge into a corporate-bureaucratic style whose virtue was its ahistoricism, its characterlessness, the fact that it seemed to symbolize nothing.[61] But a return to history (to American neoclassicism, the Peace Palace, the Palais) was impossible. The moral spectator in steel and glass was the only plausible candidate for an aesthetic of the universal after the Holocaust and European imperialism.

The ICC is currently housed in a temporary building in The Hague. Geoffrey Robertson is robust about its failings; it has

> no aesthetic qualities to compare with London's Old Bailey or the US Supreme Court or the European Court building in Strasbourg. . . . Architecture has both symbolic and practical significance: countries where justice is valued have distinct and imposing court buildings, while those where it is preordained or seen as an administrative adjunct of the state generally have courtrooms which are indistinguishable from government offices. The idea that The Hague is symbolically suitable because it is "the capital of international law" sends exactly the wrong message: this is where international law failed to thrive, or to make much of a difference, in the twentieth

century. . . . The International Criminal Court should have been located in an historic or else a specially designed building, home to the judges and the registry, but not to the prosecution.[62]

This totally fails to understand moral power. Robertson is arguing for architecture that mirrors imperial state power, echoing T. Roger Smith, who in 1873 told the London Society of Arts on his return from Bombay that British buildings should "be European both as a rallying point for ourselves, and as raising a distinctive symbol of our presence to be beheld with respect and even with admiration by the natives of the country."[63] For the architects of empire, New Delhi had to "embody the idea of law and order which has been produced out of chaos by the British administration."[64]

Compare Robertson's self-confident vision of his own moral authority with the architectural brief for the post-apartheid Constitutional Court of South Africa in Johannesburg: "What was called for was a place that would be easily accessible to ordinary citizens, and that would embody a piece of history but also reflect the hopes of a young and energetic democracy. It would have to be a site upon which a building such as a constitutional court could stand with dignity, *but without the intimidating presence usually associated with courts*."[65] All involved in designing the court understood the need to get away from the defunct European modernism Robertson proposes, to reclaim the site (a former apartheid-era prison) and create a space that integrated trials with the public realm and the everyday comings and goings of citizens. One of the architects linked "monumentalism" with the kind of state centralization that had "wrought deep destruction, pain and suffering."[66] For former prisoner and head of South Africa's Commission on Gender Equality, Thenjiwe Mtintso, the court had to be friendly, soft but serious, and "people-owned."[67]

This court has the benefit of being in South Africa for South Africans who can confer on it democratic legitimacy. Every aspect of the design and decoration process was loaded with symbolic potential, and the choice of shapes, materials, art, colors, and images all make use in one way or another of something that resonates with the South African experience. The ICC has none of these things: it is not where atrocities were committed; it is not to be integrated with affected populations (the permanent premises are on the outskirts of even The Hague); it has a mandate from 121 small and medium-size states (and a minority of the world's population); it is being paid for by Europeans; and the kind of detachment and neutrality that is seen as alienating in the South African case is seen as *a virtue* of the ICC. Its architecture, as we shall see shortly, might be very different from the Peace Palace and the Palais des Nations, but its underlying claim to legitimacy is not.

The Dutch government offered a site for a permanent ICC building of forty-six thousand square meters (with, confidently, room for expansion) close to the dunes of the North Sea coast. The original brief for this new site was

> that the premises should reflect the character of the International Criminal Court, that *there should be one site forever*, that all organs should be on one site and that the form of the building should be defined by its function. The secondary objectives are user-friendliness, adaptability, security, separation of the organs of the Court, facilities for victims, witnesses and defence, an open and welcoming character, and a high quality design.[68]

The eventual winners were a Danish firm, Schmidt Hammer Lassen.[69] Their design is below.

For the Coalition for the International Criminal Court (CICC), the ICC is a revolution in world politics. Speaking on behalf of "civil society" (the CICC is a coalition of 2,500 NGOs from 150 countries), it says:

> The new ICC premises must be an icon in a truly *potent* sense; it mustn't simply exist, it must engage. It should embody cultural and social meaning, placing us in the historical and cultural context of this new system of international justice and reflecting the importance of the International Criminal Court—an authority to help end impunity, powerful and inspiring in its actions, yet welcoming and sensitive to those involved in its proceedings.[70]

While the design of the new ICC building was to be more monumental than that of the South African constitutional court, the CICC was nonetheless aware of the need for compassion:

Fig. 9. The winning design for the new purpose-built International Criminal Court in The Hague. © Schmidt Hammer Lassen architects.

Justice is a very emotive experience for these participants; how the architecture "feels" to them will be particularly significant. Consequently, the general atmosphere should recognize and respect their histories. Given the nature of the Court's work, the design *must* address the need for secure premises, yet it should simultaneously create a dialogue with the greater community, both in its physical form and in its engagement of its surroundings. This is not to minimize the critical requirement for the integration of security concerns, but to underline that the need for security cannot and should not be the sole driver for the design; no aspect of the premises must pose a risk of re-traumatizing victims and witnesses.[71]

The winning design for the ICC can be viewed in an online video.[72] According to the architects, the building's lightness and simplicity communicate "the values of openness and transparency," while the site's parterre gardens stretch up like cladding on the sides of the main court tower. Historically, the designers say, gardens have "always existed as part of all cultures and all religions. With flowers and plants from each of the 110 [now 121] member countries the parterre garden rises up as a symbol of unity regardless of nationality and culture."

There are two principal forms of legitimation for universal humanism: the moral spectator (who fits in everywhere and belongs nowhere)
and the polyglot mix of world culture (with a little of everything). A vivid
example of the latter is the ceiling designed by Majorcan artist Miquel
Barceló for the "Chamber for Human Rights and for the Alliance of
Civilisations" (where the Human Rights Council meets) at the Palais des
Nations. Inaugurated in 2008, this ceiling displays a "lunar landscape"
made of resin painted with more than twenty different colors. The ICC
gardens are a gesture toward Barceló's "melting pot" representation of
humanism, but the modernist shapes of the building's towers are the very
essence of abstraction. The disembodied voice-over of Schmidt Hammer
Lassen's winning design video (male, soft, authoritative), puts it this way:

> When designing the new permanent premises of the International
> Criminal Court the point of departure was to communicate trust
> hope and most importantly faith in justice and fairness. The build-
> ing should have the courage to be an ambassador for the credibility
> of the ICC. The project and its architecture should be impressive
> and grandiose but should always relate to humans and the human
> scale. It is important that a formal institution like the ICC does not
> constitute barriers for people. On the contrary it must express the
> very essence of democratic architecture.

For the architects of the South African constitutional court, public space
was paramount; the building had to be an unintimidating space that was
easy to enter ("without any fanfare"), its majesty on the inside, in the
main foyer, derived from a huge open void designed to have presence
and gravitas through emptiness.[73] The initial ICC report on its permanent
premises sounds a different note:

> The premises must be unobtrusive and on a human scale, while at
> the same time symbolising the eminence and authority of the Court.
> ... The Court's premises and buildings should immediately be per-
> ceived as reflecting the Court's identity. The Court's main façade
> should serve as a timeless image symbolising its principal mission,
> i.e. to bring to justice the perpetrators of the most serious crimes
> of concern to the international community as a whole. It should

also reflect the fact that the Court is an international Court with a universal vocation and seeks a well-balanced representation of the entire international community and a place at the heart of that community.[74]

It is the court that has eminence and authority; in South Africa it is the people. The ICC has no people in any meaningful sense, except the professionals who work in international human rights and criminal justice. It is not embedded in a lifeworld. It represents "humanity," "civil society," and "the international community," empty abstractions all. In reality the ICC has a life of its own, a self-legitimating sense of its own power and a principal focus on prosecuting and punishing perpetrators. It wants to have a place "at the heart of the [international] community," but it clearly aspires to stand over and above that community as a moral spectator. To permanently subject politics to the law (as if the law was not politics by another means).

Indeed, the choice of flowers and plants to symbolize unity regardless of nationality and culture actually reinforces this symbolically, taking its authority from nature, not from the culture humans have made. Flowers and plants were here before us and will outlive us (like, its advocates hope, the ICC). Nature symbolizes the transcendence of history, of concrete humanity. It is unclear from the designs how much of the garden will be exposed and how much part of an indoor botanical garden. Either is a beautiful metaphor: any outdoor plants, given their diverse climatic origins, may struggle to survive transplanted in European soil, while botanical gardens were where European botanists preserved and grew exotic species they had transplanted from imperial colonies. This is before we even acknowledge that, historically, complex gardens were used as a form of material and symbolic power to guard space from ordinary people without the unpleasantness of walls, fences, and overt security. There will of course be plenty of security at the ICC; the cell complex is elaborate and sophisticated.

This is "frozen music," the "imposing façade" that symbolizes the moral spectator always watching, never aging, always vigilant. Even Barceló's ceiling is an abstract representation of diversity. Compare this with UNESCO's Memory of the World Register, which aims to preserve humanity's documentary heritage by collecting documents from all over

Fig. 10. The humanist international's most iconic landmark, the United Nations Secretariat building in New York. © UN Photo / Andrea Brizzi.

the world as a living archive of human endeavor.[75] UNESCO does not seek to judge them in terms of a hierarchy of value or to embed them in a chronological narrative that locates some as derivative of others. Documentary records held at Tuol Sleng Genocide Museum are on the register, as are the ICRC's POW files from the First World War.

How to symbolize humanity was a conversation rehearsed in detail in 1946 by the architects chosen to design the United Nations' headquarters in New York. Scarred by his Geneva experience, Le Corbusier lobbied privately to design the building he knew would define the 1940s, as the Palais had the 1920s.[76] This was global public architecture on the grandest scale. The ICC is the next *global* symbolic project of comparable stature. Le Corbusier declared he had been sent to New York by the French government to "defend modern architecture," but the ten-man design board he joined was put together in part to discipline him.[77] His "international style" was so titled because of an exhibition held at the Museum of Modern Art in New York in 1932. Its main principles were the use of volume (steel frames meant external walls didn't need to be supporting, enabling the use of glass to encompass vast internal space), regularity (consistency of line and angle rather than mixing different aesthetic styles), and no applied decoration (in essence, no overt symbolism).[78] The archetypal modern example of this style is the skyscraper. For Henry Russell Hitchcock and Philip Johnson, "The man who made the world aware that a new style was being born was Le Corbusier."[79] International style was also definitely European style.[80] Glass, and the idea of transparency, had been central to Le Corbusier's Palais des Nations design, in which he was already conducting "an argument between a real and ideal space."[81] Gropius's Bauhaus, too, was centrally concerned with this relationship.

Hitchcock and Johnson admired the quality of "platonic abstraction" in the international style, but they also saw the need for "living architecture." International style for them meant universal ideals, not buildings lived in under protest.[82] But Le Corbusier was committed to the Cartesian rationality of the moral spectator. For him subjects were objects about whose preferences he made standardized assumptions. He was embedding a truth about functional design in the modern world that, in its universality and categoricalness, was quintessentially European and imperial. James Scott, as a result, sees Le Corbusier's "high modernism" as "deeply authoritarian," the aim being to replace the "accidental, irrational deposit of historical practice" with a plan to tame nature through science, including the science of morals, and impose a rational social order upon it.[83]

This was pronounced in the plan to build Brasilia, whose architect, Oscar Niemeyer, was a disciple of Le Corbusier's and another member of the ten-man UN design board. Le Corbusier's emphasis on a single, rational, all-encompassing plan put the philosopher-king (the moral spectator) in the place of dictator. The "implacable authority" Le Corbusier claimed on behalf of "universal scientific truths" was self-authorizing and thus indifferent to the need for democratic legitimation.[84] The truth, not the people, authorized the plan. When extended to the city, this sort of rational plan eradicated the darkness and decay where radicalism bred.[85] Order was imposed on "chaos," and calculation and utilitarianism could be put to work.

The UN site was narrowed down first to the United States, then to the East Coast, and finally, after a last-minute intervention by the Rockefeller family in December 1946, to eighteen acres in midtown Manhattan between Forty-Second and Forty-Eighth Streets, First Avenue, and the East River (appropriately on the site of a former slaughterhouse).[86] UN

archives contain a wealth of detail about the various plans that designers and architects envisaged, some of which ambitiously contemplated a
"world capital city" built in or around New York. To avoid the farce of the
League of Nations competition (thousands of submissions, nine winners,
Le Corbusier's expulsion, nine years to build), the ten-man design board
was appointed, in February 1947, under the direction of Wallace K. Harrison, lead architect of the Rockefeller Center. At Le Corbusier's insistence,
they made a solemn declaration in April 1947 that they were a homogeneous block. It said: "There are no names attached to this work. As in any
human enterprise, there is simply discipline, which alone is capable of
bringing order."[87] Le Corbusier's influence is clear in the wording. The
time was ripe, he suggested, for the mature field of architecture to provide definitive and permanent design solutions through "applied modern
technique." One paragraph says:

> To those outside who question us we can reply: We are united, we
> are a team; the World Team of the United Nations laying down the
> plan of a world architecture, *world* and not *international*, for therein
> we shall respect the human, natural and cosmic laws.[88]

"World" we should take as a synonym for "humanity," and "international"
as a referent for "sovereign states." There are no competing plans among
the group, says the declaration: "The overriding idea must never suffer
such disfigurement."[89] This hubris is pure Le Corbusier. Aligning well with
what we know of Le Corbusier's personality, including his infuriating tendency to refer to himself in the third person (as a spectator of himself as a
historical subject), it reflects precisely a European self-confidence, border-
ing on arrogance: that architecture, just like atrocity, was a problem that
could be solved if only everyone would defer to the knowledge accrued
by Europeans themselves. The catastrophically destructive Second World
War, including the Holocaust, were in this view problems of "world history," not of distinct ideologies and political strategies employed by European national and imperialist powers. The Europeans, for some the
problem, considered themselves the solution. That solution, embodied by
Le Corbusier, was secular, universal, and categorical.

American critic Lewis Mumford immediately saw the problem. He
agreed UN architecture should ensure "he who enters these precincts

will leave part of his nationality behind him, as the Moslem faithful leave their shoes behind at the entrance of the mosque."[90] This demanded a design that symbolized the united world community in what we might term "strange space" (the sociologically empty space of the moral spectator). But Mumford saw the danger of abstraction. He warned against "freezing the whole project into a static form" rather than allowing for change. He was adamant that unity should not be "an arbitrary abstract, paper unity, to be imposed at the beginning by a single mind and never departed from, but an organic unity, imperfect as all living things are imperfect."[91] The "single mind" Mumford feared was doubtless Le Corbusier's, but in his self-confidence the indomitable Frenchman was a representative of his entire civilization.

In an interview with Gertrude Samuels of the *New York Times* in April 1947, Wallace Harrison and Le Corbusier claimed a preference for "functionalism" over "symbolism" (that the work to be done in the building should dictate its design).[92] The Palais des Nations was the reference point, a combination of fortress, temple, and palace. How modern in comparison would the UN headquarters be? The most pragmatic of all was Harrison:

> Building is a matter of stone on stone and steel on steel, air conditioning and elevators that run. The layman thinks that all we have to do is come in with a beautiful sketch, and out of that everything is going to function. Just the opposite is true. These U.N. buildings can only grow out of requirements, now and for five or ten years hence. They must have stateliness and dignity. But the question is, are we building some phony Greek temple for a Greek god, or are we building to accommodate human beings in a complex civilization?

Le Corbusier (more or less) agreed. Niemeyer and Chinese architect Ssu-Ch'eng Liang sounded unconvinced. They argued there was always a "direct psychological relationship" between political aspirations and a building's appearance. Liang in particular suggested the buildings needed to feel "un-national, expressing no country's characteristic but expressive of the world as a whole."

Samuels also records the views of Gropius, Frank Lloyd Wright, and US National Park and Planning Commission member William Adams

Delano. Wright's somewhat idiosyncratic contribution is deeply skeptical about the project, warns of the seductions of power and monumentalism, and extols the virtue of more reflective, rural space to allow a natural form of "enlightened democracy" to emerge. Delano feared a failure to adequately incorporate spirituality and tradition—to link present and past—and was averse to glass, which for him connoted neither stability nor dignity. Bauhaus founder and Harvard professor Gropius, who with Mies van der Rohe and Le Corbusier, Europeans all, dominated the world architectural scene until into the 1950s, was more nuanced. He rejected out of hand the idea that modern architecture can or should incorporate the "dead language" of the past, while praising glass as "uniquely symbolic of our civilization since it is clear, practical and beautiful." But Gropius thought the small site a mistake and felt the question of the "psychological union" of the site to be inescapable and unanswerable in merely "utilitarian" terms.[93]

By 1951 Mumford was sour on what he called "a superficial aesthetic triumph and an architectural failure," this pinnacle of Le Corbusier's style "a climax of formal purity and functional inadequacy." The modernist mantra "form follows function" (i.e., no symbolism) had become "function sacrificed to form" to produce "a new kind of academicism" that flourished because modernist buildings were easy to imitate and reproduce.[94] This was assembly-line architecture. Frank Lloyd Wright was more scathing. In a letter to Mumford he wrote: "If only the significance of architecture could be read by 'supposedly living people' they would see Hitlerism Stalinism rampant in that costly crate in which to ship Freedom to its doom: hate required, fear taught, denunciation of neighbors a public virtue, etc etc."[95]

Samuels concludes her article by asking whether the buildings will be "a living symbol of peace or another tomb of Geneva." This reflects the choice Le Corbusier offered between "academism" and "life." The former he saw as sedimented custom, blind faith, the latter as an irresistible, evolutionary force not to be denied, that of science, progress, rationality, modernity, the moral spectator rescuing us from ingrained custom. What Le Corbusier failed to realize was that he was erecting a new orthodoxy that would, in its turn, serve as "academism" for progressives. He saw not dialectic but the end of history, the "frozen music."[96] And history's end was to make the rest of the world look a lot like Europe, human rights and all.

For international style it was the primacy of the functional over the symbolic that was itself symbolic. Symbolism is not just about what was *intended*. Like Roland Barthes's "writerly texts," meaning is constructed through discourse and use, not by intention.[97] The UN's architects could see that glass and space connoted openness, simplicity, and honesty. Yet in not privileging overt symbolism, they were creating a monument to moral spectatorship. The UN secretariat was a building "from nowhere," as is the ICC. This fits perfectly with the alienating structures of law, bureaucracy, and money that condense and dissolve all human specificities into a common and commensurable currency. An aversion to overt symbolism is symbolic in itself. The aesthetic of humanity is human only in abstract. In reviewing Adam Bartos's photographs of the United Nations, which feature objects (rooms, shelves, reception desks, signs) but no people, François Debrix argues the UN is best understood as a "postmodern construct," a "structure without depth." For Debrix, all there is in Bartos's UN is "the objects themselves, the architectural eeriness of the building, and the proliferation of signs, symbols, arrows inside the edifice which are nonetheless devoid of meaning and direction."[98]

Unfreezing the Music

As evidence of an evolution in thinking about genocide memorialization from the 1990s to 2013, consider the proposed design of a Cambodia genocide museum called the Sleuk Rith Institute, the inspiration of Youk Chhang, director of the Documentation Center of Cambodia (DC-Cam) and a child survivor of the Khmer Rouge killing fields.[99] DC-Cam has been the central Cambodian NGO collecting evidence and promoting education on the Khmer Rouge period since 1997 (it was originally set up in 1995 as a satellite office of Yale University's Congress-funded Cambodian Genocide Program). Figure 11 shows a familiar neoclassical European style, designed under Chhang's direction in the late 1990s. Its Geneva-like qualities are clear. Figure 12 is the design as of 2013; as Chhang's thinking has evolved, more typically Cambodian elements have come to the fore, including the central hall named a Chor-Tean Sala (a meeting hall to celebrate six holy principles). The Sala is not a stupa, connoting death, but a celebration of life.

Fig. 11. An early design from before 2000 of the proposed Sleuk Rith Institute, Phnom Penh. © Youk Chhang, DC-CAM, Phnom Penh, Cambodia.

The museum to the genocide will be underground. Modern buildings around the Sala reflect the relationship between Cambodia and globalization, although there is a deliberate absence of the extensive glass found in European museums.[100]

In this simple shift we see the beginnings of something radical. Although DC-Cam and the Sleuk Rith Institute remain parts of a global genocide memory and justice network (many international donors support DC-Cam, which has close links to the USHMM), symbolizing what happened under the Khmer Rouge as a more distinctively Cambodian experience heralds a move to emphasize what is different and unique in each atrocity.[101] Even to make problematic the use of singular frames like "genocide" to tie together events that are very different opens up the difficulties inherent in a concept with both a "legal-political life" and an analytical, scholarly one.[102]

The singular European frame is disintegrating. Humanism has, in the form of the ICC, lifted itself free of its concrete sociological moorings. This possibility was inherent in the logic of modernity and has been intensified by the globalization of neoliberal capitalism since the 1970s.

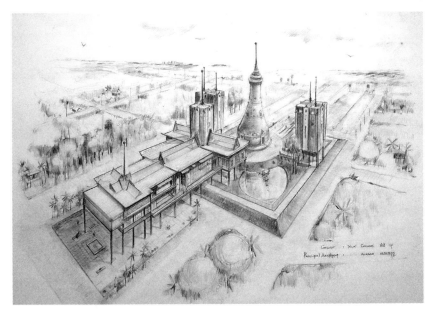

Fig. 12. A later design from around 2010 of the proposed Sleuk Rith Institute, Phnom Penh. © Youk Chhang, DC-CAM, Phnom Penh, Cambodia.

More than anything, the arrival of the United States as a serious player in global humanism after 1968 sounded the death knell for European-style secular religiosity. As with Wallace Harrison, Le Corbusier's nemesis, pragmatism would be paramount. Questions of first principle were not abandoned; they were irrelevant. What mattered was functionality: getting things done. Human rights, as with power and money, became a means to the end of globalizing neoliberal democracy.

5 HUMAN RIGHTS AND AMERICAN POWER

Prominent advocates talk confidently of an "international human rights movement," but given the vast diversity in resources, influence, and control within human rights globally, this is merely an illusion.[1] With no shared identity, concrete interest (beyond the abstract "bodily and mental integrity"), or socioeconomic circumstances, there cannot be *one movement*. The lack of priority given in the West to sustained activism on social, economic, and cultural rights is a case in point.[2] If this were truly one movement, surely its priorities would be set through some wider form of dialogue not through the executive decision of those who hold the purse strings.[3] The more reliant global humanists become on the successful functioning of the world economy to fund their expanding operations, the less likely it is that attention to social inequality will emerge. Claims to speak for "the movement" ignore the tensions between Human Rights and human rights, disguising hierarchical power and money relations within international humanism.

This does not unduly trouble international advocates, because they are only really talking to an elite audience. It can be "useful to deploy victims to change the way people see the world," argues the executive director of Human Rights Watch, Kenneth Roth, but "most of what we do is beyond the ability of the victims to follow or beyond our ability to keep victims informed."[4] This shift took place in the 1970s, the sacred moral authority of victims and survivors by then well established enough to be a deployable resource for human rights. The increasing saliency of Holocaust memory fueled this development. The agonies of contradiction, held at bay since Solferino, vanished as American advocates openly embraced the status of human rights as part of the political ideology of modern liberalism (based on democracy, the rule of law and, increasingly, the working of markets).[5] The post-Christian spiritual function of *European* human rights became increasingly redundant.

With this commitment to democracy, law, and the upside of wealth, wrapped within the constitutional tradition, American human rights advocates worried less about foundations and more about results. In the United States, said Louis Hartz, "law has flourished on the corpse of philosophy."[6] Rather than seek ultimate truths, he argued, law functioned as a pragmatic way of forging a working consensus.[7] *American* human rights followed this pragmatic logic: the question became how not what. In addition, while the United States reverberated with powerful social movements demanding civil rights, women's rights, gay rights, and environmental rights, *human rights* were an elite-level contest between liberals and conservatives over executive policy and power after Vietnam and Watergate. Human rights were not grounded in a domestic social movement, in other words, even if some advocates made the transition.[8] The American public was, by and large, a paying audience rather than a membership constituency for global rights. They rarely if ever sought international protection for domestic "human rights" abuses, and this deeply nationalist conception of the civil/human rights distinction persists.[9] Human rights were, in effect, *foreign policy* for non-Americans.[10]

Human rights became salient in the United States at the dawn of a further radical change: the neoliberal revolution. Neoliberalism opened up a "humanitarian marketplace" to organizations whose business model was increasingly about publicity and fund-raising to pay for professional global advocacy rather than to stimulate *transnational collective action*. When President Jimmy Carter at one and the same time advocated for human rights and agonized about the malaise caused by rampant consumerism, he did not see that radical individualism might make consumption and rights aspects of *the same* social transformation.[11] The reliance of human rights advocacy on middle class wealth was a problem only for the vanishing left. The 1947 founding statement of Friedrich Hayek's Mont Pèlerin Society (whose members included Milton Friedman, Ludwig von Mises, and Karl Popper) was more prescient about American human rights when it argued that free markets and human progress were twin bulwarks against tyranny. It warned of the dangers posed to "human dignity and freedom" by moral absolutism *and* moral relativism, by skepticism about the rule of law, and by "a decline in the belief in private property and the competitive market."[12] All of which—democracy, neoliberalism, national law, and the domestic-foreign divide—pitted the European secular-religiosity model of principled detachment against the pragmatic, political advocacy model that allowed, rather than resisted, alliances with the foreign policies of western governments bent on the extension of neoliberal democracy. A Global Human Rights Regime was, by the late 1990s, the result.

Human Rights and the United States

It is somewhat misleading to claim that "the drama of human rights is that they emerged in the 1970s seemingly from nowhere" (Samuel Moyn) or that "the international human rights movement has developed as a movement only during the past quarter of a century" (Aryeh Neier).[13] But these "New York stories" are right to recognize that a profound change occurred at this time.[14] Suddenly, "human rights" were politically salient in American foreign policy.[15] Stephen Cohen argues legislation had existed since 1961 that allowed Congress to pressure the executive on links between human rights and military aid; it was Henry Kissinger's intransigence about human rights that galvanized Congress in the post-Vietnam/Watergate world.[16] Even so, initial legislation was weak. Representative Donald Fraser's well-documented human rights activism in Congress after 1973 failed to create legal obligations that bound the White House. And his hearings reinforced the domestic-international split by focusing on how the United States could use human rights conditionality to pressure *other governments* to treat their citizens better, not behave better itself.[17]

President Carter's inauguration in 1977 was the turning point. He took onboard human rights for reasons of belief (albeit ambiguously at first) and strategy (the issue united liberals and conservatives against President Ford).[18] Far from welcoming this move, the career bureaucrats in the State Department resisted because it squeezed their negotiating room with client governments; they found the newly established Bureau for Human Rights a problem for similar reasons.[19] And Carter himself backed away from opportunities to push his human rights policy harder, so much so that aid policy under President Reagan was surprisingly similar.[20] Even within Congress, support for human rights was tied to other issues.[21] Liberals and conservatives both used human rights to pressure the USSR once the Kissinger-led Helsinki Final Act of 1975 had effectively legitimated Soviet control over eastern Europe.[22] Their differences flared over Latin America: Reagan-era realists and neocons supported dictators in the southern cone as essential to the fight against totalitarianism, while liberals abhorred the fact that the United States backed military regimes that tortured and disappeared their citizens. Chile and Argentina were the most contentious cases.[23]

This elite political contest was accompanied by an underlying social transformation. Lewis Mumford, whom we last met expressing skepticism about Le Corbusier's UN building, had been concerned in the Depression-era 1930s that excessive materialism was eroding the spiritual values that sustained American democracy's promise of freedom, truth, and justice. In that pre–Human Rights era, personal sacrifice and self-improvement, not materialism and capitalism, were the foundation for humanism.[24] Concerns about materialism's deleterious effects were much more acute by 1977. Daniel Bell's *The Cultural Contradictions of Capitalism*, Christopher Lasch's *Culture of Narcissism*, and Robert Bellah's *The Broken Covenant* all saw unrestrained consumption as a deeply corrosive force. These three prophets even met with a receptive President Carter in the White House, their views feeding in various ways into his famous July 1979 speech on the energy shortage and the crisis of confidence in the United States.[25]

Human rights were seen, by Carter and his advisers, as part of a response to this "malaise," as a way of putting moral purpose back into American foreign policy and of "making the country feel better about itself."[26] Carter may even have seen human rights as the ideological corollary of the civil rights movement he so admired. But in reality human rights had little popular resonance at this time. Latin America was a partial exception (in this case, transnational activism benefited from a large diaspora in the United States).[27] And political dissidence in the USSR and the question of Jewish emigration did become major elite political issues. But these did not galvanize American society in the same way as domestic social movements.

Because *global* human rights were not salient on a widespread basis, the "market" in the United States had to be constructed top-down.[28]

Supply created demand. Human Rights Watch (at first named Helsinki Watch) was the creation of three already prominent public figures in New York in 1978, for example.[29] Amnesty International had been in existence for more than fifteen years before it adopted professional marketing techniques in the United States and membership took off.[30] Many American supporters of Amnesty in the 1970s saw giving money as an equally worthy alternative to writing a letter, which was akin to heresy for European members.[31] It was the publicity these organizations gave human rights, through high-profile cases, campaigns, and celebrity support, that mobilized demand. Neoliberalism aided in this. A shrinking state sector, the search for new forms of activism, and an audience that had lost faith in radical politics made fertile ground for human rights.

Neither social change nor American foreign policy did much to invigorate international human rights law, however, and herein lies a major difference with the human rights advocacy that had gone before. In many European countries multilateral legal activism enjoyed a wider elite consensus, taking in influential parts of the state, about the desirability of global human rights *law* and *institutions* that might in some ways discipline sovereignty. The European Court of Human Rights was evidence for this. Despite its solidarity model, commitment to freeing individuals, and principled indifference to whether a regime was democratic or not, even Amnesty International from 1973 on pioneered a global Convention against Torture.[32] In the American case, the primacy of politics and the constitutional law tradition both mitigated against this.

As the world's dominant liberal democracy, committed to legitimate rule as that which was grounded in popular consent and national law, the United States was assumed by the majority of American advocates to be more progressive than other states and to have, indeed, a responsibility to export freedom, justice, and an open society.[33] Under Reagan, neocons argued that "human rights were primarily based on a set of values embedded in existing national political institutions and legal structures, of which the United States were at once the best historical example and the model."[34] Many liberal human rights advocates would have to agree. If the United States failed to honor its liberal commitments, then either an inhospitable international environment or the incumbents of state office (Nixon, Kissinger, Reagan) were at fault, not the United States itself. The foreign policy of President George W. Bush has been repudiated by liberals in exactly this fashion. The "Idea of America" is a sacred national alibi used by liberals to rationalize political failure (e.g., the use of torture and, more problematically for liberals *inside* the Obama administration such as Samantha Power, targeted assassinations).[35]

When Human Rights Watch cofounder Robert Bernstein broke with the organization in 2009 over what he saw as its anti-Israeli bias, he described the primacy of liberal democracy in the 1970s perfectly:

> At Human Rights Watch, we always recognized that open, democratic societies have faults and commit abuses. But we saw that they have the ability to correct them—through vigorous public debate, an adversarial press and many other mechanisms that encourage reform. That is why we sought to draw a sharp line between the democratic and nondemocratic worlds, in an effort to create clarity in human rights. We wanted to prevent the Soviet Union and its followers from playing a moral equivalence game with the West and to encourage liberalization by drawing attention to dissidents like Andrei Sakharov, Natan Sharansky and those in the Soviet gulag—and the millions in China's laogai, or labor camps. When I stepped aside in 1998, Human Rights Watch was active in 70 countries, most of them closed societies. Now the organization, with increasing frequency, casts aside its important distinction between open and closed societies.[36]

As human rights became Human Rights in the 1990s, Western powers came to see the utility of human rights rhetoric for legitimating foreign policy.[37] Democracy promotion became even more central to America's global grand strategy under President Clinton, the gap narrowing between what dominant states sought and what international human rights lawyers and major international NGOs demanded.[38] Trading on a legacy claim to impartiality, international humanists were in fact throwing in their lot with state power. The occupation of Afghanistan, with unprecedented closeness between NATO and humanitarian and human rights advocates, was an extreme example of this as was the intervention in Libya in 2011.

This attachment to democracy as a precondition for human rights is visible, for example, in Human Rights Watch's call to support elected

Muslim Brotherhood governments in Tunisia and Egypt. This position
received a stinging rebuke from women's organizations who accused
HRW of being apologists for regimes that denied women, gays, and religious minorities their rights.[39] A public letter from women's advocates—
organized by the Center for Secular Space—called for HRW to support
the separation of church and state and to highlight social and economic
(as well as civil and political) rights, suggesting that HRW's leadership
was still stuck in the pre-Vienna (that is, pre-1993) era when there was still
a debate about whether women's rights were human rights.[40] In response,
Human Rights Watch's senior leaders put a commitment to democracy
("constrained by international human rights law") first, followed by pressure to make sure democratically elected governments of whatever ideology supported basic human rights.

The two decades from Carter to Clinton were an exciting but uncertain time for global human rights advocates, as the worldwide legal and
judicial regime they had so long desired came tantalizingly close. A combination of post–Cold War atrocity, human rights entrepreneurialism,
growing UN self-confidence, and the "peace dividend" created a win-
dow of opportunity to build human rights infrastructure in the 1990s.
Most important of all was unipolarity: the power of the United States
as the sole global superpower could be yoked to the project of creating
precedents in international justice and humanitarian intervention by
outlawing those who committed gross human rights violations. With
the stars briefly aligned, a retributive architecture could be built. For a
generation of international lawyers trained outside the United States,
often in Europe, the chance to use a liberal hegemon to enshrine global
norms was too good to miss, even if the price was risking dependence on
American power.

Growing the Human Rights Market

Before we turn to the political institutionalization of human rights (the
construction of the Human Rights regime), the underlying social transformation from the 1970s onward that gave birth to the "humanitarian
marketplace" must be understood. I'll suggest in this and later chapters
that while the political and social power of human rights is failing, its

use as a language of justice will only increase. The ubiquity of human rights talk, campaigns, and demands is best explained not by impact but marketing. Beginning after 1977, human rights can be understood as, in effect, a new ethical brand for sale to the American, and global, middle class. This all built on the three changes Sidney Tarrow identifies as growth conditions for new social movements in the 1960s (the beginnings of the consumer generation): mass media, particularly television; more money and free time available to young people during the postwar boom years (they became "conscience constituents"); and an increase in foundation funding for new groups (in the case of human rights, particularly the Ford Foundation).[41]

Neither Amnesty International nor Helsinki Watch was self-consciously branded as a "human rights organization" at first. As press coverage grew, and membership and fund-raising increased, so a market developed in the 1980s. People could then be asked to support "human rights" rather than a specific person or issue. After the market matured in the 1990s, this logic reversed itself, and more precisely targeted human rights campaigns could be launched, the global salience of "human rights" now firmly embedded. Even by 1987, AIUSA's global rock tour was labeled "Human Rights Now!" and in 1988, when the various "Watch Committees" amalgamated, it was under the name Human Rights Watch.[42] This clearer articulation of "human rights" and the emergence of dedicated organizations committed to them consolidated a delineation between service-driven humanitarians and advocacy-driven human rights activists. Neoliberalism had opened disaster zones to nonstate humanitarian organizations, whose work increased significantly during post–Cold War complex emergencies. Money began to flow to humanitarians from government agencies, international and regional bodies, and a swelling private funding market.

Human rights organizations, skeptical at least rhetorically of states, were warier of government money (MSF, which refuses government money, once again straddles this human rights–humanitarian boundary). But both humanitarian and human rights advocates relied increasingly on a similar business model: suffering elsewhere—packaged in images, reports, videos, and campaigns—was used by professionals to increase press coverage and raise income from private and public sources. The people who paid were never likely to experience a human rights violation (or an act of violence defined as a "human rights violation"), and whether they gave for ethical or other reasons was of decreasing interest to human rights and humanitarian organizations. In sum, the scale of growth in *global human rights* and *humanitarianism* is a triumph of marketing as much as of a transcendent commitment to "humanity." People buy the product to assuage guilt or to feel good, and others do the work. You do not need to feel solidarity. None of these *human rights* activities had the kind of direct implications possessed by civil rights demonstrations in the American South or gay rights activism in San Francisco or reclaim the night marches through New York City. In each of these cases your own identity or neighborhood was at issue and your own security was often wagered.

The logic of neoliberalism is that every dollar must be free to find its maximally productive home. As American commerce and its corporate practices globalized after the 1970s, the old Amnesty International model of letter writing by small groups was overtaken by the need to increase impact. Humanists increasingly had to show *value for money*.[43] Output had often been used as a proxy for outcome in the past.[44] More laws, court cases, and reports appeared to prove that advocacy works. But this is no longer an adequate measure: empirical evidence, particularly quantitative proof, is increasingly important. Income, number of members, amount of press coverage, and number of campaigns are used as signs of growing market share when "making a difference" is so difficult to prove. Has growth in laws and organizations really delivered more than prominent and richer global human rights INGOs? Some scholars claim compliance with international human rights law is improving while others are more skeptical.[45] What is beyond doubt is that despite huge resources invested in globalizing human rights through law, courts, and campaigns, definitive evidence of their positive impact on state behavior is still so difficult to find that no scholarly consensus has been forged.[46]

If doubt remains about impact, no such reservations are possible about the growth of the humanist international. The mature results of this transformation are visible everywhere in 2013. Marketization has fueled astonishing growth, particularly in the humanitarian sector. The annual income of international humanitarian organizations is more than $15 billion a year. MSF, far from the largest player, had a recorded income for 2011 of just under $1.2 billion, of which 89 percent came from private donations (4.5 million of them). Amnesty International's annual global income in 2010 was $274 million, while Human Rights Watch, boosted by a "Global Challenge" grant from George Soros of $100 million given over ten years to fund "internationalization," reported a 2011 cash income of more than $24 million and total net assets of more than $212 million.[47] The marketing of suffering, visible on numerous international NGO websites in the pictures of victims, is the business model for almost all humanist organizations. Despite reservations that the use of child images demeans the dignity of victims and perpetuates stereotypes, attempts at self-regulation have made scant impact because innocent suffering is written into the DNA of humanism.[48]

Many international NGOs are now so big, with large staffs who have significant salary and pension entitlements, that they are locked in to this model. Money is essential, and its acquisition from the public and institutional funders, not participation, is now the mechanism for activism. Amnesty International UK, for example, recently sent an e-mail with the headline, "A woman presses send in Leeds . . . and a stoning is stopped in Iran," the accompanying commentary saying, "A man texts from Oxford. . . and a torture cell in Bahrain closes forever." It goes on: "The bus. The train. The school gate. The pub. The park. Your sofa. Now you can take action to save lives and end injustice wherever you are—using your mobile phone." Amnesty wants you to join its "Pocket Protest" where replying to the text adds your name to an urgent petition or appeal designed to protect someone in danger.[49]

Such campaigning techniques, the e-mail claims, helped free Chinese dissident Chen Guangcheng and have kept up pressure on President Obama to close Guantanamo Bay. Avaaz.Org e-mails to say "we're winning, over and over again." One example given of a successful campaign is getting European oil sanctions and Arab League sanctions against Syria. Credit is also claimed for action to block homophobic legislation in Uganda, stopping 2011's Bahrain motor racing Grand Prix, and for intervention in Libya after a million messages were sent to the United Nations (then-US ambassador to the UN, Susan Rice, publicly thanking Avaaz in a tweet).

Another Avaaz headline says, "Victory on Cluster Bombs!" after a US-led effort to weaken the 2008 Convention on Cluster Munitions was halted. It says: "Three years ago, Avaaz mobilized to help push through a global ban on cluster bombs, saving thousands of children. This year the US quietly lobbied nations to sign a new law that would have allowed their use again! Our 600,000-strong petition helped push 50 states to oppose the US's underhanded plan." In fact, as with the Rome Statute, this "global ban" does not include the United States, Russia, China, or India. Human Rights Watch also claimed some credit as part of this "powerful alliance of Norway, Austria, Mexico, and about 50 other governments, as well as several UN agencies (most notably the UN Development Programme), the International Committee of the Red Cross (ICRC) and the Cluster Munition Coalition led by Human Rights Watch."[50] This convention is noteworthy because, as HRW's report makes clear, it is about protecting civilians in conflict zones, an international humanitarian law issue taken up as a core human rights issue.[51]

Amnesty, Avaaz, and Human Rights Watch are claiming credit because their marketing model relies on selling the notion that an investment of a few dollars or the time it takes to click the "Donate Now" button will make a difference. This claim is made even though the situation in Syria worsened across 2013, there has been little accountability for human rights violations in Bahrain, and the ban on cluster munitions does not include the world's largest makers and users including the United States. Indeed, ongoing failure becomes a reason to urge supporters to give more. What are all those people pressing "send" actually doing? Is this *slacktivism*?

The essence of slacktivism is activism that is low cost, as low as clicking the mouse button or sending a text. The suspicion is that such activism would not take place if it was costlier. As a result, it does not build participatory forms of ongoing activism but provides a low-cost *alternative* to them.[52] The funding and activism models of major INGOs are increasingly concerned with this approach, which is seen as the key to the elusive youth constituency they all covet. Malcolm Gladwell has argued, however, that effective activism, such as civil rights resistance, relies on strong personal ties. Social media activism, by contrast, is marked by a low motivation threshold and weak ties reinforced by the egalitarian nature of leaderless networks. This is good for information sharing, says Gladwell, and bad for higher-cost activism.[53] This echoes research on "social distance"—people help those who are closer in some way to them more than they help others because there is some prospect of *reciprocity*.[54] Almost by definition giving to humanist organizations is a nonreciprocal activity. In local and solidarity-based rights activism an individual benefits in principle from collective success and builds up a store of goodwill for future interactions. Giving is a long-term insurance policy as the East Timorese will attest.

To what extent can individuals who, doing what they do for entertainment (surfing the Web, watching TV, logging onto Facebook, seeing what is trending on Twitter), come across an appeal to sign a petition or donate be considered witnesses to atrocity, or activists? What does shallow but wide commitment tell us about the deeper social roots (and the potential for reciprocity) of human rights and humanitarian giving? All INGOs claim that website hits and donations are activism. Although Amnesty International claims 3.2 million "members" (and aspires to 5 million), many of them are in reality only casual attendees at AI events who neither pay nor join the organization.[55] Most major humanitarian INGOs have sophisticated fund-raising operations and spend a lot of time on branding and growth.

Avaaz.Org (tagline: "The World in Action") claims more than 14.5 million members and employs forty permanent staff who have organized public protests and distributed cameras, satellite phones, and modems to democracy activists in Syria, Yemen, and Libya.[56] Avaaz petitions, whose topics are proposed and chosen democratically by members, can get five hundred thousand signatures in hours. But with no core uniting philosophy beyond "click," surely they have little scope for exercising social and political pressure? Avaaz has no votes and is not a political constituency for *any* decision maker, which deprives it of leverage. It aspires to thrive precisely in the game of sheer numbers. This makes it radically majoritarian in a narrow way, but because it is not a political community it lacks reciprocity relations between members or with beneficiaries or politicians. It is a protest of strangers. Who are these people, what do they believe in, what are they really like, and how accountable are they for their decisions? They have only mob authority. This may be the best we can hope for, but it is not sustained or sustainable ethical commitment.

Consider, finally, the YouTube sensation *Kony 2012* released by the San Diego–based NGO Invisible Children, which received nearly one hundred million hits from March to June 2012. There have been numerous complaints made about the film, ranging from the suggestion it was a front for evangelicals to the suggestion it was a money-making scheme.

Many factual inaccuracies, insensitivities, and manipulations have also been the object of intense criticism (which led the director, Jason Russell, to be hospitalized briefly after allegations about lewd public behavior blamed on temporary psychosis).[57]

The thirty-minute video is a testament to the power of the totem touching on its every aspect. At one point a group of young people are seen chanting: "We've seen these kids, we've heard their cries, this war must end, we will not stop, we will not fear, we will fight war." Kony's crimes are condemned by an animated Luis Moreno-Ocampo, at the time ICC chief prosecutor, who associates Kony with Hitler. "It's not just bad for Ugandan people, it's bad for everyone," says Ocampo, adding that we live in a "Facebook world." The video also includes a wall of head-and-shoulder mug shots of young activists exactly like the iconic museum and memorial displays. The plan was to raise awareness about Kony's crimes ("Make Kony Famous") by covering cities with posters on April 20, 2012 (Hitler's birthday), and to raise money that has built, the video claims, schools and an early warning radio network. This all seems to be evidence of some kind of impact, although the chance of catching Kony seems minimal. The day of protest failed to ignite despite the online interest.

There are already one hundred US special forces in the Central African Republic looking for Kony.[58] *Kony 2012* was designed in part to consolidate this deployment.[59] The *New York Times* reported: "Gen. Carter F. Ham, the overall commander of American forces in Africa, has a 'Kony 2012' poster tacked to his office door. As one American official put it: 'Let's be honest, there was some constituent pressure here. Did "Kony 2012" have something to do with this? Absolutely.' "[60] Is this activity evidence of a world community mobilizing to deter atrocity? The viral sensation that *Kony 2012* became obscures the fact that millions who watched it did so *because* it was a viral sensation. When activism is consumption, the audience is a "flash mob" who move quickly on to the next big thing. Their interests are not engaged, and they do not generate any political or social capital, all of which denies them a sustained voice.

This is not necessarily a problem for those who run major INGOs; they get greater freedom with casual onetime donors. More-established members tend to be vocal. Cynicism about impact is the danger. Activism via Facebook makes deeper political and economic linkages between modern life and social suffering almost completely invisible. Those who supported *Kony 2012* did not see themselves as implicated by a global system that keeps children poor and vulnerable. Evil Joseph Kony was responsible. Celebrity culture exacerbates this trend toward alienation. The giants of commercial branding also make humanitarian appearances (George Clooney, Bono, Angelina Jolie, Sting). The goods they sell are usually aspirational: watches, perfume, jewelry, high-end travel goods, human rights (a luxury good for the educated urban middle class). In *Kony 2012*, Darfur advocate George Clooney makes his obligatory appearance. Digital technology adds to this detachment because everything is mediated through a screen.[61]

Those who suffer are marginal in all of this. *Kony 2012* grounds itself on the totem by using the story of one freed child soldier befriended by the director as the motivating premise. This young boy is presented as variously damaged, grateful, and deeply innocent. The stories of thousands of boys and girls like him are "deployed" as moral fuel for a variety of international causes. With its Hollywood production values, *Kony 2012* is a sophisticated-looking campaign tool. The Human Rights Imperium can do far more with righteous anger and evil killers like Joseph Kony because righteous anger identifies and isolates a perpetrator, someone who is responsible; and thus rather than the machinery of compassion and care we get the much more powerful machinery of justice and retribution, underwritten by an expanding audience who are now consumers of the spectacle, not members who exercise voice. Slowly, movies, news, and humanitarian and human rights concerns will merge into one undifferentiated mass. Who will be the source of moral authority then? On its website, Human Rights Watch links itself to *Kony 2012* and shows its own short, moving video: *Dear Obama: A Message from Victims of the LRA*. Inevitably on the front screen is a young, forlorn-looking boy.[62] The "Support Human Rights: Donate Now" button is up and to the right.

From Confession to Profession

In this chapter I have made two claims about the transformation from human rights to Human Rights that has its roots in the 1970s. First, that a distinctly American approach to human rights based on exporting democracy and tied to the pragmatic use of liberal state power became dominant; second, that underlying socioeconomic changes, intensified by neoliberal policies, created a humanitarian marketplace where supporting humanist causes became a consumption good that fueled organizational growth. Permanent international NGOs soon meant a widening class of professional activists and advocates. These were people trained as "international human rights lawyers" or "humanitarians." Publicity also created a demand among wealthy individuals, foundations, and regular private givers to invest in human rights, which in turn boosted income, fueled supply (e.g., more campaigns), again fed demand, and so the cycle continued. Almost inevitably, major humanitarian and human rights organizations were increasingly run like businesses, with growth (in scale, not profit) as their metric.

This is a long way from 1961 when Amnesty International's pioneers saw global human rights as a spiritual mass movement for moral rearmament. In their secular religiosity they were wary of money and of politics, both things that "Americanization" threatened.[63] Some of Amnesty's US members even sought to regulate their own influence within Amnesty in the 1970s: fearing American members might erode the organization's "internationalism," they tried in vain in 1983 to appoint a Dutch former Amnesty deputy secretary general, Dick Oosting, as head of AIUSA, Amnesty's American section.[64] The effects on Amnesty of a "massive growth of individual unstructured membership" had been concerning senior leaders for years; they were particularly worried they might attract members who would pay to join but not be active.[65] In other words, membership was the antithesis of an alienated donation.

Médecins Sans Frontières was founded in France in 1971. Despite being what we would now call a "humanitarian organization," MSF mixed compassion (medical treatment) and witnessing (human rights). It was an amalgam of leftist French Red Cross doctors (led by Bernard Kouchner) who witnessed mass atrocities in Biafra in 1968 and were appalled that the ICRC expected them to stay silent, and French journalists who emphasized medical assistance to the poor and victimized.[66] Kouchner argued, before he left the organization, that MSF employees should not draw a salary and should not be provided with a pension. He also argued for more aggressive publicity about atrocities. Despite this, MSF remained close to core ICRC principles, "the idea that silence was necessary to action held by a majority of its founding members."[67]

MSF's major sections remain western European, and its charter includes the following principle, which all members are expect to honor: "As volunteers, members understand the risks and dangers of the missions they carry out and make no claim for themselves or their assigns for any form of compensation other than that which the association might be able to afford them."[68]

Human Rights Watch was not embedded in post-Christian European or leftist politics and was from the start connected with influential forces inside American national politics. It was small, law-focused, and sought to influence policy at the highest level, initially on the issue of dissidents in the Soviet Union and then increasingly on the question of torture and impunity in Latin America. One of its three cofounders, Aryeh Neier, had been head of the American Civil Liberties Union (ACLU), during which time he had been involved in several high-profile national cases, including defending the right of Nazis to march through Skokie, Illinois. Moving from the ACLU to cofound Helsinki Watch, Neier "brought my years of experience in promoting rights in the United States, and my grasp, based on that experience, of how to endow the new field of international human rights with a quality of professionalism that it previously lacked."[69]

This formulation ignores the preparation work that had already been done, by organizations like Amnesty International, to create the conditions for a global human rights market to emerge. President Carter had referenced Amnesty's signature concept, "the prisoner of conscience," and in 1977 Amnesty was awarded the Nobel Peace Prize.[70] But, once again, Neier is identifying something significant. The emergence of *American* human rights activism did mean professionalization in terms of fund-raising (the use of direct mail, for example), campaigning, lobbying, and the political use of the law.[71] And the human rights market grew accordingly at a rapid rate. The fundamental difference between Amnesty and Human Rights Watch is membership. This always gave prima facie credibility to Amnesty's claim to be a solidarity movement. Both sustained a research operation through the 1980s, but only Amnesty had to service a million or more members. Its classic model, members organized into letter-writing groups, proved unsustainable on a worldwide basis, and by the end of the 1980s members were counted as individuals, even though then, as now, one can only donate to a national Amnesty section, and some sections *still* count groups. The ongoing struggle between members and professional staff continued into the 1990s, past the point at which the "Watch Committees" were formed into Human Rights Watch.

The pivotal moment when the torch passed, when Amnesty's secular religiosity was no longer sustainable, was Rwanda in 1994. Amnesty was unable to move quickly enough because of its complex internal democracy and bureaucracy and the decades of accumulated policies and principles that framed debate about what to do, all while television footage showed the genocide in Rwanda happening. Human Rights Watch simply sent people to report on what they saw, unrestrained by the need to determine exactly how the crimes committed fitted within an organizational mandate.[72] In other words, what was once Amnesty's strength—membership—now slowed it down. One could be a fast, globally active advocacy operation or a mass movement: it was becoming harder to be both. The time was approaching when, as human rights became Human Rights, Amnesty would have to choose: global human rights organization or international solidarity movement. In the past, Human Rights Watch was very careful to distinguish itself from Amnesty, defining itself, for example, as New York–based.[73] Its current description of itself has changed radically. Gone are explicit references to distinguish it from Amnesty and to emphasize its American base. It is now "one of the world's leading independent organizations dedicated to defending and protecting human rights." HRW's "rigorous and objective investigations and strategic, targeted advocacy" raise the costs of human rights abuses and hold abusers accountable. This lays the "legal and moral groundwork for deep-rooted change," HRW standing, in its opinion, "with victims and activists."[74]

According to George Soros:

Human Rights Watch can have even greater impact by being genuinely international in scope. . . . Human Rights Watch must be present in capitals around the globe, addressing local issues, allied with local rights groups and engaging with local government officials. In five years' time it aims to have as much as half its income and a majority of its board members come from outside the United States.[75]

His $100 million donation will allow HRW to "increase its influence in emerging power centers" by employing 120 new staff (a 40 percent increase) and opening new offices in Europe, Brazil, India, Japan, and South Africa.[76] HRW has appointed former UN humanitarian chief, ex-Norwegian Red Cross head, and ex-Amnesty senior leader Jan Egeland as deputy executive director based in Oslo. By naming and shaming governments and raising money directly in their home markets, HRW hopes to extend its global reach.

Amnesty is also alert to the shifting distribution of international power, extending its operations away from London and a centralized research operation into the South under the slogan "moving closer to the ground." This has put increasing, and perhaps fatal, strain on an organization built in its core for secular religiosity as a bulwark against the endtimes.[77] In a letter to Amnesty directors in August 2010, secretary general and former UN staffer Salil Shetty stressed that "growth has no purpose other than to enhance AI's human rights impact."[78] The hope is to ally with local activists in places like South Africa, India, and Brazil. In other words, the search for a truly global membership in a world of the rising South and declining Europe has become Amnesty's primary goal.[79] "International solidarity" is, argues Shetty, what Amnesty has always stood for, along with "speaking truth to power." His "Blueprint" says:

> Our research remains world class as we amplify the voices of those whose rights are being violated. We will know when our membership is consistently growing and more active, when we are the organization of choice for staff. Our goal will be to build on the legacy of the past and create a compelling future for our movement. We have the reach, the scope, the expert knowledge, and the strategic partnerships to make this happen. We are going to join them up, respond to the changing political picture and create that global influence.[80]

The senior directors of Amnesty International and Human Rights Watch are answering the impact question differently in the era of rising multipolarity. Neither answer is about secular religiosity. Given the world in which this was necessary—one of European dominance and minimal positive law—is long since gone and that the evidence for its impact beyond the creation of symbolic global institutions is slim, should we mourn the passing of this relic of the old world?

Amnesty wants to make more noise in more places at the local level. Its management believes it can still make a major impression in Geneva and New York with localized research and campaign operations conducted by on-the-ground researchers. This looks on the face of it like a move in the direction of "human rights." The question is: does Amnesty International have the business model to sustain it? Being able to pay for and support local offices, as well as attract highly competent staffers, is one concern. Another is getting pulled into the local political equation. And perhaps more than both of these reservations, the vast majority of Amnesty's income is from a handful of western sections. Its political economy remains highly skewed toward Europe and the United States, an imbalance that will prove challenging when lines of responsibility for priority-setting become blurred. Nevertheless, Amnesty's move to disperse its centralized research and management operation in London to the South represents a pivotal test case of whether Human Rights can be transformed into locally owned and accountable human rights movements.

Human Rights Watch's approach is very different. With no membership to provide a democratic brake on its ambitions, it is ramping up its global capacity to produce authoritative information with which to "name and shame" governments. Human Rights Watch has been able to thrive without creating a membership at all. Located in New York with good access to Congress and wealthy donors, it has suffered from none of the internal angst that Amnesty is experiencing as the secular religious vision of human rights gives way to a world of resurgent sovereignty.

Yet, as Margo Picken, whose career in Amnesty began with her heading its UN office in the 1970s, reminded senior human rights advocates in 2010, René Cassin, in his speech accepting the Nobel Peace Prize in 1968 had warned them not to "keep looking for new mechanisms. Just build on what we have."[81] Picken stressed partnership, alliances, shared credit, unsung work, membership, and wariness about state power; Amnesty was, she said, about "building a following for human rights," her very language redolent of a vocation, not a profession.[82] This human rights model was about creating a real international movement. Global, hierarchical organizations are the antithesis of such collective action—they stifle diversity and discipline dissent.

How difficult it is to court power and sustain a movement is obvious from the sobering story of AIUSA's new executive director in 2012, Suzanne Nossel. On paper she was an excellent candidate for a modern American human rights INGO concerned to be taken seriously in Washington: having worked at McKinsey, the State Department (where she worked on Human Rights Council issues), the *Wall Street Journal*, and Human Rights Watch, Nossel was solidly a product of the world of elite public policy in the United States. But if the identity of the witnesser is as important as the witnessing, this was a brave choice for an organization seeking wide legitimacy outside the United States and within AIUSA's rank-and-file membership. Nossel's 2004 *Foreign Affairs* article, "Smart Power: Reclaiming Liberal Internationalism," put her squarely in the pro-democracy export tradition of American human rights advocates that includes Samantha Power, Susan Rice, Anne-Marie Slaughter, and Hillary Clinton.[83]

Nossel knew how to invoke the totem that anchors secular religiosity. In a December 2012 blog, published under her name, she imagined being a prisoner of conscience:

> Loneliness is creeping in. You've pushed beyond the limits of exhaustion. Your bones ache and tears have dried to your face. **You can't go on like this.** Then, the letters arrive. At first, just a few. Then, day by day, they grow. Soon, **beautiful messages** scrawled on **colorful paper** and decorative cards fill your world. These are letters written by people in **nearby cities and far away countries**. They are **messages of support and solidarity**, hope and inspiration, and strength and motivation **from people you don't even know**. They are messages written to both you and those who have imprisoned you. At that moment, you realize that **these aren't just letters—they are life lines.** You feel free again.

The reality is that this kind of prisoner work has been systematically sidelined as an operational priority for two decades by Amnesty's senior leadership, who see it as dated, even irrelevant, in a fast-moving world of crises, thematic campaigns, and global media. Nossel's hiring was about "smart power" not the totem. She had billboards posted on Chicago bus stops during a NATO summit in May 2012 that congratulated NATO on the progress it was making for women's rights in Afghanistan. Former secretary of state Madeleine Albright also spoke at an Amnesty "NATO shadow summit" at Nossel's invitation. Inside AIUSA there were growing concerns, particularly among its influential "country coordinators," that Nossel was undermining Amnesty's reputation for impartiality. In a Council on Foreign Relations report of May 2012, Nossel called for "normalizing the treatment of Israel" at the Human Rights Council and made it clear how strongly she felt the United States was a positive force for global human rights, US accession having in large part given the HRC "newfound credibility as a human rights watchdog."[84] In a section headed "Taking on Iran," Nossel claimed that "the council's inattention to abuses in Iran was a badge of its fecklessness."[85]

Given the reservations shared by many human rights activists about Israel's treatment of the Palestinians (and what is perceived as the United States' double-standard toward Israel) and of the ways in which successive American governments have sought to isolate Iran internationally in preparation for a possible military attack, these comments placed Nossel far too close to the official position of the American state. Many within Amnesty and AIUSA called for Nossel's resignation and she left the organization after only one year in January 2013 bound, as were the AIUSA board, by a watertight gagging agreement on public comment.

This is a cautionary tale about moral and political authority and their fundamental incompatibility. Being located within the United States, with American money as a funding base, contacts inside the state, and prominent government officials and legislative representatives as frequent interlocutors, a premium is placed on impartiality. Given we are talking about the American state, the most powerful international actor of the last seventy years, this is doubly the case. The secular religiosity that Amnesty has been trying to shed, and which Human Rights Watch never had, lies at the root of the search for moral authority.[86] Yet it survives minimally only in the classic international humanitarian organizations like the ICRC and MSF, in the Europe-based International Federation for Human Rights (FIDH) and International Commission of Jurists (of which Mary Robinson was president until 2010), and in the declining number of Amnesty members who remain skeptical about the profane worlds of state power and money. The pressure to corporatize and comply with power has affected humanitarians acutely as well, but because of their service delivery role and because they are closer to the suffering body their moral authority does not depend on the health of the Global Human Rights Regime. They can replenish themselves at source. Their moral practice comes *before* the law. The competition they face from religious actors, for whom social action is an identity-driven moral pursuit (the "why" still matters), consolidates this need to take more care with their legitimacy. Vocation cannot be entirely abandoned as a result.[87]

American-style pragmatism reaches its limits confronted with stable but resistant states or with people of abiding faith. Pragmatism's virtue may be to elide foundational questions, to put law before philosophy, but it only does this by assuming neoliberal democracy as the default position we all ought to adopt. The appropriateness of globalizing a distinction between public and private as the guarantee of an "open society" is taken as a common sense foreign-policy truth. Pragmatism relies on but hides, or ignores, this ideological claim. You and I may *prefer* neoliberal democracy, but by what *authority* can we argue everyone else is obligated to adopt it? Why should Muslims, evangelical Christians, charismatic Catholics, Jesuits, Pentecostals, Mormons, Lutherans, Hindus, Jews, Quakers, Buddhists, or Sikhs, liberalize if they choose not to? The idea of "smart power," like the creation of institutions for embedding norms, assumes we have moved beyond why to how. Critiques of human rights law and the International Criminal Court and R2P are based by American pragmatists not on their founding assumptions but on their poor design, inadequate functioning, or ineffectiveness.

In stable states with alternative social and cultural norms that enjoy legitimacy among a sizable proportion of the population, coercion and inducement are likely to be of only limited use while persuasion reaches stalemate against any authority able to effectively invoke an alternative basis for mobilization like nationalism or religion. The remaining mechanism is to create local institutions that embed, promote, and legitimate rights—that build local capacity from the inside in other words.[88] This was hard enough to achieve when liberal norms were dominant and unquestioned. Even imperial projects before the modern era of global governance frequently failed for lack of compliance. Now that there are principled challenges to the West and to liberal hegemony from several powerful states, that gaining local compliance in a world of religious diversity will require negotiation and compromise, and that secular religiosity has been successfully undermined, only human rights can succeed. Human Rights by their nature are universal, secular, and categorical. They allow no compromise, must be legitimated by nondiscriminatory authority, and must trump competing norms not authorized in a similar fashion. In a world of fractured power such an outcome is less and less likely all the time.

This reproduces the abiding tension between European and American legal traditions. Even critics of legal realism like Anne-Marie Slaughter stick closely to legal pragmatism, in which the guiding rule is "what works best" and "what really happens," rather than what is right.[89] In such a world, using force, under the guise of R2P, is always an option. As Guglielmo Verdirame points out, in Europe norms remain norms even when they are broken.[90] This is not enough to challenge the skepticism about immutable rules characteristic of pragmatic American legalism, which puts utility at the base of law's validity.[91] The law is thus an instrument. In a world where the virtues of neoliberal democracy are taken for granted this is hardly a surprise. The humanist international has made good use of American pragmatism as a result.

6 HUMAN RIGHTS EMPIRE

Human Rights have dominated humanist politics since the 1990s. The emphasis on protection and justice has enabled an increasingly ambitious interventionist infrastructure to be built and much wider claims to legitimate rule to be made. This resembles the beginnings of state formation as described, for example, by R. I. Moore:

> When rulers begin to assert themselves, and to create a recognizable apparatus of state, the earliest developments always include the appearance of a hierarchy of specialized agencies for the enforcement of order—judges, police forces, and so on—and law itself becomes coercive, imposing from above a pattern of guilt or innocence in accord with codes promulgated by the central authority, rather than mediatory, seeking agreement or compromise.[1]

The social engineering potential of high modernism inevitably appeals to all those who want to save the world, argues James Scott, while Frédéric Mégret points to the "historical irony that the international human rights movement, which started among other things as a challenge to the state's penal excesses, should end up legitimizing a huge system of criminal repression."[2] To create this system means creating an apparatus of global power that mimics the state.

This is what we are witnessing, at least as an aspiration. The increasing aversion, for example, to amnesties, or vigorous opposition to forms of local justice in Uganda and Rwanda, or the general reluctance to embrace "restorative justice" by mainstream transitional justice advocates are attempts by the Human Rights Imperium to trump existing forms of local authority in favor of universal norms.[3] Human Rights advocates want the final power to decide what are valid rules and therefore what are legitimate exceptions to those rules. In the era of the ICC and R2P, advocates believe they no longer need to take care of nurturing their own moral authority; they have power enshrined in law and institutions. If they compromise with powerful states, it is merely they hope as a transitory expedient, the soothing fiction of their eventual triumph permitting this short-term tactical concession.

Humanism's grand ambitions in the era of the ICC and R2P naturally expose its claims and practices to increasing accountability demands, yet humanists often meet scrutiny with indignation, treating doubt and doubters as heretics. But why should the custodians of humanity's sacred power not be accountable when they act in the name of us all? What stops suffering becoming an alibi for the deployment of more violence and power? The humanist "business model" uses totemic material (atrocity, suffering, heroism) as both legitimation and resource: increasingly, lives lost and endangered bring the lawyers and judicial advocates, not just the caregivers. Under the rubrics of protection and prevention, in-conflict or even preemptive action by the ICC and R2P comes to justify a permanent infrastructure of power, whether or not the alleged threat is ever likely to be realized.

International Justice and the Triumph of Human Rights

Human Rights law has slowly but surely colonized international humanitarian law.[4] In world politics, "The humanitarian law of armed conflict has been the portal through which the human-rights regimes have been admitted," argues Gerald Draper, his dating taking us back to the Tehran Conference of 1968 and the beginning of efforts by Arab and decolonizing states to use human rights to their advantage.[5] Draper is critical of what he sees as the UN-inspired confusion between international humanitarian law and human rights law.[6] But this misses the importance *politically* of "civilian" and "noncombatant" as categories of people whose claims to be protected at all times are made in the name of human rights using international humanitarian law.[7] Human Rights

Watch executive director Kenneth Roth is explicit about the organization's decision, from the early 1980s, to use Common Article 3 of the Geneva Conventions (on the fundamental protections everyone enjoys in any form of conflict) and the First Additional Protocol of 1977 (extending more protection to civilians) to legitimate its work.

> Basically, we applied those provisions to internal conflicts—recognizing that this wasn't technically right from a legal perspective but we weren't going to court. These were not legal arguments needed to convince a judge. Rather, we needed to refer to a set of norms that would persuade public opinion that certain military conduct was wrong. It we could do that successfully, it didn't matter whether the law technically applied or not. Very frequently we would use this broader principled approach to push the boundaries of the law, even where the law had not caught up.

Roth goes on: "In recent years, international tribunals have done the same thing that we were doing at an informal level in the 1980s. This has become a less radical proposition than it may have appeared in an earlier time. . . . It's the approach we used with the Landmines Convention and the Cluster Munitions Convention. It has been a very deliberate approach all the way along."[8]

Human Rights Watch's strategy was pragmatic, but its success reflects in a deeper sense the political advantages human rights have over international humanitarian law: they operate in peace *and* war, and they claim an authority more fundamental than, and a direct challenge to, that of states. Human rights law, unlike humanitarian law, is "constitutional," that is, it produces *political authority*. As Common Article 3 makes clear, human rights continue to be held by soldiers as well as civilians during war. Indeed, waging war at all is a violation of human rights.[9]

The potentially boundless scope and radical authority of human rights demands are a reason for their triumph within humanism, as is their claim to predate state formation. People going back to aboriginal antiquity *always* had human rights, if we have them. The positive law is a late recognition of timeless natural law that does not rely on state assent, state practice, or reciprocity for its normative force. While customary law gains legitimacy from, among other things, legal opinion and state practice, *jus cogens* or "compelling law" is really human rights law, inviolable and inalienable moral prohibitions on how any individual can be treated by anyone—state, armed group, or individual—in war or peace. No treaty or customary law is necessary to recognize these human rights. War is always a human rights violation waiting to be converted into a crime.

We can understand 1899's Martens Clause as a human rights claim, in other words. Recall its invocation of "the laws of humanity and the requirements of the public conscience." Morality and legality intertwined, a sacred point of origin back beyond which we need not go. The Martens Clause was even invoked in the rulings of the International Criminal Tribunal for the former Yugoslavia (ICTY).[10] Valid positive law is derived from natural law principles sanctified in a moment of creation, of "constitution," when an "unmoved mover," an unquestionable authority, a secular god, authorizes all subsequent rules. This is *global constitutional law*.[11] Theodor Meron recommends that a "solemn declaration" be made by states of "an irreducible core of human rights that must be applied at a minimum at all times," from which no derogations and reservations are possible, to cover the gray zone between forms of conflict (internal, international, etc.). His preferred guardian for this declaration is the ICRC. In other words, the end point of international humanitarian law is the recognition of fundamental norms that are applicable always, without discretion. The name of these norms is *Human Rights*.[12] For Meron, human rights and the "principles of humanity" are about humanizing humanitarian law. Even the phrase "international humanitarian law" rather than "laws of war" reflects the influence of human rights.[13] This shift begins with 1949's Geneva Conventions, and 1998's Rome Statute extends it.[14]

Herein lies the origin of the clash with American law and human rights. American pragmatists, who build norms out of existing empirical realities, cannot provide any "fundamental code of primary norms," like a "rule of recognition," that would form the basis of legal *obligation*.[15] For Europeans, the facts serve as evidence for, not *alternatives to*, norms:

> In a formal understanding of the term, a constitution is the document or even point from which all other authority is derived; it is the center of a hierarchical system in which the lower rules derive

their authority from higher ones, to the point where the constitution itself rests on an ultimate "rule of recognition" (Hart) or *Grundnorm* (Kelsen) that can be derived only from extralegal sources of legitimacy, either religious (God) or civic (the *pouvoir constituant* or people power or constitutional moment).[16]

Europeans have been building this secular source of legitimacy since 1863. But Americans already have a sanctified *national* constitution. The world is not big enough for two final authorities. By using American power and the cultural importance of the Holocaust and genocide, pragmatists believe they have done away with the need to replenish their moral authority. Their legitimacy now comes from global norms, they believe. This misconception lies at the heart of the endtimes.

International criminal justice has been the vanguard for Human Rights for three reasons. First, a temporary harmony of interests existed in the 1990s between American foreign policy and European international lawyers, who both saw the utility of a court in response to atrocity in the former Yugoslavia. Solving diplomatic problems for states is an important explanation for innovation in institutions (e.g., the referral of the situation in Sudan to the ICC under the otherwise ICC-phobic Bush administration). Second, the attraction of global judicial institutions for advocates is the possibility of accruing some serious coercive power. Third, the symbolic potential of world law and a world court that in principle holds *everyone* accountable for his or her actions as an individual under global criminal law has always been the ultimate prize for lawyers of the humanist international. The ICTY promised to be a major step in that direction.

Robbing sovereigns of the protection of the state made them subject to a higher law. Legitimating this global constitutional law means moving beyond crimes against individuals to those committed against "the international" itself. Once this move is made, humanists can define their jurisdiction as superior to that of states and claim the right to rule. "The ICC is a self-consciously innovative venture which unashamedly upholds the primacy of *jus cogens* above that of comity," in other words.[17] Law, that is, over politics (or more accurately law *as* politics). As René Provost puts it: "When the violation is taken as transcending individual harm . . . a simple individual right of action appears insufficient, and some form of collective reaction must be envisaged, very often in the form of punitive action."[18]

The global legal and judicial infrastructure is defended, consolidated, and extended by creating global punitive structures to tackle harms that attack *humanity*. In the case of *Prosecutor v. Erdemović* at the ICTY in 2006, for example, the tribunal, in sentencing, described crimes against humanity as crimes that "transcend the individual because when the individual is assaulted, humanity comes under attack and is negated. It is therefore *the concept of humanity as victim which essentially characterises crimes against humanity*."[19] Rehabilitating the international legal order when it has been breached, as at Nuremberg, and adding this knowledge to the "collective memory" are, for William Schabas, two of the criminal law's most vital functions.[20] And what of individual victims? Margaret deGuzman argues: "This reaffirmation of the legal order also addresses the victims' needs for recognition and justice."[21] But this is the metanarrative as alibi. Advocates, judges, and lawyers seek actively to build the global criminal law and judicial infrastructure, taking it as axiomatic that global law makes a difference for existing and future victims.

The ICTY's judges and prosecutors understood their role as to "promote a certain idea of international criminal justice versus what they saw as scheming and ultimately self defeating attempts to negotiate with the devil."[22] But they too schemed. The opportunity opened by US enthusiasm for ad hoc international tribunals was too good to miss. ICTY president Judge Antonio Cassese, the preeminent architect of international criminal justice, actively headhunted Richard Goldstone to be chief prosecutor. US war crimes ambassador David Scheffer refers coyly to the skepticism some might feel for a process where the chief judge "meddles so intrusively" in the selection of the chief prosecutor.[23] But examples of this close judge-prosecutor link within the ad hoc tribunals are plentiful. This was particularly the case with the ICTY and ICTR (International Criminal Tribunal for Rwanda): the Security Council statutes establishing them were so vague they gave significant leeway to activist judges like Cassese to craft rules, policies, and even the international legal definitions of crimes such as rape, torture, genocide, and crimes against humanity (leeway that was reined in when it came to the Rome Statute and the ICC).[24] International lawyers and judges were making the very law they then adjudicated upon as neutral and impartial arbiters.

The trial that started the new era was that of Duško Tadić, the first person to be convicted of crimes against humanity since Nuremberg. Tadić, a low-level operative who tortured inmates at Omarska, was first tried in

1996, with proceedings complete, after appeals, in 2000.[25] His trial drew on the Holocaust metanarrative by explicitly linking scenes from Omarska with Auschwitz. Tadić's defense counsel challenged the court's legality, but the court *itself* ruled that in its own view it was legally established.[26] The ICTY (sitting in The Hague) was seen by all its advocates as a new dawn for international criminal justice, the foundation of a wealth of innovative precedent that could then be used in building a wider and deeper body of law, case history, and institutional infrastructure. Before establishing the ICTY, the Security Council appointed law professor M. Cherif Bassiouni, who ranks with Cassese, Meron, and Goldstone as a proponent of international criminal justice, to investigate breaches of humanitarian law in Bosnia. Bassiouni's view encapsulates the humanist international's ambitions: "If the lessons of the past are to instruct the course of the future, then the creation of a permanent system of international criminal justice with a continuous institutional memory is imperative."[27]

A permanent ICC was the prize for which the ad hoc ICTY and ICTR were pathfinders. Active consideration of an international criminal court (which many humanists had desired going back to Moynier) had been under way in the International Law Commission (ILC) since 1989 following a motion from the UN General Assembly. The original General Assembly remit concerned crimes including, but not limited to, drug trafficking, which had opened a space for entrepreneurialism by members of the ILC.[28] Bassiouni helped draft the ILC motion for the General Assembly before leading a commission of experts to investigate atrocities in the former Yugoslavia.[29] The Tadić case, the first tangible result, still had restricted precedent value, because the ICTY was required to link crimes against humanity with armed conflict. Advocates succeeded in removing such a limitation from 1998's Rome Statute, a shift noted by the British Law Lords in their Pinochet judgment: most major international crimes were now within the reach of Human Rights.[30]

Rituals of Good and Evil

Humanists were well aware of the symbolic importance of the global constitutional moment after Bosnia. David Crane, chief prosecutor for the Special Court for Sierra Leone, opened his case in 2004 in Freetown with a rousing speech about the "light of truth" and "the sober and steady climb upwards towards the towering summit of justice."[31] This trope-laden hyperbole reflected the reality that post–Cold War American hegemony was a moment of unparalleled promise for humanists. Indeed, my claim is that as much as anyone the beneficiaries of international trials are international advocates. Victims are collateral damage, the raw material for building the machinery of interventionary power necessary to do good in a world of sovereigns. Advocates use the stories of victims and survivors in what are effectively show trials, or what Judith Shklar calls "political trials."[32] These are show trials not in the Soviet sense that there is manufactured evidence against the accused, but because the principal function of such rituals is to dramatize the metanarrative "on the global stage." International justice is a performance.

International criminal trials are grand ritualized spectacles that symbolize authority and power by dramatizing the archetypal myth of the hero defeating existential threats to the community.[33] Humanists must control the trial's good-against-evil narrative such that defendants do not emerge as heroes; but they must also create theater. The accused must be diminished and then convicted, but the desperately slow and sterile legalized process, the separation, in theory, of judge and prosecution, vast and complex material, the difficulty of proving direct involvement in the most heinous crimes—for example, Charles Taylor's escape from a charge of "crimes against humanity," and the conservative charges leveled at the accused in Cambodia—all make such trials problematic as spectacles.

Some (Milošević, Foday Sankoh) die before conviction; some (Saddam Hussein) are gruesomely executed, tarnishing the purity of the law; and others, Goering famously, but also Milošević, make some ground in their own defense. The trial, let us recall, is not the punishment. All too often Western legal scholars equate the two, betraying their sense that there will be no escape and that being exposed and "shamed" in this way is part of the retributive process. Acquittal must be at least a possibility for a trial to be fair. Aryeh Neier writes: "Augusto Pinochet and Slobodan Milošević are symbols of the cruelty and barbarity of the last third of the twentieth century, but they also inspired the most significant advances in international accountability for the authors of great crimes. . . . The fact that these two former heads of state were arrested on charges based on their conduct in power demonstrates the advance of international justice."[34] Yet neither was ever convicted by an international court.

When the DRC militia leader and wanted fugitive Bosco Ntaganda, fearing for his safety after he was ousted by a rival faction, surrendered in Rwanda and was transferred to the ICC in March 2013, the CICC's email announcing this fact included, buried among the triumphalism, an incongruous sentence saying: "He will at all times be presumed innocent until the case against him has been concluded." Given Ntaganda's guilt is the obvious assumption of advocates quoted throughout the email, why try him at all?[35] Why not offer him a plea bargain? The answer is, of course, to build the power of the court. What sustains the fiction that this is impartial justice is the claim that advocates and judges are fundamentally separated from each other (the former morally impartial, the latter legally impartial). But all belong to the global lobby for Human Rights. No one could have doubted that Cassese and Goldstone were on the same side in the ICTY.

For Geoffrey Robertson the Milošević trial was a success because evidence was heard and contested in open court and Milošević had ample opportunity to defend himself. The litany of trial errors Robertson lists do not detract, for him, from the trial's value. But the logic of his analysis is about convicting "tyrants" of Milošević's stature more efficiently. This is a *show trial*: the things Robertson proposes are designed to dramatize guilt.[36] Witness his outrage about the assassination of Osama Bin Laden:

> [A trial] would have been the best way of de-mystifying this man, debunking his cause and de-brainwashing his followers. In the dock he would have been reduced in stature—never more remembered as the tall, soulful figure on the mountain, but as a hateful and hate-filled old man, screaming from the dock or lying from the witness box.[37]

Surely Bin Laden would revel in the opportunity to advertise his cause? Was this not one of the Obama administration's concerns in countenancing his execution? Robertson again:

> Since his [Bin Laden's] videos exalt in the killing of innocent civilians, any cross-examination would have emphasised his inhumanity. These benefits flowing from justice have forever been foregone.[38]

If arguments like this are anything to go on, it is little wonder US Supreme Court chief justice Harlan Stone called Nuremberg a "high grade lynching party."

This alienated, translated, cumbersome legal process is advocated by humanists as the sole conception of justice. And they control its terms. The abstract formality of this sort of law robs the trial of the rage, shame, grief, and redemption that makes more immediate forms of justice so powerful for those who suffered. Once the two were more closely associated. Before the "invention" of human rights, "bodies could be mutilated in the interest of inscribing authority, and broken or burned in the interest of restoring the moral, political and religious order."[39] Slowly the court has taken on this function of the symbolic performance of good versus evil. The court has become a ritual space where sacred time operates; law unfolds here at its own pace, sacralizing the constitutional moment. Lior Barshack argues that courts do not just represent "the sacred thing"— they *are* the sacred thing, the totem, the visible body of the god. In this way, "judges are not *representatives* of totemic authority. The judge is not a *mediator*. The court is the place where the totem's distilled voice is regularly heard *directly*. The accurate juridico-theological articulation of the judge's role is that which views the judge as the law's *mouthpiece*."[40] It is in trials that we hear the transcendental authority of humanism speak. No wonder advocates pushed so hard for so long for the ICC.

For Martti Koskenniemi, the Milošević trial of 2002–2006 showed the tension in all international criminal law between punishing those individually responsible and a show trial.[41] Because the trial of a few major criminals could never adequately address the scale of suffering, other justifications are forthcoming, including unearthing the definitive truth about what happened in order that a "wounded community" may heal itself, and deterring future crimes. To achieve these goals at the national level, Koskenniemi argues, a few "show trials" might well be sufficient if supported by other mechanisms.[42] But these benefits are not possible in international justice:

When trials are conducted by a foreign prosecutor, and before foreign judges, no moral community is being affirmed beyond the elusive and self-congratulatory "international community." Every failure to prosecute is a scandal, every judgement too little to restore the dignity of the victims, and no symbolism persuasive enough to justify the drawing of the thick line between the past and the future.[43]

Disregard for these difficulties can be made comprehensible, says Koskenniemi, if we see the ICTY and Milošević's trial as about building memory for the "international community" to reinforce the narrative of progress "from Nuremberg to The Hague" and from "impunity to the Rule of Law."[44] Trials are where *suffering innocence* confronts its tormentors. Sacred power is enhanced through a form of dramatic confrontation where goodness confronts evil in a disciplined, manageable, and procedural space. Dramatization is a vital part of building authority by tying the profane world of crime and trials to the transcendent world of deep and abiding human moral truth heard in the judgment of the court. The prime institutions in this architecture of morality are the International Criminal Court and R2P.

The International Criminal Court

At the apex of international criminal justice stands the ICC. For Kofi Annan, the UN secretary-general at the time, its foundation was a major step toward realizing "universal justice," under the cover of which "the innocents of distant wars and conflicts . . . may sleep."[45] Annan, of course, has his own troubled history when it comes to saving these innocents.[46] The ICC's evolution is well recorded, as are many of the issues that affect its functioning.[47] Much of the politics around the Rome Statute were about the United States, reluctant to sign and, owing to implacable Senate resistance, unlikely ever to ratify, but also an embarrassing outlier for claims about global liberal norms and an essential component of any enforceable international regime.[48] The Rome Statute was finalized in 1998 without American assent, and a last-minute symbolic signature by outgoing president Bill Clinton in 2000 was very publicly withdrawn by George W. Bush on taking office. After coming into existence in 2002 and launching its first indictment in 2003, the ICC finally convicted its first defendant in 2012, Thomas Lubanga Dyilo, a relatively minor warlord from the Democratic Republic of the Congo

(DRC) in custody since 2005. Its most high-profile indictees—Joseph Kony of the Lord's Resistance Army in Uganda (for crimes against humanity) and Omar al-Bashir (for genocide) are still at large, al-Bashir, of course, president of Sudan.

If there is a humanist church, the ICC is its cathedral, open to criticism in practice but not in principle. It is the single most important institution on which the idea of universal humanist authority rests. But sitting in the public gallery in The Hague for the trial of another DRC strongman, Jean Pierre Bemba-Gombo, a former presidential candidate and senator, one is struck by the overwhelming mismatch between this form of international justice and local reality. The air-conditioned wood-paneled room, with sophisticated video technology, a glass viewing booth for spectators, and a general atmosphere marked, as most modern courtrooms are, by strict rules of propriety about dress, address, and procedure, is an antiseptic (that is, a purified) environment. This could hardly be further from the alleged crimes against humanity (including murder and rape) in the Central African Republic that explain Bemba-Gombo's presence in The Hague in the first place. He is charged as the military commander responsible. A large man in a good-looking suit, he sits impassively, hands folded in front of him, thinking about who knows what as the process of international justice unfolds with painful slowness in front of him. These trials are available to watch online, but even a few minutes' exposure is enough to confirm that Hague trials are like any other in a modern courtroom: sedate, forensic, and formalized.[49] They are the opposite of the violence and horror that marked the crimes themselves. All the hostility and intensity is kept within disciplined bounds. It is a slow and formal accounting, a moral power that prizes dispassion as the mark of true authority. At local and national levels there is at least a notional social contract that obligates citizens to respect the law and legal processes. But there can be no fiction of "choice" globally. Those who were victims get no say over how perpetrators are dealt with. They may not choose the death penalty. They may not simply admonish the accused. What constitutes justice is prescribed for them as a set of inflexible rules by which they are ordered to abide.

The ICC's first prosecutor, Luis Moreno-Ocampo, was not a disciplined or dispassionate man.[50] In the photographs of judges and prosecutors at the entrance to the ICC during his tenure, only Ocampo has his arms folded across his chest and a look of defiance on his face. Some of those who worked with him described his style as "erratic" and "irrational."[51] In a documentary film, *Prosecutor*, that followed his working life, Ocampo is seen at first descending from a UN helicopter in the DRC wearing a white suit.[52] The voice-over describes him as a "salesman for global justice" in a world of sovereigns. In a later scene in The Hague, Ocampo rejects the idea that his opening speech in the Lubanga trial should be a "dry recitation" of the evidence (one of his staffers fears he'll be accused of prejudice). Ocampo insists "we have to convince the world that this is awful," even if the price is being labeled "overdramatic." In other words, Ocampo's instincts—that the ICC was about the politics of the law more than the law itself—were right. Once the law is institutionalized its chief prosecutor can focus on the evidence. But "constitutional moments" are about dramatizing the authority of the court and Ocampo, for all the critique of him as a lawyer and a leader, understood this. To call him a "salesman" is not so far from the truth. As it happened, the trial's beginning was a fiasco: the first child witness recanted just as Ocampo, having made the opening statement, had left to attend the World Economic Forum in Davos.

At the conclusion to Lubanga's trial, a remarkable exchange took place between Ocampo and the British presiding judge, Adrian Fulford. This session was charged with totemic power: ninety-two-year-old Benjamin Ferencz, a prosecutor at Nuremberg and longtime advocate for an ICC, addressed the court in the name of human rights, while actress Angelina Jolie, goodwill ambassador for the UN's High Commissioner for Refugees with "know your rights" tattooed on one shoulder, and Radhika Coomaraswamy, the UN secretary-general's special representative for children and armed conflict, watched from the gallery. During the day representatives of victims were given ample opportunity to speak in court, deputy chief prosecutor Fatou Bensouda stressing that the trial had at last given voice to the innocent children the Rome Statute was designed to protect. Although Lubanga was charged with the war crimes of conscripting, enlisting, and using child soldiers in the DRC in 2002–2003, Ocampo used the summing up to try to enter new allegations on which no evidence had been heard, that of sexual violence against female child soldiers. This mirrored his opening, even though the crimes he alleged were not part of the indictment.[53] In the process he overruled one of his prosecutors and was rebuked by Fulford.[54]

Relations between the judges and Ocampo had been fraught during the trial over the question of evidence. The judges at one point dismissed the case and ordered Lubanga's release because of prosecution reliance on UN field evidence that ought to have been made available to the defense. All of these and more revelations about Ocampo's conduct are detailed at length in a well-informed 2009 article in *World Affairs* that uses words like "lunatic" and "fantasist" about Ocampo.[55] When Lubanga was sentenced, to fourteen years, the reason for not imposing a longer sentence was given as the fact that he was not charged with sexually aggravated crimes, a clear snub to Ocampo.

Things got worse with Mathieu Ngudjolo Chui, the second defendant to reach judgment phase at the ICC. Ngudjolo was acquitted by judges who found the case that he was the leader responsible for war crimes and crimes against humanity in an attack on the village of Bogoro in the Ituri region of DRC in 2003 had not been proven (again, an evidence issue). This was a revenge attack for one staged by Lubanga, in fact, on Ngudjolo's village of Zembe. More troubling still, the opening shots of the film *Prosecutor* are of Ocampo in Zembe as he explains to the people, who hold Ngudjolo in high regard, why "he led you in the wrong way; you cannot attack people and no one can attack you." Ngudjolo has been released from custody but is not allowed yet to return to the DRC until any appeal into his case is heard. He has applied for asylum in the Netherlands to prevent deportation back to the Congo. The judges stressed they did not doubt crimes were committed in Bogoro and that just because Ngudjolo was not convicted does not mean he is innocent, simply that his guilt could not be proved "beyond a reasonable doubt."[56]

At first sight this result seems to undermine the "show trial" claim. The rule of law was upheld, and Ngudjolo was acquitted, pending appeal. But this is to misunderstand the symbolic requirements of international justice. It appears to be the rule of law that is sanctified, but in reality it is the power of the law's advocates that is at issue (the triumph of good over evil). In a political world, not convicting Ngudjolo is a major failure—the story has the wrong ending. The law is in fact an instrument for advancing an ideology. Earlier architects of the ICC knew this and blurred the judicial/prosecutorial line. They wanted convictions. Ocampo knew this too and ratcheted up the charges against al-Bashir to genocide, for example, despite a lack of evidence, in order to amplify the show. Ocampo knew in an instinctive way that the ICC needs to *perform justice*, that its power is symbolic and demonstrative. But he became impatient waiting for the legal process to deliver it.

In *Prosecutor*, Ocampo talks about police-judicial cooperation becoming "normal in the world," not just within nation states. He understands, as he says, that "the referee has no fans" but does not accept that the social relations between sovereign states have a different quality from those within them and that this is what gives international justice its authority: alienation from social relations at the cost of political authority. Entering politics (using force to realize justice) is taking sides. Only the metanarrative, the alibi, sustains the idea there is neutral, impartial space. As I have stressed, this is pure ideology. You can say it as much as you want, but in a world of socially constructed norms you have to prove it. Show trials are one of the most powerful mechanisms for doing so. The assertion that such a space of "humanity" exists—with the ICC and R2P fundamentally legitimated by the *claim* that it does—is contestable like all and any other claims to be the *one true voice*.

On other occasions in the film, passion and justice are intertwined. One staffer points out how passionate was the opening statement of the Eichmann trial (in Israel where the audience was a nation being founded from the ashes of the Holocaust—*Prosecutor* also uses iconic footage of the defendants at Nuremberg). Ocampo refers movingly, with powerful video images, to the prosecutorial statement *"nunca más"* (never again) during the trials of Argentinian military leaders in which he was a prosecutor. Israel and Argentina were, as Koskenniemi puts it, "moral communities" affirming themselves. One mother in Darfur whose son was killed tells the interviewer in *Prosecutor*: "We want Omar Bashir to be tortured just like he tortured us." This passionate vision of justice is inadmissible for humanists, of course; this mother wants revenge, whereas the ICC provides retribution on behalf of the law. Another mother whose children were killed by Lubanga's forces makes it clear she supports Ngudjolo. The passion that citizens feel *within societies* does not surprise us. It takes us back to the case of South Africa, where justice is embedded in democratic mechanisms and there is a sense of being a tangible, concrete, real community with ongoing and permanent reciprocal social relations. The atrocities happened *to them* and have meaning for *their* everyday lives. The very uniqueness of universal justice is its weakness: Those who deliver it are empowered because they are strangers. Because they can never belong. Were they to become part of the struggle, they would be disqualified.

As a supreme test of the authority of the ICC, the election as Kenyan president of Uhuru Kenyatta in March 2013 could hardly be tougher. Charged with crimes against humanity as a result of postelection death squads he is alleged to have instigated in 2007, Kenyatta, Kenya's richest man and son of the nation's founder, had already appeared in The Hague in 2011 to answer a summons on the charges, even though as part of his campaign Kenyatta told electors that a vote for him was a vote of no-confidence in the ICC.[57] On March 11, 2013, the case against Kenyatta's co-accused, Francis Muthaura, collapsed. After his election, President Kenyatta's lawyers immediately sought to have his trial, due for July 2013, dropped.[58]

Kenya has been a key American ally, and aid recipient, in the war against terror and has Sub-Saharan Africa's largest American embassy. Although the Obama administration warned Kenya that "choices have consequences," having no dealings with the new president may be infeasible and may encourage him to look to China for support. Whether or not the ICC chief prosecutor Bensouda can navigate the complex local and global political implications of this case and successfully try Kenyatta is a major pointer to the ICC's institutional power and its usefulness to the international system's most powerful states. Bensouda's team argued forcefully that the case of Kenyatta would go ahead on time and with robust evidence. They know what is at stake. It is also possible a demand will be made that the trial be held in Africa to better facilitate Kenyatta's appearance while president. The implications of such a precedent for the permanent ICC premises are intriguing.

The Responsibility to Protect (R2P): Humanism Unbound?

Deploying the metanarrative ("invoking humanity") to demonize foes as "evil" and outside the civilized conscience also legitimates acts of righteous violence. This once-standard European imperial practice is replicated in "humanitarian war," the accusation of genocide in Kosovo despite scant evidence, intended to force intervention.[59] A post–Cold War decade of failed and botched "humanitarian interventions" (Somalia, Bosnia, Rwanda, Srebrenica) was capped by NATO's bombing campaign over Kosovo, which was deemed "illegal but legitimate" by an investigatory commission led by Richard Goldstone. In his investigation of NATO bombing, the *Kosovo Report*, Goldstone concluded NATO intervention was justified because "all diplomatic avenues had been exhausted and because the intervention had the effect of liberating the majority population of Kosovo from a long period of oppression under Serbian rule."[60] Antonio Cassese agreed: NATO had violated international law, but this was legitimated by the emerging norm that serious violations of human rights justified armed intervention, whatever the UN Charter said.[61] The amalgamation of Human Rights and "just war" in R2P fuses the two discourses that from the early 1970s had challenged the seemingly moribund laws of war.[62]

That NATO might legitimately act unilaterally when ethnic cleansing is taking place clashes unsurprisingly with the strong feelings of the majority of Serbs that despite 2008's Declaration of Independence, Kosovo remains part of Serbia and thus a question of national sovereignty. New Serbian president Tomislav Nikolić reiterated this claim after his election in May 2012. For him and many Serbs, the NATO intervention remains illegal *and* illegitimate. The International Commission on Intervention and State Sovereignty (ICISS) and R2P exist to tell them they are wrong. Entry to the EU will depend on their accepting this fact. President Obama dispatched New York rabbi Arthur Schneier, a Holocaust survivor, to 2012's July 9 commemoration of Srebrenica (to which as many as forty thousand people came) to rebuke Nikolić by comparing what Bosniaks suffered with what happened at Auschwitz.[63]

For Eric Posner, if the Kosovo intervention was "illegal but legitimate," then international law is merely morality.[64] Judith Shklar echoed these feelings in relation to the 1946 Tokyo tribunal, which was seen as a failure because chief prosecutor Joseph Keenan used moral and religious arguments—natural law—more than legal ones. For Posner, Keenan was simply more candid than Robert Jackson, who did the same thing at Nuremberg.[65] Indeed, Posner and Jack Goldsmith, representatives of the "realist" tradition in American international law, argue: "The appeal to law is simply the denial of self-interest."[66] The guilt of many of those charged with crimes at Tokyo was and is contested: the Indian judge at

Tokyo, Radhabinod Pal, condemned the whole proceedings as victor's justice, Emperor Hirohito and his family were exempted, and in the late 1970s the spirits of fourteen "Class A" war criminals—men who had been hanged for their crimes, including wartime prime minister General Hideki Tōjō—were enshrined at the Yasukuni Shrine that honors Japan's war dead (leading to ongoing controversies with China and South Korea).

In the case of Kosovo, retrospective legitimacy proceeds in two steps. Step one: acts are defined as legal (or illegal) *from now on* because they have been made explicitly part of treaty law or defined as part of customary law. Step two: advocates argue the acts concerned were really legal (or illegal) all the time because they were morally right (or wrong) but could not for reasons of incapacity, ignorance, or resistance be implemented. In a civilized society they *should always have been law* (and thus always really were law, "moral law"). Positive and natural law are fused in this "constitutional moment" where a "new" legal fact is created and sanctified, thereby burying its ideological origins. The sole concession to the problem of retrospective law at the ICC (no crime without law or *nullum crimen sine lege*) is that only crimes committed since January 2002 will be justiciable (which was not, obviously, the case at Nuremberg, the ICTY, or the ICTR). Anne Orford argues that we should understand R2P not as "words into deeds," as UN Secretary-General Ban Ki-moon puts it, but as "deeds into words." Legitimacy is constructed *after the fact*. For Orford:

> The responsibility to protect concept can best be understood as offering a normative grounding to the practices of international executive action that were initiated in the era of decolonisation and that have been gradually expanding ever since.[67]

This is norm entrepreneurialism: advocates build their legitimacy by turning ideology into social facts on the ground, then into law and other institutions (like the ICC), then into further facts (intervention in Libya), and so on.[68] This spiral moves from morality (natural law or the sacred) to politics (positive law or the profane), then back through morality into politics again.[69]

In the years after the end of the Cold War, calls for "humanitarian intervention" went hand in hand with those for international justice. Starting with Bosnia and Somalia, through Rwanda and Srebrenica, and finishing with Kosovo, the actual record of the international community reflected the reality that political will, operational competence, legal and moral clarity, and prospects for success were extremely variable. Humanitarian intervention in the end failed too badly too often and built up too great a wellspring of skepticism and resistance. The 1990s ended with the "illegal but legitimate" NATO bombing of Serbia (and the liberation of East Timor with the assistance of Australian troops after a pro-independence referendum vote sparked catastrophic militia violence). To make sense of NATO's attack on Belgrade, championed by Western powers, Canada sponsored the ICISS in 2001.[70] For the ICISS, the UN Security Council remained the *"rightful authority"* to undertake intervention in the name of R2P.[71] But:

> [. . . there may be] circumstances when the Security Council fails to discharge what this Commission would regard as its responsibility to protect, in a conscience-shocking situation crying out for action. It is a real question in these circumstances where lies the most harm: in the damage to international order if the Security Council is bypassed or in the damage to that order if human beings are slaughtered while the Security Council stands by.

The ICISS implicitly claims that there is a moral authority, that of humanity, over and above the Security Council. This is a political act. If this claim passed the plausibility test and was not rejected, then further innovation could be grounded on it as a precedent. The ICISS added: "If collective organizations will not authorize collective intervention against regimes that flout the most elementary norms of legitimate governmental behaviour, then the pressures for intervention by ad hoc coalitions or individual states will surely intensify."[72] This was even more daring, containing an implied threat. The report's publication, in December 2001, came at a time when the "unipolar moment" was heading into overdrive after 9/11. Things are very different now. At the time, however, what was politically problematic (western-led NATO bombing of Kosovo) could be switched into a "moral register," purified, then moved back into politics at a higher level. This is the reinforcing nature of the two-step spiral process: politics-morality-politics-morality. It relies also, of course, on seeing law as fundamentally ideological and legal claims as a form of politics.

R2P was steadily embedded after the ICISS report: in normative statements like Kofi Annan's "In Larger Freedom," by the General Assembly (World Summit Outcome Document 2005), in the secretary-general's R2P Implementation Report (2009), in the United States' National Security Strategy (2010), and in Resolutions 1970 and 1973 on Libya (February and March 2011). After Cyclone Nargis in 2008, Bernard Kouchner, French foreign minister, even pushed for humanitarian intervention in Myanmar on the basis of R2P and was rebuffed by Security Council members and others on the basis that environmental catastrophe fell outside R2P's "narrow but deep" scope (to use Secretary-General Ban Ki-moon's formulation).[73] In September 2012, at the height of the Syria crisis, the secretary-general's annual report on R2P to the UN General Assembly stressed how important it was to undertake a "timely and decisive response," mentioning once again the "brutal legacy" of the Holocaust, Cambodia, Rwanda, and Srebrenica.[74]

This report reflects both the highs and lows of the short life of R2P. Libya in 2011 was the high. UNSC Resolution 1970 (of February 2011) explicitly mentioned the failure of the Libyan government to fulfill its *"responsibility to protect* its population" and accused it of committing "gross and systematic violation of human rights," "serious violations of human rights and international humanitarian law," and "crimes against humanity."[75] This resolution imposed sanctions and travel restrictions on the Libyan government, banishing once and for all the idea that sovereignty was a "license to kill" and referred the situation to the ICC.[76] For the foremost global advocate for R2P, and cochair of the ICISS, Gareth Evans, Libya was a chance to deter future atrocities and redeem the list of international failures since 2001.[77] UNSC Resolution 1973 (passed March 2011) further authorized member states to establish a no-fly zone and take "all necessary measures" to protect Libyan civilians.[78] Before long, NATO, with the United States, the UK, and France prominent, was waging a major bombing campaign against Libyan government targets, which by October 2011 brought about the victory of rebel forces and the death of Colonel Gaddafi. This action was seemingly justified by the report of a UN Human Rights Council commission of inquiry into Libya in May 2011, a commission created by the Human Rights Council "to confirm its pre-existing belief that the Qadhafi government was responsible for serious violations of international law."[79] The commission's extension of its mandate to look at rebel and NATO crimes was not popular with the council, even though in the end the commission was tougher on Gaddafi than it was on the rebels.[80]

China and Russia had abstained on Resolution 1973. They were soon unhappy that what they claimed was support only for a no-fly zone had become, in their view, a NATO-led attempt at regime change in the interests of western states who were now providing arms and training to the rebels.[81] It is worth noting that Resolution 1970 stopped short of explicitly using the phrase "responsibility to protect" in relation to the international community, weakening the critical R2P principle that UN members had a duty to step in when a state failed to protect its people. Even 2010's National Security Strategy of the United States had accepted that "responsibility passes to the broader international community when sovereign governments themselves commit genocide or mass atrocities, or when they prove unable or unwilling to take necessary action to prevent or respond to such crimes inside their borders."[82] The resolutions on Libya did not confirm this understanding of the evolving norm, a serious drawback because it gave major powers de facto impunity. Combined with Chinese and Russian unhappiness, Libya became an exception that proved the rule: the distribution of power underlying global norms dictates their chances of effectiveness. Syria has been a test case.

From the beginning of the 2011 rebellion in Syria against President Bashar al-Assad, Russia and China have vetoed Security Council action, most recently defeating a resolution on economic sanctions in July 2012. UN efforts in Syria, notably Kofi Annan's peace plan, have all failed. Annan resigned in August 2012, angrily blaming both Assad and the divided Security Council for the lack of progress in what was by then a civil war. The Russian foreign minister, Sergei Lavrov, has consistently argued that the Security Council must not take sides in Syria, as it did in Libya, a position echoed by China. The only area of consensus has been on the possible use of chemical weapons by the Syrian government, something even Russia has reportedly warned Assad against in strongly worded private messages.[83] Certain international norms, norms that great powers see as reciprocal or strategically important, can be sustained.

Some argue R2P has already made significant progress. The debate, they say, is now about how, not whether, to protect civilians from genocide and mass atrocities: Russia, while blocking intervention, has accepted the

Syrian government has a responsibility to protect its own population and did condemn the Houla massacre.[84] The subtlety of R2P is also invoked: military intervention (to react) is only one aspect of the doctrine and a last resort. Prevention and rebuilding are equally important, and both take place far from the spotlight of international crisis. In other words, judging the future of R2P based on the Libya and Syria precedents is premature. Gareth Evans has argued that if, as seems likely, intervention comes too late for Syria, international policy makers still remain united in rejecting a return to the days of Rwanda and Srebrenica.[85] He sees hope in the idea of "responsibility while protecting," which Brazil has proposed, as a way to assuage concerns that R2P will be used for regime change. Among the specific Brazilian proposals, several seek to affirm that the Security Council must always remain in control of operations and, moreover, that it is the *only* body able to authorize the use of force.[86]

The Brazilian suggestion re-anchors R2P in the Security Council; this allows states to keep control over intervention and confirms that the Security Council is the final law-making authority in world politics. It can make and break its own rules. This will be done in the interests of global order. Sanctioning North Korea over its nuclear threats is one issue over which consensus among the P5 can be forged. This pushes us back to the realm of reciprocity and shared interests, reversing the triumph of human rights over international humanitarian law and curbing the use of NATO force in the name of Human Rights. Western nations, and especially the United States, the UK, and France, are on notice about their narrowing room for maneuver in the post-unipolar world. Rather than an affirmation, like that of Boutros-Ghali, that the age of absolute sovereignty is over, what we have now is a reaffirmation of national sovereignty and an insistence that there is no authority superior to the Security Council in terms of the use of force. It has taken two decades of expansionist humanism to get us to the point where the Security Council is reminded of powers that it has possessed under Chapter VII, Article 42, since 1945.

In its recent report *"I Wanted to Die": Syria's Torture Survivors Speak Out*, Amnesty International, after cataloging a long list of appalling abuse of detainees, says:

Amnesty International is dismayed that despite overwhelming evidence of crimes against humanity, the complete impunity at the national level and strong calls by Amnesty International, the High Commissioner for Human Rights and others, the UN Security Council continues to fail to refer the situation to the Prosecutor of the International Criminal Court.[87]

Although the court is in principle based around humanitarian law, the call to refer human rights abuses to the ICC shows the role that "crimes against humanity" increasingly plays. Genocide is a relatively infrequent crime, one that even China and the United States were prepared to accept should be subject to automatic universal jurisdiction in the Rome Statute. Rather than a crime committed by others and in some sense "of the past," crimes against humanity, now detached from "intent," "state policy," and "armed conflict," present the equivalent of a permanent global criminal code anchored in a human rights constitutional moment. Amnesty is advocating that the ICC be the supreme court for that code. This is more weight than the totem can bear. No one is tending its specific moral authority any longer. The ICC and R2P are institutions with only an imagined constituency beyond activists and advocates. With Europe declining and the United States ambivalent about any permanent multilateralism, the power that alone has made the humanist international so pervasive is waning fast. To move from pity to intervention, from moral to political authority, from the spiritual to the material, was to drink from the well of power. This is as far as human rights can go.

7 OF GODS AND NATIONS

Hubris: pride, arrogance, an overestimation of one's capabilities. The humanist metanarrative gives the impression that the success of norms lies in their inherent justness; that is, that norms are their own best advocates, their inner demand for justice persuasive in and of itself. But mobilization politically requires a lot more. The real reason that global norms have prospered is a mix of state and social power: first, the social power of the European and Western bourgeois classes through the twentieth century for whom human rights were ideological identity markers, and then, from the 1970s onward, the symmetry between the goals of the American state and the export of neoliberal democratic power. Now American influence is weakening. The distribution of power in the international system is shifting from unipolarity to multipolarity, and the institutions that are built on liberal hegemony are fatally at risk. This is one major reason for the endtimes of human rights: institutional expressions of liberal state and social power like the United Nations and the ICC are having their foundations cut away. Challenges and indifference to multilateral liberal institutions on principle, with the United States complicit, will grow. Our world will finally kill the European dream.

The ICC has so far indicted only African suspects, and even then with glaring omissions.[1] In Central Asia, government violence against opponents is endemic and transparent. The worst case is perhaps Uzbekistan, where the Andijan massacre in 2005 brought a tepid response to what appeared to be the cold-blooded murder in public by security forces of probably more than a thousand antigovernment protestors. China and Russia backed President Karimov.[2] Many Central Asian states have restricted the promotion of human rights and democracy as part of a general turn away from the West enabled by the region's strategic importance to the Russians, the Chinese, and the Americans.[3]

In the Middle East, Israel refused to cooperate with a fact-finding mission, set up by the Human Rights Council (HRC) and led by Richard Goldstone, into Operation Cast Lead (2008–2009) in Gaza, during which at least eleven hundred Palestinians died (as few as thirteen Israeli civilians and soldiers were killed).[4] Israel refused to recognize the legitimacy of the process. Goldstone claimed there was prima facie evidence that Israel had committed war crimes and crimes against humanity and recommended that the mission's findings be referred to the Security Council and the ICC prosecutor. He also cast doubt on Israel's willingness to properly investigate the allegations. A subsequent HRC panel of independent experts reported in 2011—again based on secondary and nonofficial sources, because of Israel's refusal to engage with "the Goldstone process"—that Israel was in fact investigating whether its soldiers had committed crimes.[5] Goldstone then published a *Washington Post* article accepting that civilians were not targeted as a matter of Israeli policy, something that would have been clearer, he said, had Israel cooperated.[6] A blizzard of outraged comment followed this "retraction," with the Israeli prime minister, Benjamin Netanyahu, demanding the original report be "thrown into the dustbin of history."[7] Netanyahu has called organizations supporting human rights and international law the third "strategic threat" to Israel after Iran and Hezbollah.[8]

Andijan and Cast Lead are major cases that remain off-limits to the ICC for political reasons. As Human Rights Watch puts it: "When it comes to ICC referrals, the United States, Russia, and China seem more concerned about prosecuting their enemies and protecting their friends."[9] Together with "war crimes," the catch-all category of "crimes against humanity" could cover countless other cases, given that it applies in peace and war and concerns all mass killings, whoever conducts them. The alleged murders for which Kenya's president Uhuru Kenyatta has been charged with "crimes against humanity" number just more than a thousand. This brings the threshold low enough to include many more acts of state-sponsored violence. Even if countries are not ICC signatories, cases can be referred to the prosecutor by the Security Council (it has made two referrals, Darfur and Libya). Joseph Kony is unrepresentative of the situations where violence claims most lives, even though his crimes exhibit stupefying cruelty that plays well in the narrative of good versus evil. He is a distraction from the reality that most mass killings are conducted by the state.

The metanarrative seemed so assured after Kosovo, but it is a Potemkin village, a *façade*. More plausible perhaps is the idea of "Eastphalia rising."[10] Asia has many authoritarian states that have resisted human rights advocacy on the basis of sovereignty, cultural diversity, and, more recently, counterterrorism. Linking national self-determination with cultural uniqueness is a reprise of the Asian or Confucian values debate of the 1990s, given added force by the war on terror. This is not to argue Asian societies necessarily *are* more "communitarian and obligation-oriented"[11] or that they truly possess their own unique conceptions of justice, solidarity, and governance.[12] There are countless advocates for human rights *and* Human Rights in Asia. It is to understand that the "Eastphalian" narrative helps governments in places like China, Singapore, and Taiwan "legitimize their oppressive authoritarian rule as benevolent and inherently necessary."[13] How will advocates get traction when states as powerful as China are skeptical about global liberal norms and provide funding and political cover for other states to resist? In "Eastphalia," the classic Westphalian concepts—national sovereignty and nonintervention—are combined with a challenge to "Western preferences for universal adoption of transnational principles, such as democracy, free market economics and human rights." In consequence, "The conservatism of an Eastphalian approach could radically curtail the influence of Western power and ideas that have for so long dominated the fate of humanity."[14] ASEAN's recent Human Rights Declaration, for example, "undermines, rather than affirms, international human rights law and standards," according to Human Rights Watch.[15] We look at this pushback in more detail in Sri Lanka and Cambodia.

Sovereignty is not the only basis for principled resistance. Religious zeal is back. If there is great diversity among the strongly religious about core beliefs, there is less dissent in some sensitive areas: most fundamentalists resist what they see as the attack on the "natural family" (even if they differ as to its parameters) based on traditional gender roles and heterosexuality.[16] What Clifford Bob calls "the Baptist-burqa network" is united in its opposition to the humanist alternative.[17] The "family" is also central to debates about Asian values and Confucianism; it is argued that as "a natural and biological unit," the cradle of moral learning, the family "constitutes the most fundamental and pervasive unit of social life."[18] On abortion, the pope's leadership on the "culture of life" has even been recognized by non-Catholics, particularly at the UN.[19] Religious conservatives lobby at the national level and also at the UN against what they see as a militantly secular human rights agenda, particularly on issues of women's and sexual orientation rights. "Reproductive rights" (abortion), birth control, and same-sex marriage are particularly contested.[20] Some in the Christian Right feared the ICC would become a vehicle to advance gay rights and abortion via global judicial activism, attending the Rome Statute deliberations to try to combat this possibility.[21]

Even the major human rights organizations like Amnesty International and Human Rights Watch were slow to take up LGBT rights, their role as self-appointed "gatekeepers" over what constitute Human Rights at the global level one of the ways that the high priests of the secular sacred prevent the dilution and democratization of their authority.[22] This caution is reinforced by calculations about opposition but also funding and membership. Once a gatekeeper does take up these "new" rights, they can provide significant international leverage.[23] The fight over gender and sexuality is now fused for human rights advocates who have adopted terminology that ties the two sets of claims together in the phrase "sexual orientation and gender identity" (SOGI).[24] This development expands the advocacy coalition, but it may aid conservatives, because sexuality rights create the basis for a stronger alliance among evangelicals, Catholics, ultra-Orthodox Jews, Muslims, and both "traditional values" and sovereignty discourses in the South and in Asia.

The Hollow Empire: Sri Lanka and Cambodia

Freedom House's *Freedom in the World 2011* report was subtitled *The Authoritarian Challenge to Democracy*.[25] It reported that global freedom suffered its fifth consecutive year of decline in 2010 (the longest continuous decline in the survey's forty-year history), with fewer electoral democracies and renewed repression in many countries, including China and Russia. The Economist Intelligence Unit (EIU) had the same bad news, subtitling its *Democracy Index 2011* report *Democracy under Stress*.[26] The

Arab Spring was heralded by Freedom House's 2012 report as the most significant challenge to authoritarianism since the end of Soviet communism, but it concludes that intensified repression has been more common than reform, China and Russia again prominent. Autocrats are, it argues, on the defensive, but overall "global backsliding" and a sixth consecutive year of decline is the story.

Within these surveys, Sri Lanka emerges as what the EIU terms a "flawed democracy" and Freedom House "partly free." It is neither a pariah nor a rogue state. Under the global war on terror it was the Liberation Tigers of Tamil Eelam (LTTE) who were listed by the United States as terrorists. Cambodia too is far from being an outcast, submitting itself as a candidate for a 2013–2014 Security Council seat. In the brochure for this campaign, which makes no mention of international justice or human rights, Cambodia says it is "totally committed to working tirelessly in the best interests of the international community."[27] In each case, Sri Lanka and Cambodia, we see a vision of universality that reaffirms the state and the line between domestic and international politics. China and to a lesser extent Russia provide cover for this resistance to human rights.

Sri Lanka's president since 2005, Mahinda Rajapaksa, openly defied the humanist international as he set about resolving the long-running civil war with the LTTE. An all-out offensive ended the war in May 2009 with what were described as horrific and deliberate mass killings. A panel of experts appointed by the UN secretary-general reported in March 2011 that there was strong prima facie evidence of war crimes and crimes against humanity committed mainly by the Sri Lankan army.[28] The panel described the conduct of the war as a "grave assault on the entire regime of international law designed to protect individual dignity during both war and peace." They suggested that the so-called "humanitarian rescue operation" was in fact a crime against humanity during which tens of thousands of civilians were murdered. This included heavy shelling of civilians corralled in no-fire zones and of hospitals and humanitarian sites at or near UN and ICRC facilities.

The report says that "in keeping with United Nations policy, the panel does not advocate a 'one-size-fits-all' formula or the importation of foreign models for accountability." It is, of course, doing precisely that by demanding investigations and prosecutions under international law.

That these are not considered "one-size" or "foreign" is ample evidence of the metanarrative at work. The Sri Lankan government, meanwhile, designated May 19 as "Victory Day." To meet accountability demands it established its own Lessons Learnt and Reconciliation Commission, which was widely derided (by the UN panel of experts, for example) as flawed and without independence.

Initially the Rajapaksa government had lobbied hard for its position and succeeded in heading off an independent external investigation at a special session of the Human Rights Council in May 2009. In a message to the meeting, Navi Pillay, the UN human rights high commissioner, listed a catalog of allegations against the government and LTTE almost identical to that contained in the secretary-general's report two years later (she also wanted an office of the high commissioner established in Sri Lanka). She wrote: "I would like to underscore that amnesties preventing accountability of individuals who may be responsible for war crimes, genocide, crimes against humanity or gross violations of human rights are impermissible."[29] No amnesties is a humanist norm masquerading as customary law and can hardly ground a claim of "impermissibility." But this claim is essential, as it anchors the categorical dimension of the metanarrative: no exceptions, no deals, no compromises.

In the special session itself, EU countries led by Germany and Switzerland wanted language on unhindered access for humanitarians and on the need for Sri Lanka to set up an independent investigation into human rights violations, to prosecute perpetrators and to allow for follow-up monitoring by the high commissioner.[30] Amnesty International made similar demands. But the resolution as passed (29 for, 12 against, 6 abstentions) contained none of this.[31] Afterward, Sri Lanka's UN representative, Dayan Jayatilleka, was scathing about the Europeans and their cries of "war crimes! war crimes!" saying: "And this from those who said that Iraq was harbouring weapons of mass destruction. These were people from whom Sri Lanka would not buy a used car." He called the defeat of the EU resolution "a miniature diplomatic Dien Bien Phu or Bay of Pigs for the EU."[32]

Humanists were undaunted. Bypassing the Security Council, to Russia's annoyance, they lobbied Ban Ki-moon, who set up the expert-panel investigation.[33] Former British and French foreign ministers David Miliband and Bernard Kouchner, who jointly visited Sri

Lanka in April 2009 as the war entered its final phase, wrote an op-ed in June 2011 backing the report and demanding Sri Lanka conduct a full independent inquiry. They drew attention to the restrictions journalists faced (calling it "the war without witness") and demanded the principle of R2P be honored by a UN-led monitoring effort. Otherwise, they claimed, the international human rights system's integrity would be undermined, the law itself becoming "an ass," and Sri Lanka would be prevented from taking up a "normal place" in the international community.[34]

In March 2012, the HRC reversed itself and called on the Sri Lankans to investigate war crimes and on the high commissioner for human rights to report back in a year on progress made. For this, pressure from the United States (newly elected as an HRC member and sponsor of the new resolution) and a changed vote from India were critical.[35] Sri Lanka retained its aggressive posture, denying the factual claims of crimes against humanity and challenging the right of the "international community" to make such allegations against a sovereign government fighting a counterinsurgency campaign against "terrorists." The government sent a seventy-strong team to Geneva to lobby against the resolution and condemned it afterward, with Sri Lankan delegation members saying nothing would change.[36]

This dispute is nested in a deeper transformation. The failure of the Norway-led peace process (beginning in 2002) left ill-feeling on both sides. The Sri Lankan government and Sinhalese population, for example, saw the intervention as pro-LTTE and an infringement on Sri Lankan sovereignty. This was exacerbated by the post-2004 tsunami aid effort, which brought numerous international humanitarian actors into Sri Lanka (the so-called "second tsunami"). What happens when a functioning state with significant popular support advocates norms that go against international human rights norms?[37] International humanists did not know how to talk to the Sri Lankan government, which demanded their compliance or ejected them. There can be no alignment with national policies in such situations; if the metanarrative is to mean anything it must be accepted as *the* system.[38] In Sri Lanka it is not: organizations like MSF eventually complied with the restrictions placed on them (which essentially meant dropping human rights), unable to get any political leverage from inside or outside to pressure the government.[39]

But the wider shift was strategic; increasing support from China (and to a lesser extent Iran and Russia) gave Sri Lanka an exit option from western funding and alternative political support. By 2009 China's annual assistance to Sri Lanka was reportedly more than $1 billion, and the arms sales dimension proved vital to the eventual defeat of the LTTE.[40] Sri Lanka is a key asset for China in its bid for a network of deepwater ports in South Asia. China and Russia, both with separatist concerns of their own, made it clear during the endgame of the war that they would veto any attempt to put the issue on the agenda of the Security Council.[41] Data suggest that support within the UN for EU human rights positions has been declining rapidly since the 1990s at the same time as an increasing number of General Assembly votes have gone in accordance with China's stance.[42] The current isolation of China and Russia at the General Assembly over Syria is largely due to the issue-specific Western-Arab coalition that is unlikely to become a lasting feature of UN deliberations. It was only with serious US diplomatic pressure that a tougher resolution on Sri Lanka was passed through the HRC in 2012, the lesson being that if the United States does not invest politically, little will happen.[43]

A further US-led resolution at the HRC in March 2013 condemning Sri Lankan human rights violations during and since the end of the war still stopped short of setting up an independent international investigation into alleged war crimes and crimes against humanity.[44] This was despite the fact that China and Russia are no longer on the council. What leverage there is on Sri Lanka for advocates comes from the chance a Commonwealth Heads of Government meeting set for Colombo in November 2013 will be cancelled. Yet the government of Sri Lanka has continued to call its ending of the war a "humanitarian rescue operation."[45] The UN meanwhile undertook an internal investigation of its Sri Lanka response that recorded numerous failures of its own, including, for example, that "some senior staff [in Colombo] did not perceive the prevention of killing of civilians as their responsibility."[46] It referred, depressingly, back to failures similar to those during the Rwandan genocide in 1994. It expressed with great clarity the deeper problem:

The single most effective UN action to protect civilians from gross human rights violations is early and robust political consensus among UN Member States in favour of protection: the combined

political will alone of the international community has dramati-
cally positive effects in encouraging parties on the ground to
change their conduct and protect civilians. But, conversely, the single most significant factor that limits the UN's ability to adequately
address such situations is the difficulty Member States have, especially at the Security Council, in reaching an early and qualitatively
adequate political consensus on a situation.[47]

The question of political will brings us to Cambodia. The Extraordinary
Chambers in the Courts of Cambodia, or ECCC, provides an even longer-
running example of successful resistance to the humanist international.
Prime minister Hun Sen has successfully manipulated international justice since the mid 1990s, skillfully exploiting the lack of leverage of the
UN and humanist advocates to realize domestic political goals. Here a
major effort to bring to justice those who took part in genocide and crimes
against humanity during the Khmer Rouge (KR) years 1975–1979 in Cambodia has so far produced just one conviction—but for all his crimes, the
ex-head of S-21 torture center Kaing Guek Eav, alias "Duch," was not a
senior KR leader and had no role in planning or undertaking the Cambo-
dia-wide policies that resulted in the deaths of at least 1.5 million Cambodians. One conviction is derisory when the killings in Cambodia dwarf
those in Bosnia, where the ICTY has completed proceedings in more than
120 cases. Cambodia's mass killings are more comparable to Rwanda in
terms of scale (while still twice as large) but were far more organized
and elaborate, making the KR period the nearest modern comparison we
have to the Holocaust. The ECCC is often referred to as a modern-day
Nuremberg.

    Initially Hun Sen supported an international tribunal to try
Khmer Rouge senior leaders, writing to the UN as early as 1988 (even
mentioning Nuremberg) proposing eight names for a trial.[48] He hoped
to end the KR insurgency by trying top leaders while reintegrating those
below into the political system.[49] Despite a cool reception internationally,
he pressed on. In June 1997, with co–prime minister Prince Norodom
Ranariddh, he wrote to the UN requesting assistance in establishing
an ad hoc tribunal like the ICTY. In sole control by 1998, Hun Sen privately assured two of the three top KR leaders still at large, Nuon Chea
and Khieu Samphan, that they would not be tried *internationally* if they

unconditionally surrendered, which they duly did, appearing publicly with Prime Minister Sen, who now said it was time to "dig a hole and bury the past."[50] By this time, however, the UN and United States were keener on an international trial, putting them at odds with Sen's revised preference for a Cambodian trial in accordance with his promise to Chea and Samphan. This question, international versus domestic, is still the point at issue for the court.

Over many more tumultuous years, agreement was reached and a court established (formally in 2006). UN Secretary-General Kofi Annan favored an out-of-country court with a majority of international judges; Hun Sen favored the reverse.[51] Many states were also concerned about costs, given the spiraling budgets of the ICTY and ICTR.[52] Annan and his legal advisers walked away from the process in 2002, and even after being forced back by the General Assembly, Annan remained forthright about the lack of respect for the rule of law in Cambodia.[53] Human Rights Watch called the final agreement "deeply flawed."[54] But without compliance from Hun Sen or serious external pressure, the UN could achieve no more.

The first trial, 001, saw Duch convicted in July 2010 and sentenced in 2012, after appeal, to life imprisonment. He had been in custody since 1999. This case proved to be straightforward compared with 002, the trial of Chea and Samphan, along with Ieng Sary and his wife, Ieng Thirith. Thirith's trial was soon halted because of her Alzheimer's while in March 2013, Ieng Sary died at age 87 having never been convicted. Trial 002, fraught with internal problems, had been split by the court into separate cases, beginning with the events following the seizure of power by the Khmer Rouge in April 1975 when Phnom Penh and other cities were forcibly evacuated, with huge loss of life. The advantage of this was the prospect, now thwarted, of a conviction before any of the remaining defendants died or were invalided; the drawback was that the hope for a full public accounting of KR atrocities would in the end be reduced to one specimen case that fails to scratch the surface of KR crimes.

Hun Sen, adamant that 002 will be the last trial, has worked tirelessly to stop the two remaining cases, 003 and 004, from going ahead. Cases 003 and 004 involve KR leaders like the air force and navy heads, Sou Met and Meas Muth, who are accused of war crimes and crimes against humanity.[55] Case 004, according to Douglas Gillison, includes "Ta An," who in 1977 was allegedly responsible for ordering the mass killing of Cambodia's ethnic Cham community, the basis for the main charge of genocide during the KR period.[56] Hun Sen's government consistently argues more trials would destabilize Cambodia and that the defendants in cases 003 and 004 are not "senior leaders" (the ECCC's jurisdiction also covers those "most responsible"). In October 2010 Hun Sen told Ban Ki-moon unequivocally he would not allow further trials, and he demanded the UN shut down its human rights office and sack its head of mission, a longtime advocate for Cambodian human rights, Christophe Peschoux (Peschoux left soon afterward; the office remains open). Already some senior government officials have refused to respond to summonses in relation to case 002.

In April 2011 the coinvestigating judges (international judge Siegfried Blunk and national judge You Bunleng) announced the closure of investigations into case 003, shocking many internal staff and rights activists. Both Blunk and You Bunleng came in for withering criticism from advocates, who alleged they had succumbed to political interference.[57] The Open Society Justice Initiative (OSJI) claimed that You and Blunk, by questioning whether the ECCC had jurisdiction, were using "an absurd legal ruse aimed at justifying the shelving of Cases 003/004 to satisfy Cambodian government political will."[58] International co-prosecutor Andrew Cayley challenged their decision in public by releasing details of 003 (even though Sou Met and Meas Muth had not at that point been formally named) and alleging that the cases had not been properly investigated. His national co-prosecutor Chea Leang, having been an opponent of cases 003 and 004 from the very beginning, publicly disagreed with him. In the face of organized resistance, the international community was impotent. OSJI commented: "The United Nations and international donors have done nothing more than repeat general statements affirming the importance of judicial independence, while taking no concrete action to defend the principle."[59] After much internal wrangling, Judge Blunk resigned in October 2011.[60]

Anne Heindel, a legal adviser to DC-Cam, is adamant that "they can't use the provisions of national law to subvert a treaty."[61] What she means is "they are not supposed to." But of course if Hun Sen can successfully manage the process to the point that the UN and its members lose the political will to pay the spiraling costs, then after a single verdict in 002 the court will close. Ban Ki-moon's efforts to prevent this outcome have been ineffectual.[62] It is unlikely that many senior UN personnel will rue its passing. Seeta Scully argues that we should judge the ECCC in terms of its success in laying the groundwork for social change in Cambodia, even if from a human rights perspective it is a failure. But this assumes what works best in Cambodia, rather than building the humanist international's power and authority, is the main aim of global advocates.[63]

What these examples show is that against a patient and determined sitting government only injecting significant external diplomatic pressure makes a difference. By far the most successful trial is the ICTY. But that is in Europe, based in The Hague, detached from the control or influence of any Balkan government, and involves all the major players, particularly the United States and the EU. It had concentration camps as a powerful stimulus, and it came just at the moment when the Cold War ended and the "peace dividend" was available.

Nested Norms and Competing Authorities

The humanist international was born on a continent where Christianity was the dominant religion across all social classes and where the majority of the world's Christians had lived for a thousand years.[64] And yet Europe was secularizing. For a while longer Christianity's legacy filled in the substance of "civilized conscience." The global population has quadrupled since 1910, and the increase in Christians (who have more than trebled) has almost kept pace, Christians now 32 percent rather than 35 percent of the global population. But whereas in 1910 Europe had 66 percent of the world's Christian population, by 2010 that had fallen to 26 percent. Now the majority of the world's Christians live in the Americas (37 percent), sub-Saharan Africa (24 percent), and the Asia-Pacific (13 percent).[65] This mirrors the shift in population during the same period.

This has at least two implications: the obvious one of a decentered Europe and the less obvious one that the secularizing trend is either not manifest or works differently where, from the beginning, spiritual diversity was a fact of life (Africa and Asia) or where religious observance has bucked the secularizing trend (the United States). In sub-Saharan Africa the growth in Christians in the last century has been extraordinary (from under 9 million to more than 516 million people). Whereas 9 percent of sub-Saharan Africans were Christian in 1910, that number is now 63 percent.

In the Asia-Pacific region the number has grown from 28 million to 285 million (raising the share of the Asia-Pacific population that is Christian from 3 percent to 7 percent). Muslims make up a smaller percentage of the global population (23 percent), but this share is projected to rise (to 26 percent) by 2030.[66] Nevertheless, the distribution of the world's Muslims will not change radically. The vast majority are in the Asia-Pacific (62 percent), with 20 percent in the Middle East and North Africa and 15 percent in sub-Saharan Africa. The number for Europe is under 3 percent. Demographics also favor religion. In Islam and ultra-Orthodox Judaism, but also in fast-growing Christian religions like Mormonism and Pentecostalism, parents tend to have more children, and those children tend to keep their faith and marry within their religion, compared with the children of liberal religious parents.[67] Even in Europe this dynamic may be at work.[68]

At issue is not the theoretical, logical, or conceptual compatibility of human rights with, say, Islamic law or Protestant evangelism. To the extent that all are ongoing conversations about meaning we can envisage consensus. For example, in their report *CEDAW and Muslim Family Laws*, the Malaysia-based Musawah movement "for equality in the family" argues convincingly that CEDAW (Convention on the Elimination of All Forms of Discrimination against Women) and Islam have compatible principles of "equality, fairness and justice."[69] The difficulty with Islam in the context of women's rights is the fusion of state and religious power, they argue. They skillfully show how progress could be made by distinguishing Shari'ah law from *fiqh*, or "understanding," defined as "the process by which humans attempt to derive concrete legal rules" from the Qur'an and the Sunnah of the Prophet.[70] *Fiqh* is about interpretation and thus allows temporal and cultural change to occur. This account is totally convincing but politically inert. How will religious conservatives who derive influence, political power, and status from their literalist interpretations, much like conservative justices on the US Supreme Court, be won over if they are immune to *principled persuasion*? They understand what human rights advocates are saying; they are just not moved by it to change their existing principled beliefs. If they do not share the same sense of what conscience requires as the ICRC founders did, what will shift their position? The answer is: political leverage. Pressure from within (e.g., from an evolving middle class whose economic and social interests may converge around rights) and from without (international pressure from states, which can reward or punish compliance in areas like trade and military alliances).

The reason the struggle at the global level matters so much is that it is here that meta-norms are set—and the most meta of all is that which sees all international norms as *necessarily* universal, secular, and categorical.[71] There are clearly "multiple modernities" and "multiple secularisms."[72] This is conceptually and empirically obvious. But in political terms the key issue is the way Christian doctrine, biblical literalism, Islamic law, or Hindu tradition can be *interpreted and used* to advance ideological projects that are not consistent with universality. The most important implication of this is for the two forms of *global* or meta-secularism: the UNESCO model and the moral spectator (everything or nothing). For path-dependent colonial and political reasons we now know well, it is the latter—the moral spectator—that has grounded the international system. It has held all other claims to authority and validity subordinate to it.

Ask yourself: could any international treaty or convention that was universal be formally authorized by a deity? Could a universal liberal norm ever treat some human beings differently on principle because of some aspect of their identity? The moral authority of global humanism (and thus of human rights) is constitutively secular, universal, and nonnegotiable. In Europe this is self-evident. The Council of Europe's 2005 resolution on religion and women describes religion's influence as "rarely benign," adding that "freedom of religion cannot be accepted as a pretext to justify violations of women's right [*sic*], be they open or subtle, legal or illegal, practised with or without the nominal consent of the victims-women."[73] It is much simpler to sell the metanarrative with a mass murderer like Ratko Mladić in the dock, but the Council of Europe's framing—religious authority *cannot prevail* when it comes to women's rights—reveals the active moral project that underlies global justice shorn of show trials and tactical compromises like "the culture of human rights" (this "culture" is the UNESCO model and implies some form of syncretic melting pot). Religious opponents are under no illusions; they know they are locked in an ongoing struggle over the authority to determine how we will live. When it comes to the "natural family," choices about sexuality, marriage, birth control, and abortion quickly become binary. In a truly humanist world, all individuals have the right to express their sexual orientation and gender identity exactly as they choose. What argument consistent with humanism could possibly make an alternative case? The ultimate sovereignty of the liberal individual is the revolutionary promise of human rights.

The stirrings of modern conservatism in both Christianity and Islam can be found in the same 1970s that spawned the human rights revolution.[74] Accelerating social and economic liberalization in the 1960s (e.g., consumerism and women's and gay rights) brought forth an equal and opposite reaction in the form of neoconservatism, evangelism, and Islamism among other conservative religious and social movements. The struggle between secular norms and religious authorities has only intensified since. By 1994 the UN's International Conference on Population and Development, while clear that abortion should not be promoted as a method of family planning, had established "reproductive rights" in international discourse (the so-called Cairo Consensus). In Beijing in 1995, the UN Fourth World Conference on Women's "Platform for Action" had stressed that "reproductive rights embrace certain human rights that are already recognized in national laws, international human rights documents and other consensus documents. These rights rest on the recognition of the basic right of all couples and individuals to decide freely and responsibly the number, spacing and timing of their children."[75]

Yet we are living in the era of rollback. One recent example was at the 2012 Rio+20 sustainable development conference, where language on reproductive rights was deleted from the final outcome document at the last minute after heavy lobbying by the Christian Right led by the Vatican. Savio Carvalho, director of Amnesty International's Demand Dignity program, said "the mere fact that we have to advocate for the inclusion of human rights is absurd."[76] But only for advocates. The idea that rights are the orthodoxy and religious prescriptions on gender and sexuality are illegitimate challengers shows how deep secular humanist assumptions go. There was a further extended struggle at 2013's Commission on the Status of Women simply to get an agreement by consensus (lacking any legal force) condemning violence against women. An alliance of the Vatican, the Muslim Brotherhood, and Russia sought to insert language on religion, culture, and tradition that is diametrically opposed to the moral thrust of human rights. As a Muslim Brotherhood statement asserted: "This declaration, if ratified, would lead to complete disintegration of society, and would certainly be the final step in the intellectual and cultural invasion of Muslim countries, eliminating the moral specificity that helps preserve cohesion of Islamic societies."[77]

CEDAW, drafted in 1981, is one of the most widely ratified international treaties and a foundational moment for women's rights advocates. But the treaty is subject to numerous reservations lodged by states (naming articles by which they refuse to be bound), especially to Article 16 relating to marriage and family relations, which is expressed entirely in the language of rights.[78] Even the United States has not ratified CEDAW (although it was signed by President Carter in 1980); and while the Senate Foreign Relations Committee has approved the treaty twice, it was always with a significant "no" vote and only with "reservations, understandings and declarations." There has never been a Senate floor vote.[79] This is before we even get to those Islamic states considered to be the most resistant, many having only signed using the reservation mechanism.[80] There was no mention of "reproductive rights" in the Millennium Development Goals ("maternal health" replaced "reproductive health") and in the World Summit Outcome Document of 2005, and no major women's conference was organized for 2005, ten years after the previous one.[81] The momentum for women's rights is meeting stiffer resistance. By 2013 the focus of CEDAW advocates was on getting more women into senior political leadership positions, an acknowledgment that changing the law may be less important than changing the personnel who interpret it.

UN Women, a new UN "entity" designed to amalgamate several existing programs, became operational in 2011. Advocates hoped that under the leadership of former Chilean president Michelle Bachelet, appointed at under-secretary-general level, UN Women would extend the work of the United Nations Population Fund (UNFPA), the most outspoken development agency pressing for reproductive rights. The campaign to get more women into leadership positions is being spearheaded by UN Women drawing on the Rio+20 Outcome Document that allows "temporary measures" to advance the cause of women's empowerment. Bachelet praises CEDAW as "living law" but is frank about rollback:

How else can we explain that today, across the world, the sexual and reproductive rights of women are still being questioned on a daily basis? In Rio, just a couple of weeks ago, it took massive concerted efforts from UN Women, UNFPA, civil society and other partners to ensure that the Member States recommit in the Outcome Document to the Cairo Platform for Action and recognize explicitly the importance of sexual and reproductive health for sustainable development. Not long before that, at the CSW [Commission on the Status of Women], we had seen how some quarters were trying to question the clear commitments for sexual and reproductive health and reproductive rights made in Cairo and Beijing.[82]

The Vatican made clear its position on Rio+20 in advance, avoiding the language of "human rights" entirely (preferring "principles" and "pillars") and only mentioning "rights" briefly to refer to collective rights like that to development, a healthy environment, and peace.[83] Responsibilities (i.e., duties) also make an appearance. The Vatican argued:

It is also important to acknowledge and enhance the role of the family, the basic cell of our human society and "the natural and the fundamental group unit of society," as mentioned in Art. 16 of the Universal Declaration of Human Rights. In addition, it is the principle of subsidiarity's last line of defence against totalitarianism. For it is in the family that the fundamental process of education and growth begins for every person, so that the principles mentioned above can be assimilated and passed on to future generations. For that matter, it is within the family that we receive our first, decisive notions about truth and goodness, where we learn what it means to love and to be loved, and so, in concrete, what it means to be a person.[84]

There is little indication in his record that the new pope, Francis I, will be noticeably more liberal even with his Jesuit background. This is a serious challenge to humanism.[85] Most of the church's Rio contribution was framed in terms of "human dignity." This is language human rights advocates themselves have started to use in the hope it will provide precisely the deeper grounding in "natural law" that positive legalized human rights lack. But the "protection of human dignity" can lead us in various directions, many of which are paternal and conservative.[86] We find a similar tension within the current HRC discussions on "traditional values," where dignity again makes an appearance. The language of "traditional values," pushed particularly by the Russian government with support from China, mirrors that of "Asian values."[87]

The initial Russian-backed Human Rights Council resolution of 2009 called for a study on the contribution traditional values make to human rights promotion. An eighteen-member HRC advisory committee was asked to report on how "a better understanding and appreciation of traditional values of dignity, freedom and responsibility could contribute to the promotion and protection of human rights."[88] This request sounded alarm bells for human rights advocates, who insisted the negative impact of tradition and culture be included. They feared the beginning of an attempt to question the universality of human rights.[89] The first draft of the study in February 2012 confirmed some of these concerns, stressing positive aspects of tradition and showcasing the importance of institutions like the family. The subsequent draft then veered too far the other way for some member states, and at an HRC meeting in August 2012 the advisory committee was asked to resubmit the study in 2013.[90] Russia pushed ahead anyway at the HRC (before its three-year term ended in December 2012) and won a vote in September 2012 on a resolution that stressed the role "traditional values" could play in securing human rights.[91] By March 2013, Egypt had joined the fray, tabling a resolution on "the protection of the family."[92] Advocates saw this kind of pushback, and that at the CSW days earlier, as part of an organized campaign by conservative national and religious forces to weaken human rights language.[93] The first step is to insert terms into UN documents that establish rival ideas to those of human rights and to delete language that is seen as too human rights friendly.

Ultimately this is a dispute over the political implications of authority claims from above (the supply side) and below (the demand side). For religious authorities, what women (or LGBT activists) want is not definitive. It is for a higher authority to decide what it is permissible for them to have. Humanist claims to moral authority are directly challenged by this assertion. Sometimes this debate takes on a consequential tone over what provides more sustainable development, better health outcomes, and so on. But underlying it is a normative face-off. Amanda Klasing, a women's rights researcher at HRW, says of Rio: "It's hard to understand why language on reproductive health and rights could cause such problems at a conference dedicated to seeking solutions for the earth's currently unsustainable development."[94] The depth of the (misplaced) self-confidence of the humanist international is transparent in her assertion.

Competition from religious authorities is even more pronounced locally. States may not have the means of exercising influence in favor of global norms either. As Sonia Harris-Short points out, the state is frequently willing to accept human rights conventions as the price of membership in the global system (only the United States and Somalia have not signed the Children's Rights Convention, for example) but unable to effect changes in local social practice.[95] Much work has been done on what is called "vernacularization," that is, the ways in which local people interpret and customize rights and those "translators" who assist them.[96] But the idea of translation targets the purity of the classic humanist vision, which allows no room for compromise about who enjoys rights (everyone) and which rights people have (all of them). Only tactical concessions in the service of the final authority of the international can be made. This makes "local sacredness" a profane sphere for humanists, one where "politics" must be played only to get compliance, rather than one where sacred narratives of equal value meet. This turns local subjects into the *objects* of international human rights intervention. The humanist international struggles to take local interests seriously, as have development specialists through decades of work. The expertise of internationals is based on already knowing what needs to be done. When experts face empowered locals who have competing normative beliefs, things quickly reach stalemate. One of the reasons faith-based organizations, even foreign churches, have been effective is their capacity to work in environments where faith is still highly meaningful.[97]

In Naz Modirzadeh's Words:

Despite the movement's increasing sophistication, human rights NGOs remain unsure of how to address questions of Islamic law when it conflicts with international human rights law. Islamic leaders, on the other hand, are often unequivocal in their belief that specific areas of substantive Islamic law conflict with specific aspects of human rights law, and that *Shari'a* law should govern in such instances. Modern proponents of Islamic law regard their prescriptive rules for society as God-created alternatives to human rights law and as a parallel path to justice and emancipation. Human rights advocates, conversely, appear deeply uncomfortable about acknowledging the apparent contradiction between human rights norms and Islamic law. When they do acknowledge the conflict, human rights proponents seem unable to articulate a coherent response.[98]

The difficulty historically of eradicating the practice of female circumcision or female genital mutilation (FGM) is an object lesson to the hubristic. Nothing could seem on the surface more like a human rights abuse than FGM, but despite colonial and missionary activism and law, postcolonial condemnation, and several decades of INGO activism, it remains deeply entrenched and legitimate among millions of African women who see it not as a physical assault on their daughters and granddaughters but as both an identity marker and a key requirement for marriage. Despite more than a century of efforts under Christianity and secular humanism, "none of these struggles has fully established self-determination over basic bodily integrity for tens of millions of women and girls, in the private sphere still unreached by the global rise of rights."[99] The metanarrative says clearly: free these girls to be their natural selves. In order to do that, global rights also desires to reach inside the intimate sphere of the women concerned, turning their bodies into a battleground for universal humanism.

The Return of Great-Power Politics

The implacable resistance of China and Russia to the extension of R2P and the ICC signals the return of an old norm, one that unravels a century of humanism in the name of sovereignty and nonintervention. Who will, who can, defend humanism? Not Europeans, who have no capacity alone or in concert to exercise political influence globally and are increasingly riven by internal nationalist and economic tensions.[100] In a *Foreign Affairs* article titled "The Crisis of Europe," Timothy Garton Ash anchors his narrative in the 1943 Warsaw Ghetto uprising and the picture of a child with hands held high in surrender. It is one of the Holocaust's iconic child photos.[101] With the euro's failure, the lack of a unifying external Soviet-like threat, the power of a Germany increasingly indifferent to Europe's weaker states, and waning US engagement, the fact that "the greatest single driving force of the European project since 1945, personal memories of war, has disappeared" takes on even greater significance.[102] "Europe" as a collective entity is now treated with something like contempt by China, claims Ash.[103]

The only hope for political pressure to support global liberal norms is from the United States. But its record is deeply unsettling. It has advocated global liberal norms while refusing to be bound by them. Even periods of greater American multilateralism have been marked by a feature they share with times of isolationism or expansionism: *Whatever international institutional arrangements evolve, the United States will not recognize a supranational authority as possessing in principle or practice superior political or moral authority to its own constitutional democratic process.* On this stark truth the ultimate hopes of the humanist international will be dashed. Sometimes a congruence of objectives has drawn the United States into military intervention and thereby appeared to advance global norms like R2P for a brief moment. More commonly, it has been a frontier state in setting the "no entangling commitments" standard for great-power aspirants like China and India: joining the ICC comes to seem like something a state does because it is too weak to say no. This is the world the United States has bequeathed as its hegemony wanes. With containing China increasingly central to US strategic concerns, the diplomatic capital necessary to push through human rights norms, often begrudgingly given anyway, will be unavailable when it impacts negatively on maintaining alliances with states who fear, or seek, Chinese influence. As the 2012 US strategic defense review puts it, in italics, *"we will of necessity rebalance toward the Asia-Pacific region."*[104] Perhaps even a race to the bottom will emerge as human rights conditionality is sacrificed to strategic containment goals.

The United States was the prime mover behind the ICTY and ICTR, but these were ad hoc and temporary courts (setting no precedent) and of narrow geographical and chronological jurisdiction (meaning no ongoing obligations). Moreover, they had political utility as a form of action short of intervention. They may be seen as "customary law" by advocates, but when the dominant powers in the international system reject this interpretation without reservation, that view is little more than a hopeful fantasy. While it is true the long-hoped-for ICC was catapulted to the top of the human rights agenda by the innovation of the ad hocs, this was no incremental evolution for the United States but a whole different game. US ambassador for war crimes David Scheffer spent much of his time in Washington under Secretary of State Madeleine Albright lobbying for a treaty that would enable the United States to join the ICC. His perseverance and ingenuity are visible on every page of his memoir.[105] And President Clinton's last act in office was to have Scheffer sign the treaty. But the implacable opposition within the Senate and Pentagon to American assent was always likely to prevail.

The counterargument to ICC assent, embodied in the formidable shape of Senator Jesse Helms, was about loss of sovereignty and risks to American soldiers. It seemed natural to senators and the Joint Chiefs of Staff that the American negotiating position include protections for these. But the Rome Statute was a treaty designed to disallow reservations. The message was: accept the superior authority of international law or do not join the court. Scheffer's efforts were, as his own account makes clear, an exercise in futility. Albright does not mention the ICC in her memoirs, and President Clinton became fully engaged, despite years of briefing from Scheffer, only after reading a *New York Times* op-ed.[106]

Helms and the Pentagon forced a negotiating position on Scheffer that would, if agreed, have gutted the ICC. Most important was the demand that the national state of a suspect would have to agree to his or her prosecution by the ICC—a demand designed to protect US soldiers. A further deeply contentious issue was whether the ICC would have *automatic jurisdiction* over all the crimes the statute prohibited: genocide was uncontroversial, but war crimes and crimes against humanity were far more conceivable crimes. These are the planks of universal jurisdiction. Without Security Council control, any citizen of the United States could in principle be charged with war crimes or crimes against humanity and his or her extradition demanded to The Hague. This is the ICC's purpose: to hold states, the United States first among them, to a superior nondemocratic international judicial authority. When the United States' last-ditch proposals were defeated at Rome, other delegates stood, cheered, and applauded because they had prevented the United States from killing the treaty with what they saw as self-serving demands.[107] This is less of a problem with R2P, of course, because the lack of a treaty and the central role accorded to the Security Council create enough discretion for great powers to either use the "doctrine" (Libya) or not (Syria). R2P has no independent authority or force. Scheffer's conclusion was: "The era of American leadership in the arena of international justice had passed."[108] It was *very* short.

George W. Bush's combative neoconservative ambassador to the UN, John Bolton, described unsigning the Rome Statute in May 2002 as "my happiest moment at State," the only real objection he claimed coming from "sundry High Minded Europeans."[109] The name of The Hague even had the dubious privilege of being linked to the American Service-Members Protection Act, passed by the US Congress in 2002 to authorize measures up to and including using armed force to rescue US and allied personnel who might be detained by the ICC.[110] In reality, neocon, Senate, and even Pentagon reluctance to hamper American power takes us back at least as far as the Senate's rejection of the Genocide Convention in 1950 as part of an attempt to "block the international human rights movement in general."[111] Even as Clinton told Scheffer to sign the Rome Statute, he told his successor, President George W. Bush, not to submit the treaty, with its "significant flaws," to Congress. President Barack Obama has made no effort to re-sign the statute, has not closed Guantanamo Bay, and has greatly increased the use of drones in targeted killings. He is widely assumed to have been indifferent to or even supportive of Osama Bin Laden's assassination, and we have seen how his attorney general, Eric Holder, defended the administration through "lawfare" against claims it illegally killed a US citizen, Anwar al-Awlaki, in Yemen.

Today, the more multipolar balance of power and counterterrorism strategies that have established new norms of permissibility in terms of the exercise of power internationally, combined with current economic distress (and joblessness) and domestic ideological shifts within the United States to the right culturally and politically, make the outlook bleak for American liberalism abroad. The conservative position is encapsulated by John Fonte in his book title *Sovereignty or Submission? Will Americans Rule Themselves or Be Ruled by Others?*[112] In the liberal wing of the American foreign policy establishment, the talk has been of a "concert of democracies" and "forging a world of liberty under law."[113] For liberals, the neocon "vision of world order is based on unrivalled American military might and a cultivated belief in American exceptionalism."[114] But both neocons and liberals root human rights in democracy. They differ on methods (on whether to deploy force unilaterally or multilaterally). And liberals do not argue the United States should claim an exemption *on principle* from the international norms it advocates for everyone else. But the virtues of American-style neoliberal democracy and the upside of using American power are accepted positions across the US human rights spectrum. Andrew Moravcsik outlines four reasons why the United States continues to hold a "paradoxical" view in relation to human rights: external power, democratic stability, conservative minorities, and veto groups.[115] Moravcsik says the United States is the only advanced industrial country that has all four, and all of these reasons, together and separately, militate against permanent embedded multilateralism.

In other words, the last great hope for humanist internationalism is an illusion. The United States, democratic, liberal, and successor to the great heritage of the Western enlightenment, has avoided becoming embroiled in alliances and commitments that would constrain it. Its gaze firmly fixed now on Asia, and the opportunities and threats that a rising China creates, it has neither the desire nor the need to back the humanist international. R2P is a meaningless doctrine without US support, and the ICC is a European vanity project. Neither will be the scene of great-power politics in the decades ahead. All eyes will be fixed on the Security Council and on the competition for allies between the United States and China. What might this world, of the endtimes of Human Rights, look like? That is the question to which we turn in the final chapter.

THE NEO-WESTPHALIAN WORLD

"Romans before the fall were as certain as we are today that their world would continue for ever substantially unchanged," says Bryan Ward-Perkins. "They were wrong."[1] What followed in Europe was the Dark Ages. We are not going to regress that far. Nor will there be a neo-medieval turn—national-territorial states are too powerful and global social relations too extensive to be fully undone.[2] Rather, we are entering a *neo-Westphalian* world. That is, a world of renewed sovereignty, resurgent religion, globalized markets, and the stagnation or rollback of universal norms about human rights. The core modernizing assumption, that history brings secularism, a sense of oneself as an individual rights holder, and the erosion of collective beliefs and loyalties, is fracturing alongside the Western power that sustained it.[3]

The meta-rules were, until the twentieth century, written and enforced by Europe and upheld for much of the twentieth century by Europe and the United States and the armies of secular humanist experts they trained. But there is no longer a *singular* "lifeworld" at the global level. American power has disguised this fact for thirty years. Now that the United States is being forced to retrench, the diplomatic muscle necessary to globalize human rights will be increasingly unavailable. This brings us to the "endtimes" in two senses; the failure of "Human Rights" as a set of hegemonic norms that all accept on the basis they are secular, universal, and nonnegotiable, and the final demise of the European dream of one world under a secularized Christian god. We are living through the last days of secular religiosity on which effective claims to "impartiality" have relied since 1863.

The global system is now religious *and* secular, Christian *and* Islamic (*and* Hindu *and* Jewish etc), about human rights *and* traditional social hierarchies, about sexual orientation and gender identity *and* sexism and homophobia. *Both* liberal *and* authoritarian democracy will be permanent features of our world, as will women's rights *and* patriarchy. We have entered an era of multipolar authority where what is "normal" or "appropriate" no longer has one answer. Traditional values and conservative religious doctrine will not be outposts, like the Barbary Pirates, waiting for the "universal modern" to arrive. They will be global-level alternative discourses to Human Rights. Liberal power cannot prevail in an international order of dispersed and more evenly empowered sovereigns. Of course, ideological, technological, or environmental change could transform our world beyond all recognition in twenty, fifty, a hundred years. And then universality might become feasible again. But no state or society, for the foreseeable future, will be able to turn diversity into universality, not through coercion or inducement or persuasion. Only the Human Rights Imperium is still trying.

The ICC and R2P will be used by states to solve political problems, not to change the world. The ICC's true tragedy is that it is a court that cannot conceivably exercise political jurisdiction over great powers, creating a permanent two-tier justice system in which strong states use global institutions to discipline the weak. The soothing alibi that advocates tell themselves is "History is with us!" How, otherwise, is the obvious reality that China, Russia, and the United States will never be subject to an R2P intervention or an ICC case tolerable? Great powers even recognize each other's implicit right to veto a client state's investigation at the ICC (Israel, Sri Lanka, Syria). Such reciprocal arrangements create a self-interested incentive for cooperation. The ICC and R2P are simply more elaborate forms of organized hypocrisy.[4] After the embarrassing Livni affair in London, the UK government acted to rollback universal jurisdiction.[5] Other European governments soon followed.

Whether to use R2P or the ICC will be decided on the grounds not of justice but expediency, in other words. The UN's internal report into its shocking Sri Lanka failure says: "The concept of a 'Responsibility to Protect' was raised occasionally during the final stages of the conflict, but to no useful result. Differing perceptions among Member States and the Secretariat of the concept's meaning and use had become so contentious as to nullify its potential value. Indeed, making references to the Responsibility to Protect was seen as more likely to weaken rather than strengthen UN action."[6] Has there been a more obvious case for R2P than the imminent killing of as many as forty thousand stranded civilians by the Sri Lankan government? Before long, transparent inequity will doom R2P, while the interminable delays and partiality of the ICC will turn it into the League of Nations, a museum to European hubris trying a collection of African warlords and occasionally heads of state. The ICC is "Europe's court for Africa" because many African states are too fractured politically to resist. The French-led, non-R2P intervention from January 2013 to stop Islamist power spreading south in Mali is a textbook example of how Africa remains Europe's "moral laboratory" when great power interests are not at stake. Several African indictees are in The Hague because removing them from power by collaborating with the ICC suited their opponents, some of whom could just as easily have been charged. This does not mean that Lubanga, Bemba Gombo, and Ntaganda are not guilty of appalling crimes. It should give us pause for thought, however, when we call this *global* justice.

The decline of Human Rights is good news for classic humanitarianism. Humanitarian norms based on reciprocity will persist because they serve a useful function for combatants and present no challenge to the authority of states. The ICRC's current definition of *protection* is human rights based: "All efforts aimed at obtaining full respect for the rights of the individual and of the obligations of the authorities / arms bearers in accordance with the letter and the spirit of the relevant bodies of law."[7] But in reality the ICRC has survived precisely by *not* speaking out about human rights, a path MSF has also taken in relation to recent crises, and R2P (to which it is opposed).[8] Being silent is an ironic shift for MSF, given its origins. It is also a smart one: in a world that is all about profane politics, making credible claims to be impartial becomes both harder and more valuable. Things look bright for faith-based humanitarians for the same reason. Where there is a lot of moral "noise," clear ethical purpose, commitment, and transcendent nonpolitical legitimation become a focal point for mobilization. This means downplaying Human Rights. Cooperation with the ICC led to the expulsion of thirteen INGOs from Sudan in 2009, but most faith-based organizations were allowed to stay. Those secular agencies that negotiated to return dropped mention of "protection," code for human rights, from their information material and websites.[9]

The crisis work that international humanitarians do is also self-sustaining because of the logistical advantages, expertise, and resources they can deploy at short notice. A properly functioning global humanitarian regime is like a social insurance policy for the world. A supply of tents, tarpaulins, blankets, high-nutrient food, medicine, and search-and-rescue services remains on hand for those who need it. Major humanitarian INGOs—so-called multi-mandate organizations—have until now done relief *and development* work, however. And they have increasingly defined development as "rights based."[10] For many postcrisis societies, getting the internationals out before the human rights and justice phase kicks in will become imperative. New money from the Gulf for Islamic states will help in this. This money is not conditional on human rights; it is legitimated by *zakat*, compassion, Islamic solidarity, and resource politics. Libya's transitional government was adamant, for example, that it did not need an East Timor–style UN-led transitional government, and money from the Gulf helped make this stand successful. Getting traction for human rights in post-Gaddafi Libya looks uncertain as a result.

The Old New World

The best hope for human rights may lie with shale gas. If the United States can achieve the degree of energy independence some predict, its freedom of maneuver will expand.[11] A more assertive foreign policy, in which human rights figure more prominently, will become possible once more. Without shale gas, however, securing energy supplies and sea lanes, containing China, protecting the "homeland" from terrorism, and restructuring the US economy to maintain national competitiveness will be paramount. Unless the United States, still first among equals, commits resources to socializing new powers in human rights norms, there will be no incentive for those rising states to comply with what are already deeply contested universal rules, unless they see it as in their own interest to do so.

But shale gas is a distant future, while neo-Westphalia is now. The single most important change we are experiencing is the move to multipolarity.[12] It creates "an authority crisis in today's liberal order" where the question, as American hegemony wanes, is: Who can legitimately act on behalf of the international community?[13] As we have seen, the United States has been a poor ally when it comes to embedding global liberal norms outside the economic realm. Recent arguments for a "concert of democracies" are transparently self-interested. When power was there, the will was not, and the will is there now only because power is dissipating.[14]

Of the futures John Ikenberry outlines for our rapidly transforming world, the alternative to Liberal Internationalism 3.0 (in which human rights survive in a "flatter" world of eroding sovereignty norms) and Liberal Internationalism 2.5 (in which the United States still leads but as first among equals) seems to be disorder.[15] But a neo-Westphalian world is one where sovereignty does not erode further, liberal trade rules continue on a reciprocal basis, and major inter-state security problems like nuclear proliferation are collectively discussed. The critical move is a separation of political from economic liberalism. This means a world where the United States ceases to export democracy and focuses on maintaining an open set of trading relationships with clients and allies who are wary of China. American military power will remain unrivaled but also largely unused except as a deterrent.[16] If this picture is wrong, if American primacy persists, and if globalizing neoliberal democracy retains its place within US foreign policy, then the Global Human Rights Regime might continue to expand. Embedding democracy will likely, other things being equal, have greater long-term impact on concrete human rights observance than any number of multilateral Human Rights institutions.

But these "ifs" rely on the preferences of states not on humanist advocacy. If the American state changes its priorities, it can simply create an exception for itself and its allies.[17] The so-called pivot in American foreign policy toward Asia and away from the Middle East and Europe suggests just such a radical priority shift. So does the stress laid on "Asia-Pacific" economic cooperation, a formulation that may one day lead to a free-trade area that excludes China but includes Latin America, Japan, South Korea, South East Asia, and Australia. In former secretary of state Hillary Clinton's words: "It is becoming increasingly clear that, in the 21st century, the world's strategic and economic center of gravity will be the Asia-Pacific, from the Indian subcontinent to western shores of the Americas."[18] Clinton stressed that economics rather than politics were "front and center" in this new world. And human rights are politics. Despite the intensity of American efforts to contain China, there is not necessarily a deep-seated tension between these two powers. The deep clash of ideologies or civilizations that many have predicted seems absent, and there is certainly no new Cold War. China seems fully prepared to be part of a world that continues to grow on capitalist principles, as long as the monopoly of the Chinese Communist Party is not threatened. Ultimately, liberal rights in the United States and community rights in China are compatible, provided the market flourishes.

This is the true legacy of the transformation since the 1970s: human rights in the end were subsumed by the politics of American power and market-based democratic liberalism. Secular religiosity, the European legacy, was the cornerstone of an active effort to construct a plausible metanarrative of impartiality. Prior to the modern era, humanists had stood as spiritual guardians outside the prevailing global regime of politics and money. The leverage offered by the huge resources of the US state and the power of neoliberalism facilitated the global spread of human rights as an ideology and cultural practice of middle-class liberals. Allying with power was too good an offer to resist. But this is a one-way journey. Once authority is converted from moral to political there is no alchemical process that can fully reverse it. Once Human Rights, no longer sacred, are considered dispensable allies of power, they are left to rely on international institutions and their funding markets to survive. The language of human rights will not disappear any time soon for precisely that reason. The question of what difference they make—what impact they achieve—will only become more insistent.

The Last Rights

At the local level the language of human rights is often deployed, frequently by rights activists and groups trying to leverage their local power by linking with global INGOs. But this adoption is often instrumental and transitory: it makes human rights one language among others, and a conditional one, used for its capacity to create alliances between those whose substantive beliefs differ, and to connect with transnational networks. In terms of social mobilization, however, these rights are no different in terms of status from other languages of solidarity, identity, and entitlement, ranging from "civil liberties," "justice," "freedom," "fairness," and "peace" to "dignity, "decency," "equality," "love," and "grace." Often change comes, as we know, through local civil society organizations in alliance with transnational activists.[19] Or through specific local initiatives like the prime-time television show *Police Case* in Sierra Leone, funded in part by the Open Society Foundations, to raise awareness about women's rights issues.[20] Such a program may fare well even as global liberal norms fail, because it is funded independently. But without resources from an indigenous middle class or a diaspora sending remittances, and with significant pushback, cases like Sierra Leone remain permanently dependent on private philanthropy. Moreover, where the human rights frame is contested, local organizations will need to widen networks to include those who are not exclusively secular and who might object to some human rights.

When Human Rights discourses are embedded in global institutions—norms, laws, courts, trials, conditional aid, international campaigns, funding—they begin to assume power in their own right, whatever their impact on the ground. This is when human rights becomes Human Rights. Now local social movements must reckon with the power of the humanist international and its resources just as weak states must be wary of great powers. If gatekeepers like Human Rights Watch or Amnesty International or the ICRC do not adopt an issue, its chances of reaching a global audience are slim.[21] Global organizations gain funds, access, and influence because they claim a specific authority as the sole legitimate representatives of universal moral norms. They colonize local claims to this end.

If the meaning of what "human rights" are becomes openly contested within the "human rights movement," then the power of advocates to be *the*, not *a*, moral authority relies on nothing more than political and market power and their strategic placement as gatekeepers. This process is underway. The accountability, impact, and responsibility of INGOs is being tested, their transparency and democratic legitimacy increasingly scrutinized. When religious and nationalist movements speak, they speak for millions; when international NGOs speak, their narrow funding base makes them little more than the private foreign policies of middle-class professionals.

Maybe the expanding middle class *is* the answer.[22] After all, high-quality global brands like "Human Rights" and "Louis Vuitton" and "Apple" are ubiquitous in the best districts of all major global cities. Human rights may thrive as aspirational Western norms that have the status of "cultural capital," much like the explosion in China of interest in Western classical music.[23] Indeed, perhaps the *culture* that will tie disparate national classes together will be that of capitalism, a world of normative diversity and converging consumption where elites in Europe, China, India, Brazil, Russia, and the United States align with their shared interest in capital accumulation and protecting their own rights by sustaining a humanist culture. Human rights advocacy therefore becomes a status symbol signaling membership in the transnational capitalist class.[24] But if human rights depend on the *intensification* of capitalism, there is little hope for economic, social, and cultural rights. Indeed, advocating for human rights abroad is one way to avoid the consequences of domestic social and economic rights entitlements, which could in principle be enforced through taxes and legislation.

One might make this claim stronger: more affluence, more social inequality, more human rights talk. This is not the message of the metanarrative. Better to focus on the unimaginable cruelties inflicted by Mladić and Kony and Taylor or the Islamists in Mali. Civil and political human rights, rights of association, representation, and protection of private life, disguise the growth of social inequality under globalization. The demands from Egyptian protesters in 2011 were for bread, dignity, and justice; a jobless stagnant economy was critical to the initial mobilization phase. Collective and violent political action was necessary to realize gains, not decades of protest by Human Rights advocates against a government kept in power by American aid. Social justice issues, let alone women's rights and Islam, lack the clear-cut good-versus-evil narrative global advocates like. They prefer to concentrate on torture, state crimes, and mass atrocity, building early warning systems and transitional justice mechanisms and spreading lessons learned about preventing genocide and crimes against humanity. Everyday discrimination and violence, that which constitutes 99 percent of the oppression people suffer, and where the need is greatest, comes a distant second. No one is building a universal court for that.

Activist UN bodies will also meet stiffer resistance. What choice will agencies like UN Women and the UNFPA have when there is ineffectual diplomatic and financial support from Western states? Meeting their objectives as operational agencies will entail more compromise, and compromise means the end of the categorical nature of rights. If UN agencies need to work with or through local actors, including national governments and religious organizations, this will narrow the room for human rights advocacy. Particularly in Islamic states, where religion and the state are fused, getting access for the UN or INGOs will require negotiation. No visa means no entry. No legitimacy means no access. That visa may be conditional on a promise not to mention rights. The Sri Lankan government used visa politics against UN and INGO staff during their attack on Tamil civilians; the Sudanese government simply threw the INGOs out. Maternal mortality is perhaps the future: it sparked a Millennium Development Goal that was so successful internationally because religious and secular actors could both support keeping women alive either to have more children or to exercise their reproductive rights.

How will the UN High Commissioner for Human Rights fare if states on the Human Rights Council block the investigation of their allies or push through resolutions on traditional values and reject those on sexual orientation and gender identity? Europe's "fading power to set the rules of the game" was evident on the HRC almost as soon as it was established; EU members had to threaten to withdraw completely in 2007 to stop China from blocking human rights monitoring efforts in Belarus and Cuba.[25] Indeed, creating the Human Rights Council in 2006 to replace the widely derided Commission on Human Rights meant updating membership to the detriment of EU influence.[26] The United States initially refused to run for membership of the HRC; without it, getting an initial resolution condemning Sri Lanka for shelling trapped civilians proved impossible.

Having UN agencies forced to adopt a tactical logic will do nothing to defend the principle that global norms are universal, secular, and categorical. In this respect, putting all the eggs of women's rights in the UN Women basket may be an error; it creates one large target on which the attentions of religious and sovereignty-driven actors can focus. It also assumes senior Western and UN officials will support women's rights in a serious way. If the US Supreme Court overturns *Roe v. Wade*, the pressure on reproductive rights at the international level will intensify. Forcing abortion rights into the open will mobilize traditionalists and the faithful against humanism's legion of rights, relief, and development experts. Even the mighty Gates Foundation has discovered that gender, sexuality, and sex are politically treacherous. Through their "polio infrastructure," Bill and Melinda Gates aim to distribute contraception to hundreds of millions of girls and women worldwide. Melinda Gates called the lack of access to family planning for many women a "crime." Resistance was immediate and intense, her attackers calling this a "blatant attack on morality."[27]

Beyond Denial

The shift to multipolarity will reinforce the peace and security focus of the Security Council and split human rights off as a sideshow in Geneva, Old Europe, where the stakes are far lower for states. The use of classic techniques of state control (censorship, surveillance, draconian punishment, police violence, torture, reprisals) is endemic in both Russia and China and far from unknown in Western states, the United States counterterrorism policies after 9/11 having challenged many American ideals and civil liberties.[28] Authoritarian measures in China and Russia have intensified, not weakened, since the Arab Spring.

But Global Human Rights rollback may yield a perverse gain: more honesty. Russia and China make no effort to disguise their principled indifference to the suffering of other sovereign nationals or their willingness to target dissidents who resist them. Nonintervention, they argue, is too valuable a principle to lose. They are raising no one's expectations that a savior is coming. Maybe Tiananmen Square in 1989 was the moment when the new world came into view exactly as the old Cold War world was ending. The outrage of American officials at the refusal of China and Russia to support tougher action in Syria must be weighed against the long list of cases where the United States, the United Kingdom, and France have used violence or supported repressive governments to meet their own policy goals. We might begin, in the American case, with Mobutu in the DRC, Pinochet in Chile, the Khmer Rouge in Cambodia, and Mubarak in Egypt. For many observers, the Chinese and

Russians protect their clients in exactly the same way the United States protects Israel and Saudi Arabia. All great powers seek to realize their national interests, but only in the case of the United States and Europe is this routinely dressed up in the language of moral progress.

This is how two of the foremost advocates of liberal internationalism, Ikenberry and Slaughter, introduce their report, "Forging a World of Liberty under Law":

> The basic objective of U.S. strategy must be to protect the American people and the American way of life. This overarching goal should comprise three more specific aims: 1) *a secure homeland*, including protection against attacks on our people and infrastructure and against fatal epidemics; 2) *a healthy global economy*, which is essential for our own prosperity and security; and 3) *a benign international environment*, grounded in security cooperation among nations and the spread of liberal democracy.[29]

These are American scholar-practitioners who claim to believe in global norms. The purpose of a "concert of democracies" is to keep America safe and allow Americans to prosper. There is no commitment on principle to the idea of *global* norms, only a commitment to globalize *American* norms. Isn't this just neoconservatism? How are liberal internationalists and neocons distinct when both support spreading liberal democracy via R2P and the use of force if necessary? Why should China, Russia, or India behave any differently? It is the prerogative of a great power to be a hypocrite, but the United States may be more hypocritical than the new great powers, particularly China. One basis proposed for choosing members of the Human Rights Council, suggested by Human Rights Watch, was the number of UN rights treaties ratified and reporting requirements met. But it transpired that the United States might be excluded as a result.[30]

In the neo-Westphalian world there will be future mass atrocities and even genocides. If they happen in Africa, there might even be some kind of intervention, provided (a) there is no prospect of serious resistance, and (b) no great power protects the state concerned. Mali in 2013 was an example. If there are mass atrocities in Asia, nothing will be done about them unless China and maybe India and Russia feels their security is threatened. If President Karimov continues murdering Uzbeks, there may be Chinese and Russian pressure to cease. It will not be because of any norm but because it affects trade, investment, and energy supplies. The same is true when Saudi Arabia attacks its own, or Bahrain's, citizens. The United States shows great tolerance for strategically important allies. Counterterrorism is a discourse that gives state killing more legitimacy than it has had for decades. Sanctions will happen only if and when the three major players, China, Russia, and the United States, find their interests aligned.

The Last Rites

Neo-Westphalia means more politics, less morality, and less Europe. The Human Rights Council is in Geneva and the ICC is in The Hague because they are "European" institutions. The fact that Europe pays the majority of the UN's budget and gets so little leverage in return is a sign of just how far political power has shifted.[31] Europe's preeminent political philosopher, Jürgen Habermas, in his aptly titled *The Divided West*, argues that the response of the Bush administration to 9/11 threatens to derail the "constitutionalization of international law." This law is, for Habermas, the great achievement of the Europe-led Kantian project.[32] But the battle was lost long before Bush. Europe's political decline began in 1945 after the atrocity of the Holocaust. We are living through the end of its ideological power, embedded until recently in the norms that underwrote the idea of a universal system headed by secular multilateral organizations—the League of Nations, the United Nations, the International Criminal Court.

That there is genuine global solidarity is a conceit of human rights advocates in Geneva, New York, and London. A political and moral economy keeps the global and the local irrevocably apart. The "middle," global civil society, is unstable precisely because the financial flows, and therefore the setting of priorities, tend to be all one way. Global and local do not share the same lifeworld in terms of the risks and dangers that are an everyday fact of life. There is no real reciprocity, the "gift" from one side unreturnable by the other. Or so I have argued.

One might point out that the example of the Mothers of the Plaza de Mayo in Argentina did as much in the 1980s to build the Global Human

Rights Regime as Amnesty, Human Rights Watch, and the wide array of international human rights jurists, lawyers, and advocates. Or that key figures of the humanist international came from the South, most notably José "Pepe" Zalaquett (Chile), Juan E. Méndez (Argentina), Wilder Tayler (Uruguay), and Alex Boraine (South Africa). But all except Boraine made their international reputations working for or through Amnesty or Human Rights Watch.[33] And the Mothers of the Plaza de Mayo, while highly influential, continue to focus on social justice issues within Argentina. They have no seat at the top table in Geneva or New York. As early as 1988, the claims of global justice (in the shape of Aryeh Neier) clashed with the needs of local communities (Chile's Zalaquett) at the Aspen Institute's now famous November conference termed *State Crimes: Punishment or Pardon*. In the 1990s with the ad-hocs, the Rome Statute, and the vastly expanded transitional justice lobby, the argument for global justice won out.[34]

Lowercase human rights, a nonhegemonic language of resistance allied to a variety of causes and motivations, has no preset future. In the amateur 1970s, the gap between Western human rights activists and those working against dictatorial regimes, while real, was nonetheless narrower. There were no plush offices or high salaries. There was more of an ethic of sacrifice, born of the vocational nature of the work. Time, money, personal security, and peace of mind were often jettisoned to aid others. Longtime senior Oxfam activist Tony Vaux argues: "In order to understand the person in need and his or her full social, economic and political context, we need to obliterate our own self."[35] This is extreme, but the personal costs paid by Amnesty International's pioneering staff were real enough.[36] The growth of a Global Human Rights Regime has created a wider gap between what people face on the ground and those who claim solidarity with them in Western capitals. This works in the opposite direction to the lessons some evangelical churches are learning, their missionaries conceived of as "servants" not "leaders" in local settings.[37] The political economy of churches and diasporas—the permanent channeling of resources in a serious and sustained way throughout a transnational network—is another potential avenue for a more equitable distribution of power. Perhaps George Soros should have given his $100 million not to Human Rights Watch but to human rights organizations in the South to spend as they chose, much as the Ford Foundation is now doing.

There has always been a strong link between sacrifice and secular religiosity. But the function of sacrifice—to affirm solidarity and commitment and to accrue moral authority—has been lost. The classical heroes of the humanist international, those who enter the public consciousness, are increasingly out-of-date: Dunant, Nightingale, Barton, Jebb, Nansen, Lemkin, Wallenberg, Bernadotte, Hammarskjöld. Humanitarian aid worker Fred Cuny is one of the few, and he is idealized as a result. Some recent Nobel Peace Prizes (again, awarded by Europeans) have gone to institutions: MSF, the UN's Peacekeeping Forces, and even the EU. President Obama has also received one. Many have gone to those whose advocacy work is national, even though they have international resonance. But who are the international equivalents of Mohammed Bouazizi, the Tunisian street vendor whose self-immolation in protest at his unfair and petty treatment by local police officials sparked the Arab Spring? The humanist international, in an era of laws and trials and corporate fund-raising, is starved of heroes of this caliber. Will there ever be a statue of Bouazizi in Geneva or New York?

Underneath the global institutions of power the humanists have built lies a residual intuition about waning moral authority. It is too late to rescue it, but sacralizing the work of heroes of the international provides some solace as an antidote to the gap between rhetoric and reality. The first "global state funeral" was held for Sergio Vieira de Mello, the nearest we have to a recent hero of the humanist international, the heavy symbolism of his mourning a sign of how much advocates need their sustaining myths to keep the alibi from fracturing. But the sanctification of de Mello, last seen by us in East Timor in 1999, may well be a sign not of what is to come but of what has been lost.

As Kofi Annan's special envoy to Iraq, de Mello was assassinated on August 28, 2003, in a suicide truck bombing at the UN building (the Canal Hotel) in Baghdad that claimed a total of twenty-three lives. He is the archetypal humanist advocate, having worked as a troubleshooter in East Pakistan, Cambodia, Mozambique, Lebanon, Bosnia, Rwanda, Kosovo, and East Timor, as well as being the UN's emergency relief coordinator and, in his last permanent posting, UN high commissioner for human rights. He had an MA in philosophy and wrote a PhD on the legal-political concept of supranationality. A moving documentary, *Fight to Save the World: Sergio*, about his life and final hours based on a book about him by the ubiquitous Samantha Power, records that as he lay dying under the post-explosion rubble of his office his last words to his rescuers were: "Don't let them pull the mission out."[38] It was a sentiment worthy of a hero. Opposite the nondenominational meditation space at the entrance to the UN complex in New York, the tattered and bomb-damaged UN flag from the Canal Hotel is proudly displayed with the words "Fallen in the cause of peace" underneath. A plaque records the bombing, the loss of life and serious injuries, and the fact that the blast "ripped this flag." Nearby is a bust of Count Folke Bernadotte, an earlier hero.

In the week following his death, de Mello's body was first flown back to Brazil after a brief memorial service at Baghdad Airport. His coffin, draped in a blue and white UN flag, was lifted by six pallbearers, including his bodyguards, onto a Brazilian air force jet. His legal wife and two sons accompanied the coffin, even though his fiancée, Carolina Larriera, was living in Baghdad with him and had waited, frantic, outside the rubble of his collapsed office for hours desperate for him to survive. The US's Iraq administrator, Paul Bremer, wept. In Brazil, three days of mourning were declared, and a memorial service was held in Rio de Janeiro attended by Annan, among others. At the memorial service, the secretary-general had this to say of his envoy:

> We cannot accept that Sergio had to die at this time, in this way, or that anything good can come of it. We cannot accept that all his brilliance, his energy, his devotion to his staff and his loyalty to the ideals of the United Nations, have been so abruptly taken from us. Indeed we can imagine nothing more cruel, or pointless, or unjust. But when we contemplate his sacrifice, and that of the comrades who died with him—when we remember that they gave their lives for principle, and peace, and reconciliation—then we, too, can hold our heads a little higher; and we are proud to work for the same Organisation that they served. Sergio, my friend, you have entered that Pantheon of heroes that the United Nations wishes it did not have. You will shine for ever among our brightest.[39]

A few months before his death, addressing the fifty-ninth session of the UN Commission on Human Rights de Mello had told delegates that "security" and "protection" were first and foremost human rights issues, and that the attempt by states after 9/11 to curb civil liberties had to be resisted:

We cannot compromise our hard-won human rights to give states a free hand in fighting terrorism. There, again, we draw a line. Well established international norms—the right not to be detained arbitrarily or imprisoned indefinitely, the right to due process of law, an impartial jury and an impartial judge, to legal representation, to be free from inhumane and degrading treatment—these norms are under siege today. We have to draw a line and defend them.[40]

He went on:

The culture of human rights must be a popular culture if it is to have the strength to withstand the blows that will inevitably come. Human-rights culture must be a popular culture if it is to be able to innovate and to be truly owned at the national and sub-national levels.[41]

Commenting the day after his death, Amnesty International's secretary general, Irene Khan, said: "If Sergio's death is to have any meaning, Iraq must be a building site for human rights—it must not be allowed to become a wasteland. Truth and justice for the Iraqi people was Sergio's goal. The principles that he held so dear in life must not be sacrificed now."[42]

From Brazil, de Mello's body was flown to Geneva, the international city, for a second service and burial. UN flags were at half mast. About five hundred people filled St. Paul's Roman Catholic Church while loudspeakers broadcast the service to those outside. According to the BBC: "Candles flickering on the altar in the church symbolised each victim of the attack, with Vieira de Mello's wife, Annie, and their two adult sons, Adrien and Laurent, lighting the 23rd candle in his memory."[43] The BBC reported:

The coffin was carried out of the church to the sound of John Lennon's song Imagine for burial at the Cemetery of Kings. The cemetery is a resting place reserved in Geneva for figures who have marked international history, including the theologian Jean Calvin and writer Jorge Luis Borges.[44]

Even after his interment, further memorial services were held, and in 2007, outside the Palais Wilson in Geneva and in front of survivors of the bombing, former secretary-general Annan and new high commissioner for human rights Louise Arbour (former chief prosecutor of the ICTY) unveiled a bust of de Mello.[45] Finally, in December 2008, the anniversary of de Mello's death was designated World Humanitarian Day.[46] It is intended to "honor all humanitarian and the United Nations and associated personnel who have lost their lives in the cause of duty and those who have worked in the promotion of the humanitarian cause."[47] Religions thrive on martyrs, and for martyrs the manner of their death and its commemoration are vital. As de Mello's son Adrien explained in St. Paul's Church: "His assassins did not really kill him because his legacy and ideals of helping people live on in each of us."[48]

De Mello's work made no difference whatsoever to success or failure in Iraq. The contribution of the UN was minimal. Indeed, it did pull out, as de Mello feared, for a year. The reasons for the war, the political and military strategies used in prosecuting it, its outcome, the failure of the United States to seek a final Security Council resolution for fear of a veto from Russia and/or China, and maybe even France, the fallout for neocons in the United States, for the "imperial" Bush presidency, the massive death toll, the increasing influence of Iran, the damage done to Western legitimacy, and the recruiting success for radical Islamist groups—none of this had anything to do with the UN and the humanist international. The massive violence the United States deployed in response to 9/11 was the defining feature of the first decade of the twentieth century.

The scale of de Mello's commemoration is an attempt to invigorate the metanarrative, to canonize a secular saint.[49] The moral power of de Mello's exemplary sacrifice is palpable for anyone raised in the liberal humanist tradition. His story, as told through *Sergio*, is certainly very moving. But the world he represented, one of overambitious, unaccountable, alienated, and largely ineffectual Human Rights is a global alibi for a world in which sovereignty and religion are back. Once the Human Rights Regime became dependent on the successes of liberal power and money and abandoned its secular religiosity, the eclipse of its moral authority at the global level was only ever a matter of time. The classic humanist space of impartiality—of a space that was not politics, money or power—has foundations that will crumble regardless of how deep they pour the concrete for humanity's new palace in the sand dunes of The Hague.

acknowledgments

For institutional support in the research and writing of this book I am grateful to the Leverhulme Trust for a remarkably generous Major Research Fellowship and to SOAS, University of London, for allowing me to take extended leave. All of my colleagues in the Politics and International Studies Department at SOAS deserve recognition for carrying any extra burden my absence entailed, and in particular I would like to thank Fiona Adamson, Felix Berenskoetter, Laleh Khalili, Mark Laffey, Matthew Nelson, Rahul Rao, and Leslie Vinjamuri.

During the book's long gestation numerous conversations and suggestions helped form my understanding. In particular I would like to thank: Fiona Adamson, Daniel Attas, Elazar Barkan, Louis Bickford, Clifford Bob, Peter Brett, Youk Chhang, Phil Clark, David Cohen, Claudio Cordone, Matthew Craven, Michelle Dockery, Antonio Donini, Mark Duffield, Christopher Hall, Laura Hammond, Steve Heder, Cathy Huser, Peter Katzenstein, Edward Keene, Tim Kelsall, Martti Koskenniemi, Paavo Kotiaho, Susan Lee, Jennifer Llewellyn, Jens Meierhenrich, Robert Murtfeld, Matthew Nelson, Norah Niland, Daniel Philpott, Anne Orford, Margo Picken, Rahul Rao, James Ron, Amaia Sanchez Cacicedo, Ole Jacob Sending, John Sidel, Jack Snyder, Bertrand Taithe, Dorothy Q. Thomas, Lars Waldorf, Peter Walker, Rob Waygood, Thomas Weiss, Lynn Welchman, and Tom Young. For those I have neglected to remember, please accept my profound apologies. Of all of these people, I owe a particular debt to Steve Heder.

I received outstanding research assistance from Gerasimos Tsourapas and Sami Everett at SOAS. Roger Haydon proved once again to be an inspired and inspirational editor whose provocations and vision improved the argument and text at every stage. The companionship of

Daniel Attas and Rob Waygood deserves particular mention, as does the support and forbearance of my wife Helen Jenkins and my children Ellie Hopgood and Lucas Hopgood, whose patience during my many absences from home and periods of withdrawal were of inestimable importance in helping me to finish the book. I could not have done it without them. My final debt is to three people whose engagement with the project from the beginning has also been indispensable. Michael Barnett has been a pathfinder in constructing an engaged critique of humanism on its many dimensions; his deep insight, unwavering support, and friendship have been invaluable. There is no one like Janice Gross Stein: her fierce intuition and boundless energy have no equal as a motivating force. Finally, Leslie Vinjamuri has been the other half of a five-year dialogue about every aspect of this book. She may disagree profoundly with much of its analysis, and conclusions, but our conversations have significantly shaped whatever virtues the argument may have. For this long and selfless contribution I cannot begin to thank her enough. None of those mentioned above is responsible in any way, of course, for the final result.

abbreviations

ACLU	American Civil Liberties Union
AI	Amnesty International
AIUSA	Amnesty International United States of America
ASEAN	Association of Southeast Asian Nations
CEDAW	Convention on the Elimination of All Forms of Discrimination against Women
CICC	Coalition of ICC Supporters
DRC	Democratic Republic of the Congo
ECCC	Extraordinary Chambers in the Courts of Cambodia
EIU	Economist Intelligence Unit
FGM	female genital mutilation
FIDH	International Federation for Human Rights
HRW	Human Rights Watch
ICC	International Criminal Court
ICHRP	International Council for Human Rights Policy
ICISS	International Commission on Intervention and State Sovereignty
ICRC	International Committee of the Red Cross
ICTR	International Criminal Tribunal for Rwanda
ICTY	International Criminal Tribunal for the former Yugoslavia
IHL	international humanitarian law
ILC	International Law Commission
INGO	international nongovernmental organization
KR	Khmer Rouge
LGBT	lesbian, gay, bisexual, and transgendered
LTTE	Liberation Tigers of Tamil Eelam
MoMA	Museum of Modern Art, New York

MSF	Médecins Sans Frontières (in the United States, Doctors without Borders)
NATO	North Atlantic Treaty Organization
NGO	nongovernmental organization
OHCHR	Office of the High Commissioner for Human Rights
OSJI	Open Society Justice Initiative
POC	prisoner of conscience
R2P	responsibility to protect
SCSL	Special Court for Sierra Leone
UDHR	Universal Declaration of Human Rights
UN	United Nations
UNFPA	United Nations Population Fund
UNGA	United Nations General Assembly
UNIFEM	United Nations Development Fund for Women
UNSC	United Nations Security Council
USHMM	United States Holocaust Memorial Museum

notes

Preface

1. East Timor Action Network (ETAN), "Human Rights and the Future of East Timor: Report on Joint UNTAET Human Rights Unit and East Timor Jurists Association workshop held in Dili, 7–8 August 2000," http://www.etan.org/issues/9-00reprt.htm.

2. Commission for Reception, Truth and Reconciliation in Timor-Leste (CAVR), "Chega! The CAVR Report," http://www.cavr-timorleste.org/en/chegaReport.htm.

3. See Allan Nairn, "U.S. Support for the Indonesian Military: Congressional Testimony," *Bulletin of Concerned Asian Scholars* 32, nos. 1–2 (2000): 43–47, http://criticalasianstudies.org/assets/files/bcas/v32n01.pdf.

4. Human Rights First, "Indonesia: Ghosts of Past Abuse Haunt Political Ambition of Prabowo Subianto," http://www.humanrightsfirst.org/2012/09/12/indonesia-ghosts-of-past-abuse-haunt-political-ambition-of-prabowo-subianto/.

5. John M. Miller, "10 Years after Timor's Independence, Where Is the Justice?" East Timor Action Network (ETAN), http://www.etan.org/news/2012/04justice.htm.

6. For example, from the practitioner side, Aryeh Neier, *The International Human Rights Movement: A History* (Princeton, NJ: Princeton University Press, 2012), and from the academic side, Kathryn Sikkink, *The Justice Cascade: How Human Rights Prosecutions Are Changing World Politics* (New York: W. W. Norton, 2011).

7. See Margaret E. Keck and Kathryn Sikkink, *Activists beyond Borders: Advocacy Networks in International Politics* (Ithaca, NY: Cornell University Press, 1998).

8. CAVR, "Chega! The CAVR Report," http://www.cavr-timorleste.org/en/chega Report.htm.

9. The tension between Catholics and Muslims in East Timor was a key social and political cleavage throughout the struggle against Indonesian imperialism.

10. Several excellent critical histories of the origins of human rights have been written recently: see, for example, Stefan-Ludwig Hoffmann, ed., *Human Rights in the Twentieth Century* (New York: Cambridge University Press, 2011), including Hoffmann's introductory chapter, "Genealogies of Human Rights." Also Akira Iriye, Petra Goedde, and William I. Hitchcock, eds., *The Human Rights Revolution: An International History* (New York: Oxford University Press, 2012), and Samuel Moyn, *The Last Utopia: Human Rights in History* (Cambridge, MA: Belknap Press of Harvard University Press, 2010).

11. Stephen Hopgood, *Keepers of the Flame: Understanding Amnesty International* (Ithaca, NY: Cornell University Press, 2006).

12. See James C. Scott, *Two Cheers for Anarchism* (Princeton, NJ: Princeton University Press, 2012).

13. On transnational advocacy networks, see Keck and Sikkink, *Activists beyond Borders* and Sally Engle Merry, *Human Rights and Gender Violence: Translating International*

Law into Local Justice (Chicago: University of Chicago Press, 2005). On the importance of local institutions to increase compliance with global norms, see Thomas Risse, Stephen C. Ropp, and Kathryn Sikkink, eds., *The Persistent Power of Human Rights: From Commitment to Compliance* (Cambridge: Cambridge University Press, 2013) and Emilie M. Hafner-Burton, *Making Human Rights a Reality* (Princeton, NJ: Princeton University Press, 2013).

14. Carl Schmitt, *Political Theology*, trans. George Schwab (Chicago: University of Chicago Press, 1985).

15. On the importance of innocence in the development of the laws of war, see Helen M. Kinsella, *The Image before the Weapon: A Critical History of the Distinction between Combatant and Civilian* (Ithaca, NY: Cornell University Press, 2011).

16. Josef L. Kunz, "The Chaotic Status of the Laws of War and the Urgent Necessity for Their Revision," *American Journal of International Law* 45, no. 1 (1951): 37.

17. Hopgood, *Keepers of the Flame.*

18. East Timor Action Network (ETAN), "Human Rights and the Future of East Timor," http://www.etan.org/issues/9-00reprt.htm.

19. Jamie Fly and Robert Zarate, "Now Is Not the Time to Show a Lack of Resolve on Libya," *Foreign Policy Initiative* (June 2011), http://www.foreignpolicyi.org/content/fpi-bulletin-now-not-time-show-lack-resolve-libya-0.

20. See Vladamir Pustogarov, "Fyodor Fyodorovich Martens (1845–1909)—A Humanist of Modern Times," *International Review of the Red Cross*, no. 312 (1996), http://www.icrc.org/eng/resources/documents/article/other/57jn52.htm

21. Universal Rights Network, "UN Secretary-General's Remarks at the Funeral of Sergio Vieira de Mello," http://www.universalrights.net/heroes/display.php3?id=67. The Human Rights Council replaced the Commission on Human Rights in 2006.

22. KESTA (Klibur Estudantes OAN-Timor Australia), "Statement of H. E. President Kay Rala Xanana Gusmão on the death of Sergio Vieira de Mello," http://groups.yahoo.com/group/KESTA/message/4233.

23. For an example of this process in action, see the Ford Foundation's effort to bring "southern hemisphere voices into the global human rights dialogue." See "Ford Awards Seven Human Rights Organizations $1 million Each to Become Global Leaders," http://www.fordfoundation.org/newsroom/news-from-ford/651.

1. Moral Authority in a Godless World

1. On risks to aid workers see Abby Stoddard, Adele Harmer, and Victoria Di Domenico, "Providing Aid in Insecure Environments: 2009 Update," Humanitarian Policy Group Brief 34, April 2009. On religion and secularism in international politics, see Elizabeth Shakman Hurd, *The Politics of Secularism in International Relations* (Princeton, NJ: Princeton University Press, 2008) and Jack Snyder, ed., *Religion and International Relations Theory* (New York: Columbia University Press, 2011).

2. One of the main drafters of the Universal Declaration of Human Rights in 1948, René Cassin (winner of the Nobel Peace Prize in 1968) knew at the time they were deferring for the sake of consensus all the difficult questions about the authority of human rights so as not to "delve into the nature of man and of society and to confront the metaphysical controversies, notably the conflict between spiritual, rationalist, and materialist doctrines on the origins of human rights." Quoted in Joseph R. Slaughter, *Human Rights, Inc.* (New York: Fordham University Press, 2007), 47.

3. Max Weber, "Science as a Vocation," in *From Max Weber: Essays in Sociology*, ed. H. H. Gerth and C. Wright Mills (London: Kegan Paul, Trench, Trübner, 1947), 155.

4. Moses Moskowitz, known in UN and Jewish circles in New York as "Mr. Human Rights," criticized Amnesty International's organizational growth precisely because it

threatened to build "a new Tower of Babel." Quoted in Samuel Moyn, *The Last Utopia: Human Rights in History* (Cambridge, MA: Belknap Press of Harvard University Press, 2010), 123. Also Samuel Moyn, "Empathy in History, Empathizing with Humanity," *History and Theory* 45 (2006): 408.

5. By the Dutch prime minister, as quoted in Geoffrey Robertson, *Crimes against Humanity: The Struggle for Global Justice*, 3rd ed. (London: Penguin Books, 2006), 466.

6. "Architectural Design Competition for the Permanent Premises of the ICC: Statement to the Jury," Coalition for the International Criminal Court, October 30–31, 2008. The CICC is quoting Mies van der Rohe.

7. Gareth J. Evans, *The Responsibility to Protect: Ending Mass Atrocity Crimes Once and for All* (Washington, DC: Brookings Institution Press, 2008).

8. Jan Egeland, *A Billion Lives: An Eyewitness Report from the Frontlines of Humanity* (New York: Simon & Schuster, 2008), 215. Egeland, also a former chair of Amnesty International in Norway and secretary general of the Norwegian Red Cross, touches on several important humanist tropes even in his subtitle.

9. Roger Normand and Sarah Zaidi, *Human Rights at the UN: The Political History of Universal Justice* (Bloomington: Indiana University Press, 2008), 8.

10. Ruti G. Teitel, *Humanity's Law* (New York: Oxford University Press, 2011); Kathryn Sikkink, *The Justice Cascade: How Human Rights Prosecutions Are Changing World Politics* (New York: W. W. Norton, 2011).

11. United Nations Security Council, *An Agenda for Peace: Report of the Secretary-General pursuant to the Statement Adopted by the Summit Meeting of the Security Council on 31 January 1992*. June 17, 1992.

12. See Teitel, *Humanity's Law*, 39.

13. Livni was deputy prime minster and foreign minister in Israel during Operation Cast Lead (2008–2009), an Israeli bombing campaign against Gaza that led to allegations of war crimes and crimes against humanity.

14. Frédéric Mégret points out the irony that "the apex of the human rights movement [the ICC] comes in the form of a tribunal that is not a human rights tribunal properly so called": see "The Politics of International Criminal Justice," *European Journal of International Law* 13, no. 5 (2002): 1265.

15. See Stuart Ford, "How Leadership in International Criminal Law Is Shifting from the U.S. to Europe and Asia: An Analysis of Spending on and Contributions to International Criminal Courts," *Saint Louis University Law Journal* 55 (2010).

16. Jean-Marie Henckaerts, "Study on Customary International Humanitarian Law: A Contribution to the Understanding and Respect for the Rule of Law in Armed Conflict," *International Review of the Red Cross* 87, no. 857 (2005): 187. See also Yves Sandoz in the foreword to a 2005 ICRC report on customary law: "The Geneva Conventions have been universally embraced. The rules of IHL represent a kind of common heritage of mankind, with its roots in all humanitarian cultures." Yves Sandoz, foreword, in *Customary International Humanitarian Law*, vol. 1, *Rules*, ed. Jean-Marie Henckaerts and Louise Doswald-Beck (Cambridge: Cambridge University Press, 2005), xvii.

17. Antonio Cassese, *International Law*, 2nd ed. (Oxford: Oxford University Press, 2005), 396.

18. H. L. A. Hart, *The Concept of Law* (Oxford: Clarendon Press, 1961), 92.

19. Karl Popper, *The Open Society and Its Enemies*, 4th ed., 2 vols. (London: Routledge & Kegan Paul, 1962). The idea of an open society has become influential in contemporary humanism through the philanthropy of the financier George Soros.

20. Pierre Bourdieu, *Language and Symbolic Power* (Cambridge: Cambridge University Press, 1991), 42.

21. The defining feature of natural law for my purposes is that it grounds rights in an authority that transcends and overrules human authority, including positive law. To claim for rights that they are rooted in natural law or natural justice is to trump the

190 NOTES TO PAGES 7–12

day-to-day political process with an unanswerable reference to a superior position of judgment. Hence the critical importance of creating a unique space, to which all in theory defer, of impartial authority.

22. Stephen Gardbaum, "Human Rights and International Constitutionalism," in *Ruling the World: Constitutionalism, International Law, and Global Governance*, ed. Jeffrey L. Dunoff and Joel P. Trachtman (Cambridge: Cambridge University Press, 2009), 237 and 241–42.

23. Theodor Meron, *The Humanization of International Law* (Leiden: Martinus Nijhoff, 2006), 370.

24. See Teitel, *Humanity's Law*, 9.

25. Lynn Hunt, *Inventing Human Rights: A History* (New York: W. W. Norton, 2007), 75. See also Michel Foucault, *Discipline and Punish: The Birth of the Prison* (London: Penguin, 1991).

26. Guillaume Daudin, Matthias Morys, and Kevin H. O'Rourke, "Globalization, 1870–1914," Department of Economics Discussion Papers, no. 395 (Oxford: University of Oxford, 2008), 2. This is also my source for the data on prices, capital, and migration.

27. Karl Marx, *Selected Writings*, ed. Lawrence H. Simon (London: Hackett, 1994).

28. On "base" and "superstructure" see Ernesto Laclau and Chantal Mouffe, *Hegemony and Socialist Strategy: Towards a Radical Democratic Politics*, 2nd ed. (London: Verso, 2001).

29. Michael N. Barnett, *Empire of Humanity: A History of Humanitarianism* (Ithaca, NY: Cornell University Press, 2011), 52–53.

30. Ibid., 49, and also Margaret C. Jacob, *Strangers Nowhere in the World* (Philadelphia: University of Pennsylvania Press, 2006), 126–27.

31. ICRC, *International Red Cross and Red Crescent Museum Catalogue* (Geneva: ICRC, 2000), 17.

32. See Henry Dunant, *A Memory of Solferino* (Geneva: Henry Dunant Institute, 1985).

33. Pierre Boissier, *History of the International Committee of the Red Cross: From Solferino to Tsushima* (Geneva: Henry Dunant Institute, 1985), 13–16.

34. Friedrich Nietzsche, *The Gay Science*, trans. Josefine Nauckhoff (Cambridge: Cambridge University Press, 2001), 120. This question is asked by a madman doomed Cassandra-like to spread news of god's death to a skeptical audience he accuses of being god's murderers, a man deemed mad because he has a lit lantern in daylight, an unsubtle metaphor for the failure of the Enlightenment.

35. Émile Durkheim, *The Elementary Forms of Religious Life*, trans. Carol Cosman (Oxford: Oxford University Press, 2001), 166.

36. Part of the wider story of modernity is the problematizing of these social identities both by denaturalizing them and by rendering visible the silences they conceal (about gender, race, and sexuality, for example).

37. Helen M Kinsella, *The Image before the Weapon: A Critical History of the Distinction between Combatant and Civilian* (Ithaca, NY: Cornell University Press, 2011): 16, 151.

38. Luc Boltanski, *Distant Suffering: Morality, Media and Politics* (Cambridge: Cambridge University Press, 1999), 29. He goes on: "The public sphere thus presupposes the existence of a detached, casual observer who can survey the peculiarities of society in the way that the geographer, cartographer or painter inspired by the cartographic ideal surveys the peculiarities of the landscape." See also Didier Fassin, *Humanitarian Reason: A Moral History of the Present* (Berkeley: University of California Press, 2012), 9–10; and on "social death" and authority see Orlando Patterson, *Slavery and Social Death: A Comparative Study* (Cambridge, MA: Harvard University Press, 1985).

39. Adam Smith, *The Theory of Moral Sentiments* (Minneapolis, MN: Filiquarian Publishing, 2007), 171.

40. As Martha Nussbaum puts it, "becoming a citizen of the world is often a lonely business": see Martha C. Nussbaum, "Patriotism and Cosmopolitanism," in *For Love*

of Country? A New Democracy Forum on the Limits of Patriotism, ed. Martha C. Nussbaum and Joshua Cohen (Boston: Beacon Press, 2002), 15. See also Georg Simmel, "The Stranger," in *On Individuality and Social Forms: Selected Writings*, ed. Donald N. Levine (Chicago: University of Chicago Press, 1971), 146. On the relationship between money and objectivity see Georg Simmel, *The Philosophy of Money* (London: Routledge, 1978), 436–37, and Stephen Hopgood, "Moral Authority, Modernity and the Politics of the Sacred," *European Journal of International Relations* 15, no. 2 (2009). See also Jeri Laber, *The Courage of Strangers: Coming of Age in the Human Rights Movement* (New York: PublicAffairs, 2002).

41. Zygmunt Bauman, *Modernity and the Holocaust* (Cambridge: Polity, 2000), 27–28. For Bauman it is in the Holocaust that the contradiction at modernity's heart—its destructive potential and capacity for violence—was fully revealed.

42. Mark Mazower, *No Enchanted Palace: The End of Empire and the Ideological Origins of the United Nations* (Princeton, NJ: Princeton University Press, 2009), 122–23.

43. Jack L. Goldsmith, "Mea Culpa: Lawfare," *Lawfare: Hard National Security Choices* (blog), September 8, 2011, http://www.lawfareblog.com/2011/09/mea-culpa-lawfare/. Goldsmith talks of the need to "do one's best to win the war over law." See also David Kennedy, *Of War and Law* (Princeton, NJ: Princeton University Press, 2006), and David Luban, "Carl Schmitt and the Critique of Lawfare," Georgetown Public Law and Legal Theory Research Paper, no. 11–33 (2011).

44. See Philippe Sands, *Torture Team: Rumsfeld's Memo and the Betrayal of American Values* (London: Palgrave Macmillan, 2008).

45. Charlie Savage, "Secret U.S. Memo Made Legal Case to Kill a Citizen," *New York Times*, October 8, 2011.

46. See the Coalition for the International Criminal Court website, http://www.coalitionfortheicc.org/.

47. The critical website "ICC Watch," which "monitors the International Criminal Court's threat to civil liberties and national autonomy," claims that accession states comprise only 27 percent of the world's population (adding in for good measure that westerners, particularly Europeans, dominate the ICC staff); see the ICC Watch website at http://www.iccwatch.org/iccfaq.html.

48. See Leslie Vinjamuri, "Deterrence, Democracy, and the Pursuit of International Justice," *Ethics & International Affairs* 24, no. 2 (2010).

49. See the petition "Letter to Board of Directors, Amnesty International–USA," *Went 2 the Bridge* (blog), July 11, 2012, http://went2thebridge.blogspot.co.uk/2012/07/letter-to-board-of-directors-amnesty.html.

50. On the idea of a "lifeworld" see Jürgen Habermas, *The Theory of Communicative Action*, vol. 2, *A Critique of Functionalist Reason* (Cambridge: Polity Press, 1995), 125.

51. Edward T. Linenthal, *Preserving Memory: The Struggle to Create America's Holocaust Museum* (New York: Columbia University Press, 2001).

52. Ibid., 86–88, 94.

53. Largely the work of one man, Raphael Lemkin; see John Cooper, *Raphael Lemkin and the Struggle for the Genocide Convention* (London: Palgrave Macmillan, 2008).

54. On Martens, see Kinsella, *The Image before the Weapon*, chap. 5.

55. See Gerd Oberleitner, *Global Human Rights Institutions* (Cambridge: Polity Press, 2007), 173.

56. Mary Robinson and the former Norwegian prime minster Gro Harlem Brundtland, both members of "The Elders," made clear their frustration at this reverse, "Rio + 20 Is Not the Response We Need to Safeguard People and the Planet," *The Elders*, June 21, 2012, http://theelders.org/article/rio20-not-response-we-need-safeguard-people-and-planet. See also Sandeep Bathala, "Pop at Rio + 20: Reproductive Rights Missing from Outcome Document—Assessing the Disappointment," June 22, 2012, *NewSecurityBeat* (the blog of the Environmental Change and Security Program of the Wilson Center).

2. The Church of Human Rights

1. For the eighteenth-century origins of this sensibility and the "humanitarian narrative" (a feeling of concern and responsibility for the pain and suffering of ordinary people) see Thomas W. Laquer, "Bodies, Details, and the Humanitarian Narrative," in *The New Cultural History*, ed. Lynn Hunt (Berkeley: University of California Press, 1989). For a recent discussion of some of the themes in this chapter see Katherine Davies, "Continuity, Change and Contest: Meanings of 'Humanitarian' from the 'Religion of Humanity' to the Kosovo War," *Humanitarian Policy Group*, August 2012. The best introduction by far to the history of humanitarianism is Michael Barnett, *Empire of Humanity: A History of Humanitarianism* (Ithaca, NY: Cornell University Press, 2011).

2. Carl Schmitt, *Political Romanticism*, trans. Guy Oakes (New Brunswick, NJ: Transaction Publishers, 2011), 13. Also John F. Hutchinson, *Champions of Charity: War and the Rise of the Red Cross* (Boulder, CO: Westview Press, 1996), 203.

3. On Calvin and human rights see John Witte Jr., *The Reformation of Rights* (Cambridge: Cambridge University Press, 2007).

4. See David Brion Davis, *The Problem of Slavery in the Age of Revolution, 1770–1823* (New York: Oxford University Press, 1999); Robin Blackburn, *The American Crucible: Slavery, Emancipation and Human Rights* (London: Verso, 2011); Margaret E. Keck and Kathryn Sikkink, *Activists beyond Borders: Advocacy Networks in International Politics* (Ithaca, NY: Cornell University Press, 1998), chap. 2.

5. David Brion Davis, *Slavery and Human Progress* (New York: Oxford University Press, 1984), chap. 3, and Ethan A. Nadelmann, "Global Prohibition Regimes: The Evolution of Norms in International Society," *International Organization* 44, no. 4 (1990): 495. Many of the Quakers involved were also highly successful businessmen: Thomas L. Haskell, "Capitalism and the Origins of the Humanitarian Sensibility, Part 1," *American Historical Review* 90, no. 2 (1985): 346.

6. Barnett, *Empire of Humanity*, 64–66.

7. That states would use voluntary medical services to evade responsibility for their own troops was the basis of Florence Nightingale's objection to the ICRC: see Hutchinson, *Champions of Charity*, 40–41.

8. On the bourgeois public sphere see Jürgen Habermas, *The Structural Transformation of the Public Sphere* (Cambridge, MA: MIT Press, 1989).

9. Émile Durkheim, *The Elementary Forms of Religious Life*, trans. Carol Cosman (Oxford: Oxford University Press, 2001), 166.

10. Émile Durkheim, *Sociology and Philosophy*, trans. D. F. Pocock (London: Routledge, 2010), 58.

11. On innocence and the laws of war, see Helen M Kinsella, *The Image before the Weapon: A Critical History of the Distinction between Combatant and Civilian* (Ithaca, NY: Cornell University Press, 2011).

12. François Bugnion, *The International Committee of the Red Cross and the Protection of War Victims* (Oxford: Macmillan/ICRC, 2003). This picture first appeared with the caption "War's most innocent victim" in a story on the ICRC in the *National Geographic* of November 1986 under the headline "A Little Humanity amid the Horrors of War," written by Peter T. White with photographs by Steve Raymer.

13. Cornelio Sommaruga, "Foreword: Mirror of Humanity: Experience and Conscience," in Bugnion, *International Committee*, xxv. Sommaruga says "his," but it is not obvious the child is male. I retain the male pronoun for the sake of consistency.

14. Mark Drumbl, *Reimagining Child Soldiers in International Law and Policy* (Oxford: Oxford University Press, 2012), 9.

15. For classic earlier Red Cross posters idealizing "the greatest mother in the world" see Hutchinson, *Champions of Charity*, 276–79.

16. Drumbl, *Reimagining Child Soldiers*, 154.

17. Caroline Moorehead, *Dunant's Dream: War, Switzerland and the History of the Red Cross* (London: HarperCollins, 1998), 17.

18. Hutchinson, *Champions of Charity*, 21.

19. Moorehead, *Dunant's Dream*, 176.

20. Jean-Claude Favez, *The Red Cross and the Holocaust*, trans. and ed. John Fletcher and Beryl Fletcher (Cambridge: Cambridge University Press, 1999), 286.

21. André Durand, *From Sarajevo to Hiroshima: History of the International Committee of the Red Cross* (Geneva: Henry Dunant Institute, 1984), 146 and chap. 4; also Hutchinson, *Champions of Charity*, chap 6.

22. David P. Forsythe, *Humanitarian Politics: The International Committee of the Red Cross* (Baltimore: Johns Hopkins University Press, 1977), 8–9; J. D. Armstrong, "The International Committee of the Red Cross and Political Prisoners," *International Organization* 39, no. 4 (1985): 618–19, and David P. Forsythe and Barbara Ann J. Rieffer-Flanagan, *The International Committee of the Red Cross: A Neutral Humanitarian Actor* (London: Routledge, 2007), 29–30.

23. Habermas, *Structural Transformation*; also Sidney Tarrow, *Power in Movement: Social Movements and Contentious Politics*, 2nd ed. (Cambridge: Cambridge University Press, 1998), 43–53; Haskell, "Capitalism and the Origins of the Humanitarian Sensibility, Part 1"; and Joseph R. Slaughter, *Human Rights, Inc.* (New York: Fordham University Press, 2007).

24. Habermas, *Structural Transformation*, 28.

25. See Laquer, "Bodies, Details," on the importance of scientific reports like autopsies and case studies for embedding the humanitarian narrative.

26. Jürgen Habermas, *The Theory of Communicative Action*, vol. 2, *A Critique of Functionalist Reason* (Cambridge: Polity Press, 1995), 125.

27. Durand, *From Sarajevo to Hiroshima*, 179–80. See also White, "Little Humanity," *National Geographic*, November 1986, 650.

28. Habermas, *Structural Transformation*, 56 (italics in original).

29. Pierre Boissier, *History of the International Committee of the Red Cross: From Solferino to Tsushima* (Geneva: Henry Dunant Institute, 1985), 194.

30. Ibid., 351–52.

31. Ibid., 277–78; Hutchinson, *Champions of Charity*, 203–4.

32. For a discussion of how constructivist conceptions of "humanity" elide its racist dimensions see Robert Vitalis, "The Graceful and Liberal Gesture: Making Racism Invisible in American International Relations," *Millennium—Journal of International Relations* 29, no. 2 (2000).

33. Boissier, *History*, 344.

34. In Karl Marx and Friedrich Engels, *The Communist Manifesto*, ed., with introduction and notes, by Gareth Stedman Jones (London: Penguin, 2002).

35. Thomas L. Haskell, "Capitalism and the Origins of the Humanitarian Sensibility, Part 2," *American Historical Review* 90, no. 3 (1985): 557. See also John Ashworth, "The Relationship between Capitalism and Humanitarianism," *American Historical Review* 92, no. 4 (1987).

36. Haskell, "Capitalism and the Origins of the Humanitarian Sensibility, Part 2."

37. See Bertrand Taithe, "The Red Cross Flag in the Franco-Prussian War: Civilians, Humanitarians and War in the 'Modern Age,' " in *War, Medicine and Modernity*, ed. Roger Cooter, Mark Harrison, and Steve Sturdy (Stroud, UK: Sutton Publishing, 1998).

38. Paulo Malanima and Oliver Volckart, "Urbanisation, 1700–1870," Centre for Economic Policy Research (2010), 20.

39. Durkheim, *Sociology and Philosophy*, 68–69.

40. Durkheim, *Elementary Forms of Religious Life*, 237.

41. Moorehead, *Dunant's Dream*, 12.

42. Boissier, *History*, 37. Dunant changed his name from "Henry" to "Henri," but the ICRC has retained the original spelling. Dunant's statement is remarkably similar to that of Amnesty International founder Peter Benenson a hundred years later in 1961; see Stephen Hopgood, *Keepers of the Flame: Understanding Amnesty International* (Ithaca, NY: Cornell University Press, 2006), 56–57.

43. Hutchinson, *Champions of Charity*, 14–20.

44. See the ICRC edition available at International Committee of the Red Cross, "A Memory of Solferino," ICRC Resource Centre, http://www.icrc.org/eng/resources/documents/publication/p0361.htm. Lytton Strachey's famous description of Nightingale is highly suggestive of the wider social contradictions her class faced. Under her watchful gaze, "The reign of chaos and old night began to dwindle; order came upon the scene, and common sense, and forethought, and decision, radiating out from the little room off the great gallery in the Barrack Hospital where, day and night, the Lady Superintendent was at her task. Progress might be slow, but it was sure": *Eminent Victorians* (London: Penguin, 1986), 122.

45. Moorehead, *Dunant's Dream*, 57. At the exhibition he shared a gold medal with Moynier and Dufour, although Moynier shunned him. See also Boissier, *History*, 203–6. Strachey is frank about Nightingale's highly demanding personality, her "demonic possession": *Eminent Victorians*, 111. She, Moynier, and Dunant all died in 1910.

46. Forsythe and Rieffer-Flanagan, *International Committee of the Red Cross*, 8.

47. Boissier, *History*, 69; Moorehead, *Dunant's Dream*, 50.

48. See Cornelio Sommaruga, "Gustave Moynier, Builder of the Red Cross," *International Review of the Red Cross* 29, no. 272 (1989): 485.

49. Available for download from, intriguingly, the US Army Judge Advocate General's School Library: see *International Review of the Red Cross,* April 1963, third year no. 25, http://www.loc.gov/rr/frd/Military_Law/pdf/RC_Apr-1963.pdf.

50. Ibid.

51. Boissier, *History*, 64.

52. The idea of neutrality owed a great deal to Dunant's friend, the Dutch medical officer Dr. J. H. C. Basting. The two men announced the idea together at a statistical conference in Berlin; Boissier, *History*, 61.

53. Boissier, *History*, 67.

54. The red cross was quickly adopted for commercial purposes by various private enterprises: Baptiste Rolle and Edith Lafontaine, "The Emblem That Cried Wolf: ICRC Study on the Use of the Emblems," *International Review of the Red Cross* 91, no. 876 (2009): 761, http://www.icrc.org/eng/assets/files/other/irrc-876-rolle-lafontaine.pdf.

55. Taithe, "Red Cross Flag," 27. As Taithe points out, the shelling of Paris during the war brought women and children, the "archetypal innocents," into the field of battle, fueling good-versus-evil narratives. During the war, gendered images of threats to women and children on the German side, particularly from "bestial" French African soldiers, were used for propaganda purposes: see Christine G. Krüger, "German Suffering in the Franco-Prussian War, 1870–1871," *German History* 29, no. 3 (2011): 415.

56. "Betancourt Rescuer Wore Red Cross," BBC News, July 17, 2008. FARC stands for the Revolutionary Armed Forces of Colombia.

57. François Bugnion, "The Red Cross and Red Crescent Emblems," *International Review of the Red Cross* 29, no. 272 (1989): 412. There is no evidence the red cross was chosen as an inversion of the Swiss flag; Boissier, *History*, 77; Hutchinson, *Champions of Charity*, 142–43.

58. Hutchinson, *Champions of Charity*, 143.

59. Boissier, *History*, 304–5.

60. Bugnion, *International Committee*, 37–38. The use of the red crescent if anything reinforces the underlying religious dimension to both symbols: Bugnion, "Red Cross," 418. The Ottoman Red Cross was run by Christians; see Boissier, *History*, 304–5. Also Barnett, *Empire of Humanity*, 82.

61. Hutchinson, *Champions of Charity*, 6.

62. Forsythe and Rieffer-Flanagan, *International Committee of the Red Cross*, 51. The Iranian Red Cross had its own symbol, the red lion and sun, prior to 1980, since when it has used the red crescent.

63. Rolle and Lafontaine, "Emblem That Cried Wolf," 769.

64. Ibid., 763.

65. Ibid., 761. Both IHL and the emblem receive their moral power through association with the totem, which is entirely absent in this formulation. It is the suffering of the innocents that empowers both. As the totem cannot be owned, quarantining its power in this way, while understandable, is doomed to fail. Despite protestation, anyone *can* make use of it (see 762).

66. Ibid., 763.

67. "As experience has amply shown, misuse of the emblem, even in isolated cases of only one kind, inevitably leads to a general decline in its authority and therefore in the protection of those entitled thereto": Antoine Bouvier, "Special Aspects of the Use of the Red Cross or Red Crescent Emblem," *International Review of the Red Cross* 29, no. 272 (1989): 440.

68. "Study on the Use of Emblems: Operational and Commercial and Other Non-Operational Issues," ICRC Resource Centre, December 6, 2011, http://www.icrc.org/eng/resources/documents/publication/p4057.htm.

69. Boissier, *History*, 117–19.

70. Ibid., 299.

71. François Bugnion, "From Solferino to the Birth of Contemporary International Humanitarian Law," *International Committee of the Red Cross*, April 2009. The 1863 Lieber Code that codified behavioral rules for Union soldiers during the American Civil War was a parallel attempt to regulate conflict. Its author, Francis Lieber, had been born in Berlin and left Europe only in his late twenties.

72. Martti Koskenniemi's phrase to describe Jellinek's argument for the self-legislation of the will, in *The Gentle Civilizer of Nations: The Rise and Fall of International Law, 1870–1960* (Cambridge: Cambridge University Press, 2001), 200.

73. Boissier, *History*, 327.

74. Hutchinson, *Champions of Charity*, 324–25, 333, chap. 6; Moorehead, *Dunant's Dream*, chap. 10.

75. Hutchinson, *Champions of Charity*, 280.

76. Georg Simmel, "The Stranger," in *On Individuality and Social Forms: Selected Writings*, ed. Donald N. Levine (Chicago: University of Chicago Press, 1971).

77. Koskenniemi, *Gentle Civilizer*, 47.

78. Ibid., 51–54. Also Boissier, *History*, 234–35.

79. Koskenniemi, *Gentle Civilizer*, 78.

80. See Krüger, "German Suffering," and Christopher Keith Hall, "The First Proposal for a Permanent International Criminal Court," *International Review of the Red Cross*, no. 322 (1998).

81. Boissier, *History*, 282–83.

82. Koskenniemi, *Gentle Civilizer*, 39–41.

83. Vladimir Vasilievich Pustogarov, "Fyodor Fyodorovich Martens (1845–1909)—a Humanist of Modern Times," *International Review of the Red Cross* 36, no. 312 (1996).

84. Bugnion, *International Committee*, 107, also 156–57.

85. This was tied to the ICRC–American Red Cross internecine struggle, which included ARC head Davison creating a League of Red Cross Societies as a peacetime rival to the ICRC: Hutchinson, *Champions of Charity*, 301, chaps. 6 and 7.

86. See Durand, *From Sarajevo to Hiroshima*, 99–102, and Donald I. Buzinkai, "The Bolsheviks, the League of Nations and the Paris Peace Conference, 1919," *Europe-Asia Studies* 19, no. 2 (1967): 259.

87. Keith David Watenpaugh, "The League of Nations Rescue of Armenian Genocide Survivors and the Making of Modern Humanitarianism, 1920–1927," *American Historical Review* 115, no. 5 (2010): 1319.

88. Carl Schmitt, *The Nomos of the Earth* (New York: Telos Press, 2003), 241.

89. Charles Howard Ellis, *The Origin, Structure and Working of the League of Nations* (Clark, NJ: Lawbook Exchange, 2003), 19. This comment was first written in 1928 as the institution in which Ellis placed so much faith was about to fail catastrophically.

90. Rachel E. Crowdy, "The Humanitarian Activities of the League of Nations," *Journal of the Royal Institute of International Affairs* 6, no. 3 (1927). Crowdy headed the League's Social Questions Section.

91. Buzinkai, "Bolsheviks." Lenin called the League the last hope of "bourgeois ideology."

92. George W. Egerton, "Collective Security as Political Myth: Liberal Internationalism and the League of Nations in Politics and History," *International History Review* 5, no. 4 (1983): 504. Writer Vera Brittain was nearer the mark with her comment that the League was to "cure our fearfulness and fortify our steps" (506–7).

93. Mark Mazower, *No Enchanted Palace: The End of Empire and the Ideological Origins of the United Nations* (Princeton, NJ: Princeton University Press, 2009), 21.

94. Ibid., 82. The League's first secretary general, from 1919–1933, was Eric Drummond, an Eton-educated Foreign Office official who eventually succeeded to the hereditary title of Earl of Perth.

95. Watenpaugh, "League of Nations," 1327, 1334.

96. Gary Jonathan Bass, *Stay the Hand of Vengeance: The Politics of War Crimes Tribunals* (Princeton, NJ: Princeton University Press, 2000), 99–100.

97. Ibid., chap. 4.

98. Schmitt, *Nomos of the Earth*, 261–62.

99. It was through the Paris-based International Federation for Human Rights (FIDH), formed 1922 with the motto "Peace for human rights," that Cassin called in 1927 for an international criminal court and an international declaration of rights. Cassin was involved in what was probably the first explicitly human rights NGO, the League of Human Rights (LDH), established in 1898 in Paris to defend Captain Alfred Dreyfus, the Jewish French officer falsely accused and imprisoned for treason; see "The Founding of the League of Human Rights," Dreyfus Rehabilitated, at http://www.dreyfus.culture.fr/en/the-aftermath-of-the-affair/the-struggle-for-human-rights/the-founding-of-the-league-of-human-rights.htm. The LDH was refounded as the International League of Human Rights by Roger Baldwin (ACLU pioneer) with various émigrés after 1942 in New York. On Lauterpacht see Mazower, *No Enchanted Palace*, 130.

100. For a compelling argument that ICRC intervention in Russia was an attempt to turn humanitarian rights into universal rights see Kimberly A. Lowe, "Humanitarianism and National Sovereignty: Red Cross Intervention on Behalf of Political Prisoners in Soviet Russia, 1921–1923," *Journal of Contemporary History* (forthcoming).

101. Armstrong, "International Committee of the Red Cross and Political Prisoners," 623–25.

102. Bugnion, *International Committee*, 108.

103. David P. Forsythe, "Human Rights and the International Committee of the Red Cross," *Human Rights Quarterly* 12, no. 2 (1990): 265.

104. Durand, *From Sarajevo to Hiroshima*, 134–35.

105. Armstrong, "International Committee of the Red Cross and Political Prisoners," 626–27.

106. Forsythe and Rieffer-Flanagan, *International Committee of the Red Cross*, 76.

107. See Emily Baughan, " 'Every Citizen of Empire Implored to Save the Children!' Empire, Internationalism, and the Save the Children Fund in Inter-war Britain," *Institute of Historical Research* (2012). Linda Mahood notes the feminist origins of the Save the Children Fund and gives a more accurate picture of Jebb than the one provided in various hagiographies about her, beginning with *The White Flame*, put together by her sister Dorothy in 1931 to perpetuate the heroic myth of Eglantyne as a "martyr for child welfare":

see Linda Mahood, "Eglantyne Jebb: Remembering, Representing and Writing a Rebel Daughter," in *Women's History Review* 17, no. 1 (2007).

108. Moorehead, *Dunant's Dream*, 288.

109. Durand, *From Sarajevo to Hiroshima*, 162–66; Barnett, *Empire of Humanity*, 93.

110. Durand, *From Sarajevo to Hiroshima*, 167.

111. Ibid., 165.

112. Carl Schmitt, *Political Theology*, trans. George Schwab (Chicago: University of Chicago Press, 1985), 37.

113. Moorehead, *Dunant's Dream*, 241.

3. The Holocaust Metanarrative

1. John F. Hutchinson, *Champions of Charity: War and the Rise of the Red Cross* (Boulder, CO: Westview Press, 1996), 346–55.

2. Jean-Claude Favez, *The Red Cross and the Holocaust*, ed. and trans. John and Beryl Fletcher (Cambridge: Cambridge University Press, 1999).

3. The Third Reich threatened "the disintegration of European civilization itself": Mark Mazower, *No Enchanted Palace: The End of Empire and the Ideological Origins of the United Nations* (Princeton, NJ: Princeton University Press, 2009), 123.

4. See Zygmunt Bauman, *Modernity and the Holocaust* (Cambridge: Polity Press, 2000).

5. Lawrence Douglas, *The Memory of Judgment: Making Law and History in the Trials of the Holocaust* (New Haven, CT: Yale University Press, 2001), 39–41. The phrase "explode the limits of law" is Hannah Arendt's as cited by Douglas.

6. Bauman, *Modernity and the Holocaust*.

7. Jean-François Lyotard, *The Postmodern Condition: A Report on Knowledge* (Manchester: Manchester University Press, 1984).

8. Roland Barthes, "The Death of the Author," *Aspen*, nos. 5–6, 1967, http://www.ubu.com/aspen/aspen5and6/threeEssays.html.

9. See Stefan-Ludwig Hoffmann, ed., *Human Rights in the Twentieth Century* (New York: Cambridge University Press, 2011) and Akira Iriye, Petra Goedde, and William I. Hitchcock, eds., *The Human Rights Revolution: An International History* (New York: Oxford University Press, 2012). Also Samuel Moyn, *The Last Utopia: Human Rights in History* (Cambridge, MA: Belknap Press of Harvard University Press, 2010); Mazower, *No Enchanted Palace*; and Elizabeth Borgwardt, *A New Deal for the World: America's Vision for Human Rights* (Cambridge, MA: Belknap Press of Harvard University Press, 2005).

10. Gary Jonathan Bass, *Stay the Hand of Vengeance: The Politics of War Crimes Tribunals* (Princeton, NJ: Princeton University Press, 2000), 99–100; Carl Schmitt, *The Nomos of the Earth* (New York: Telos Press, 2003), 261–62. On some of the many mass atrocities committed by European imperial states see Dan Stone, ed., *The Historiography of Genocide* (London: Palgrave Macmillan, 2008).

11. Douglas, *Memory of Judgment*, 41. Also Émile Durkheim, *The Division of Labor in Society* (New York: Free Press, 1984), 43.

12. Helen M. Kinsella, *The Image before the Weapon: A Critical History of the Distinction between Combatant and Civilian* (Ithaca, NY: Cornell University Press, 2011), 111–12.

13. Kerwin Lee Klein, "On the Emergence of *Memory* in Historical Discourse," *Representations*, no. 69 (Winter 2000): 139.

14. Ibid., 137.

15. Aryeh Neier, *Taking Liberties: Four Decades in the Struggle for Rights* (New York: Public Affairs, 2003), xvii.

16. But see James E. Young, *The Texture of Memory: Holocaust Memorials and Meaning* (New Haven, CT: Yale University Press, 1993), 287–89; Tony Judt, *Postwar: A History of*

Europe since 1945 (London: Vintage Books, 2012), 808–20; and Deborah E. Lipstadt, *The Eichmann Trial* (New York: Schocken Books, 2011), 189–94.

17. See Hannah Yablonka, "Holocaust Survivors in Israel: Time for an Initial Taking of Stock," in *Holocaust Survivors: Resettlement, Memories, Identities*, ed. Dalia Ofer, Françoise Ouzan, and Judy Tydor Baumel-Schwarz (New York: Berghahn Books, 2012).

18. Hannah Arendt, *Eichmann in Jerusalem: A Report on the Banality of Evil* (London: Penguin Books, 2006), 4–5; but see also Lipstadt, *Eichmann Trial*, 63.

19. Douglas, *Memory of Judgment*, 105–6.

20. Lipstadt, *Eichmann Trial*, 188; Peter Novick, *The Holocaust in American Life* (Boston: Houghton Mifflin, 1999), 113. For a highly critical argument about how the Nazi holocaust became "the Holocaust" see Norman G. Finkelstein, *The Holocaust Industry: Reflections on the Exploitation of Jewish Suffering*, 2nd ed. (London: Verso, 2003).

21. Peter Novick, *The Holocaust and Collective Memory* (London: Bloomsbury, 1999), 110.

22. Ibid., 133.

23. Émile Durkheim, *The Elementary Forms of Religious Life*, trans. Carol Cosman (Oxford: Oxford University Press, 2001), 237.

24. Finkelstein dates this to 1967's Six-Day War and argues it was a way for Jewish organizations in the United States to cement the thickening US-Israel strategic relationship; Finkelstein, *Holocaust Industry*, 19–24. For Novick, it was the 1973 Yom Kippur War that was decisive, allied to the broadcast of the NBC miniseries *Holocaust* in 1978 that thoroughly pressed the Holocaust into the public consciousness, an event embraced by much of organized Jewry but hated by Elie Wiesel, whose view of the uniqueness and sacredness of the Holocaust is without equal in intensity and influence; Novick, *Holocaust in American Life*, 151, 209–12.

25. Fabrice Weissman, "Silence Heals . . . ," in *Humanitarian Negotiations Revealed: The MSF Experience*, ed. Claire Magone, Michaël Neuman, and Fabrice Weissman (London: Hurst, 2011), 179.

26. See Eleanor Davey, "From tiers-mondisme to sans-frontiérisme: Revolutionary Idealism in France from the Algerian War to Ethiopian Famine" (unpublished manuscript, Queen Mary, University of London, November 2011). The grandparents of Bernard Kouchner, MSF founder, died in Auschwitz: Michael N. Barnett, *Empire of Humanity: A History of Humanitarianism* (Ithaca, NY: Cornell University Press, 2011), 145.

27. See the analysis and citations in Klein, "On the Emergence of *Memory* in Historical Discourse."

28. See Richard J. Goldstone, "From the Holocaust: Some Legal and Moral Implications," in *Is the Holocaust Unique? Perspectives on Comparative Genocide*, 3rd ed., ed. Alan S. Rosenbaum (Boulder, CO: Westview Press, 2009), 48. Goldstone was the first chief prosecutor of the International Criminal Tribunal for the former Yugoslavia (and for Rwanda) from 1994 to 1996, chairman of the Kosovo inquiry that coined the phrase "illegal but legitimate" to describe NATO's bombing of Serbia that led to the idea of a Responsibility to Protect, and wrote the UN-commissioned Goldstone Report in 2009 that examined alleged war crimes in the Gaza War of December 2008–January 2009.

29. Goldstone, "From the Holocaust," 52.

30. David Scheffer, *All the Missing Souls: A Personal History of the War Crimes Tribunals* (Princeton, NJ: Princeton University Press, 2012); Jonathan Glover, *Humanity: A Moral History of the Twentieth Century* (London: Pimlico, 2001), xi.

31. James Orbinski, *An Imperfect Offering: Dispatches from the Medical Frontline* (London: Rider Books, 2008), 21–25.

32. Geoffrey Robertson, *Crimes against Humanity: The Struggle for Global Justice*, 3rd ed. (London: Penguin Books, 2006), 248–49. He begins his book with a transcript of BBC television journalist Richard Dimbleby's words on first entering Belsen (but on Belsen see Snyder, *Bloodlands*, 311–12). For an insightful review of Robertson's book see Frédéric

Mégret, "The Politics of International Criminal Justice," *European Journal of International Law* 13, no. 5 (2002).

33. Eyewitness accounts about the defendants' response to the film diverge: see Douglas, *Memory of Judgment*, 25–26, and also John Tusa and Ann Tusa, *The Nuremberg Trial* (London: BBC, 1995), 160–61.

34. Telford Taylor, *The Anatomy of the Nuremberg Trials: A Personal Memoir* (London: Bloomsbury, 1993), 334–37, and Tusa and Tusa, *Nuremberg Trial*, 278–88, where they give a devastating account of Jackson's weakness in examining Goering.

35. Tusa and Tusa, *Nuremberg Trial*, 169.

36. Johannes Morsink, "World War Two and the Universal Declaration," *Human Rights Quarterly* 15, no. 2 (1993): 358.

37. Ibid., 400–401.

38. Moyn, *Last Utopia*, 7.

39. See Borgwardt, *A New Deal for the World*, 226–29.

40. G. Daniel Cohen, "The Holocaust and the 'Human Rights Revolution,'" in Iriye, Goedde, and Hitchcock, *Human Rights Revolution*," 58, 68 (his italics).

41. "Declaration of the Stockholm International Forum on the Holocaust," Task Force for International Cooperation on Holocaust Education, Remembrance, and Research, January 28, 2000. In 2004 the United Nations adopted its first Statement of Commitment commemorating the Holocaust.

42. Cohen, "Holocaust," 53.

43. United Nations General Assembly, "Resolution Adopted by the General Assembly on the Holocaust Remembrance (A/RES/60/7, 1 November 2005)," November 1, 2005. UNESCO set up its own Holocaust education program in 2007.

44. See Scott Straus, "Darfur and the Genocide Debate," *Foreign Affairs* 84, no. 1 (2005).

45. See Save Darfur, "The Genocide in Darfur—Briefing Paper," June 2008. Human Rights Watch (along with International Crisis Group and Amnesty International) resisted calling Darfur a genocide, but its executive director Kenneth Roth is on the board of advisers of the Save Darfur Coalition (along with John Prendergast, Juan E. Méndez, and David Scheffer), while former AIUSA executive director William F. Schulz is on the board of directors.

46. See Mahmood Mamdani, "The Politics of Naming: Genocide, Civil War, Insurgency," *London Review of Books* 29, no. 5 (2007): 5.

47. United Nations, *Report of the International Commission of Inquiry on Darfur to the United Nations Secretary-General* (2005), p. 4.

48. Save Darfur, "What Has Happened to Darfur?"

49. The Senate's rejection for forty years of the Genocide Convention was based on a refusal to be bound by international law, not on indifference in principle to genocide and certainly not to the Holocaust which continues to have tremendous political salience in the United States.

50. Madeleine Albright and William Cohen (cochairs), *Preventing Genocide: A Blueprint for U.S. Policymakers* (United States Holocaust Memorial Museum, American Academy of Diplomacy, and the United States Institute of Peace, 2008). At several points (e.g., 75, 98–99) they explicitly link their call for prevention to the UN World Summit's 2005 commitment to R2P.

51. Ibid., xix.

52. Ibid., xv. The report is inevitably quiet about the long history of implacable Senate resistance to the Genocide Convention, which was only ratified in 1988. See Elizabeth Borgwardt, "'Constitutionalizing' Human Rights: The Rise and Rise of the Nuremberg Principles," in Iriye, Goedde, and Hitchcock, *Human Rights Revolution*.

53. United States White House Office of the Press Secretary, "Presidential Study Directive on Mass Atrocities," August 4, 2011.

54. See Maria Otero, "Remarks at a Briefing to the Diplomatic Community on the Atrocities Prevention Board," April 23, 2012, and Megan Slack, "Join the Conversation: Honoring the Pledge of 'Never Again,'" April 20, 2012, and also the response of the Auschwitz Institute, "Auschwitz Institute Praises U.S. Creation of Atrocities Prevention Board," April 23, 2012.

55. "Vice-President Biden's Address in Honor of Tom Lantos," United States Holocaust Museum, February 24, 2011. Lantos was sheltered by Raoul Wallenberg, one of the pantheon of heroes of the humanist international.

56. Timothy Snyder, *Bloodlands: Europe between Hitler and Stalin* (New York: Basic Books, 2010), viii.

57. Didier Fassin and Richard Rechtman, *The Empire of Trauma: An Inquiry into the Condition of Victimhood* (Princeton, NJ: Princeton University Press, 2009), 17, 18.

58. Ibid., 72. They see "trauma" after 1945 being "repositioned" to represent universal human experience as well as subjective suffering, something I argue had been happening for nearly a century by this stage.

59. Joseph R. Slaughter, *Human Rights, Inc.* (New York: Fordham University Press, 2007), 107.

60. Arendt, *Eichmann in Jerusalem.* See the introduction by Amos Elon, "The Excommunication of Hannah Arendt," which details the campaign against her; and also Lipstadt, *Eichmann Trial*, chap. 6.

61. Roméo Dallaire, *Shake Hands with the Devil: The Failure of Humanity in Rwanda* (London: Arrow Books, 2004); Samantha Power, *A Problem from Hell: America and the Age of Genocide* (New York: Harper Perennial, 2002); Scheffer, *All the Missing Souls*; William Shawcross, *Deliver Us from Evil: Warlords and Peacekeepers in a World of Endless Conflict* (London: Bloomsbury, 2000); Dan Bortolotti, *Hope in Hell: Inside the World of Doctors without Borders* (Buffalo, NY: Firefly Books, 2004).

62. See Christopher R. Browning, *The Origins of the Final Solution: The Evolution of Nazi Jewish Policy, 1939–1942* (London: Arrow Books, 2005), 428–33 for a summary, and passim. According to Snyder, fourteen million civilians and prisoners of war were killed in the "bloodlands" between Nazi Germany and Soviet Russia (Ukraine, Belarus, the Baltic states, and Poland) between 1933 and 1945, more than half of whom were deliberately starved to death; *Bloodlands*, xiv and 407–12.

63. The vast literature on this question turns on the relationship between moral and empirical uniqueness. On the latter, the "second generation" of genocide studies has concluded de facto that the Holocaust is the one incontrovertible case of "genocide." In a recent review of major works on genocide, the Holocaust was the only case all analyses had in common: Scott Straus, "Second-Generation Comparative Research on Genocide," *World Politics* 59, no. 3 (2007): 496–97.

64. Daniel Levy and Natan Sznaider, *The Holocaust and Memory in the Global Age* (Philadelphia: Temple University Press, 2006), 4. See also Jeffrey C. Alexander, "On the Social Construction of Moral Universals: The 'Holocaust' from War Crime to Trauma Drama," *European Journal of Social Theory* 5, no. 1 (2002), and Anson Rabinbach, "From Explosion to Erosion: Holocaust Memorialization in America since Bitburg," *History and Memory* 9, no. 1/2 (1997).

65. See the many references on "analogy to the Holocaust" in Power, *Problem from Hell*, 604; also Mégret, "Politics of International Criminal Justice," 1272. Lawrence Eagleburger, deputy and then acting US secretary of state during the early years of the Yugoslav conflict, was particularly affected by revelations of atrocities in Bosnia. All the books Mégret reviews see Bosnia in 1992 as the pivotal moment when things changed. See also Nozick, *Holocaust in American Life*, 251–53; Power, *Problem from Hell*, 251–78; and Roy Gutman, *A Witness to Genocide* (New York: Macmillan, 1993).

66. Alan E. Steinweis, "The Auschwitz Analogy: Holocaust Memory and American Debates over Intervention in Bosnia and Kosovo in the 1990s," *Holocaust and Genocide Studies* 19, no. 2 (2005): 279.

67. Scott Straus, "Identifying Genocide and Related Forms of Mass Atrocity," USHMM Working Paper, October 7, 2001, p. 1.

68. M. Cherif Bassiouni, "Crimes against Humanity," in *Crimes of War 2.0: What the Public Should Know*, ed. Roy Gutman, David Rieff, and Anthony Dworkin (New York: W. W. Norton, 2007), 135–36.

69. Alexander, "On the Social Construction of Moral Universals"; Rabinbach, "From Explosion to Erosion"; Novick, *Holocaust in American Life*; and Levy and Sznaider, *Holocaust and Memory in the Global Age*.

70. Cohen, "Holocaust," 62.

71. See Dan Stone, "Raphael Lemkin on the Holocaust," *Journal of Genocide Research* 7, no. 4 (2005); Power, *Problem from Hell*, chaps. 4 and 5; Mazower, *No Enchanted Palace*, chap. 3.

72. Mazower, *No Enchanted Palace*, 128–32.

73. Comparison to the Holocaust could also of course have the perverse effect of raising the bar too high to justify interventions short of genocide: see Power, *Problem from Hell*, 434.

74. Lizette Alvarez, "At Memorial in Bosnia, Clinton Helps Mourn 7,000," *New York Times*, September 21, 2003, and "Clinton Unveils Bosnia Memorial," BBC News, September 20, 2003.

75. "Clinton Unveils," BBC News.

76. Steinweis, "Auschwitz Analogy," 283.

77. See Yang Jisheng, *Tombstone: The Untold Story of Mao's Great Famine* (New York: Allen Lane, 2012), and Frank Dikötter, *Mao's Great Famine* (London: Bloomsbury, 2012).

78. Makau Mutua, *Human Rights: A Political and Cultural Critique* (Philadelphia: University of Pennsylvania Press, 2002), xi.

79. Ibid., x.

80. Moorehead, *Dunant's Dream*, xxxi.

81. Favez, *Red Cross and the Holocaust*, 84.

82. Ibid., 91. This bears strong resemblance to Amnesty International's reasoning over its relative inaction during the Rwandan genocide: Stephen Hopgood, *Keepers of the Flame: Understanding Amnesty International* (Ithaca, NY: Cornell University Press, 2006), 137–39.

83. These are the words in December 1942 of Carl J. Burckhardt, longtime ICRC member and president from 1945 to 1948: Favez, *Red Cross and the Holocaust*, 278.

84. Favez, *Red Cross and the Holocaust*, 86–88; Moorehead, *Dunant's Dream*, xxv–xxxi.

85. Judt, *Postwar*, 84, 813.

86. François Bugnion, "Dialogue with the Past: The ICRC and the Nazi Death Camps," ICRC Resource Centre, November 5, 2002.

87. Moorehead, *Dunant's Dream*, xxx.

88. Favez, *Red Cross and the Holocaust*, 282.

89. Gerd Oberleitner, *Global Human Rights Institutions* (Cambridge: Polity Press, 2007), 173.

90. Martti Koskenniemi, *The Gentle Civilizer of Nations: The Rise and Fall of International Law, 1870–1960* (Cambridge: Cambridge University Press, 2001), 53–55.

91. Mary Ellen O'Connell, *The Power and Purpose of International Law: Insights from the Theory and Practice of Enforcement* (Oxford: Oxford University Press, 2008), 9.

92. Mark Goodale, *Surrendering to Utopia: An Anthropology of Human Rights* (Palo Alto, CA: Stanford University Press, 2009), 10.

93. Sonia Harris-Short, "International Human Rights Law: Imperialist, Inept and Ineffective? Cultural Relativism and the UN Convention on the Rights of the Child," *Human Rights Quarterly* 25, no. 1 (2003): 181.

94. Pierre Schlag, "Law as the Continuation of God by Other Means," *California Law Review* 85, no. 2 (1997): 440.

95. Judith N. Shklar, *Legalism: Law, Morals, and Political Trials* (Cambridge, MA: Harvard University Press, 1964), 2.

96. "When Legal Worlds Overlap: Human Rights, State and Non-State Law," *International Council on Human Rights Policy*, 2009. The ICHRP recently closed owing to lack of funding.

97. Robertson, *Crimes against Humanity*, 626.

98. J. A. Lindgren Alves, "The Declaration of Human Rights in Postmodernity," *Human Rights Quarterly* 22, no. 2 (2000): 491.

99. Lyotard, *Postmodern Condition*, 22–23.

100. Rosenbaum, *Is the Holocaust Unique?* 16–17.

101. D. D. Guttenplan, *The Holocaust on Trial* (New York: W. W. Norton, 2002), 290.

102. Rosenbaum, *Is the Holocaust Unique?* 17.

103. Ibid.

104. Bruce Robbins, *Feeling Global: Internationalism in Distress* (New York: NYU Press, 1999), 4.

105. Ibid., 62–63.

106. Judt, *Postwar*, 804. He actually means *western* Europe, problems continuing in the post-Communist East: 820, 826–28.

4. The Moral Architecture of Suffering

1. Channel 4 films, *Sri Lanka's Killing Fields*, broadcast June 14, 2011. The phrase "killing fields" links Sri Lanka with the genocide in Cambodia.

2. Dix has gone on to raise funds and coauthor a graphic novel to publicize Sri Lankan crimes during the war's final phase; see http://www.thevanni.co.uk/intro/.

3. David Scheffer, *All the Missing Souls: A Personal History of the War Crimes Tribunals* (Princeton, NJ: Princeton University Press, 2012), 12.

4. Jan Egeland, *A Billion Lives: An Eyewitness Report from the Frontlines of Humanity* (New York: Simon & Schuster, 2008), 79.

5. François Bugnion, *The International Committee of the Red Cross and the Protection of War Victims* (Oxford: Macmillan/ICRC, 2003), xxxviii.

6. Samantha Power, *A Problem from Hell: America and the Age of Genocide* (New York: Harper Perennial, 2002), xi–xiii.

7. See Janet Jacobs, "Gender and Collective Memory: Women and Representation at Auschwitz," *Memory Studies* 1, no. 2 (2008): 214, and the many relevant works she cites therein.

8. Costas Douzinas, *The End of Human Rights: Critical Legal Thought at the Turn of the Century* (Oxford: Hart Publishing, 2000), 187.

9. Bertrand Taithe, "Pyrrhic Victories? French Catholic Missionaries, Modern Expertise, and Secularizing Technologies," in *Sacred Aid: Faith and Humanitarianism*, ed. Michael Barnett and Janice Gross Stein (New York: Oxford University Press, 2012), 169.

10. These words come from the contemporary voice-over of the ICRC digital video set *Humanitarian Action and Cinema: ICRC Films in the 1920s*, ICRC, Memoriav, and Jean-Blaise Junod, 2005. Orphans are a central category in Islamic aid as well, the Prophet Muhammad an orphan himself.

11. James Orbinski, *An Imperfect Offering: Dispatches from the Medical Frontline* (London: Rider Books, 2008); Claire Bertschinger and Fanny Blake, *Moving Mountains* (London: Doubleday, 2005); Lilie Chouliaraki, *The Spectatorship of Suffering* (London: Sage, 2006); John S. Burnett, *Where Soldiers Fear to Tread: A Relief Worker's Tale of Survival* (New York: Bantam Books, 2005); Jan Egeland, *A Billion Lives*; Kenneth Cain, Heidi Postlewait, and Andrew Thomson, *Emergency Sex and Other Desperate Measures* (London: Ebury Press, 2006); Alison Brysk, *Global Good Samaritans: Human Rights as Foreign Policy* (Oxford: Oxford University Press, 2009).

12. Readers may have been attracted to *The Endtimes of Human Rights* for a similar reason.

13. Marianne Hirsch, "Projected Memory: Holocaust Photographs in Personal and Public Fantasy," in *Acts of Memory: Cultural Recall in the Present*, ed. Mieke Bal, Jonathan Crewe, and Leo Spitzer (Hanover, NH: University Press of New England, 1999), 13.

14. Ibid., 21.

15. The idea of a "magic trace" is from Didier Fassin and Richard Rechtman, *The Empire of Trauma: An Inquiry into the Condition of Victimhood* (Princeton, NJ: Princeton University Press, 2009), 72.

16. Edward T. Linenthal, *Preserving Memory: The Struggle to Create America's Holocaust Museum* (New York: Columbia University Press, 2001), 216; Raul Hilberg, *The Destruction of the European Jews*, 3rd ed. (New Haven, CT: Yale University Press, 2003).

17. Linenthal, *Preserving Memory*, x.

18. Ibid., 212–14. See also Edward T. Linenthal, "The Boundaries of Memory: The United States Holocaust Memorial Museum," in *American Quarterly* 46, no. 3 (1994): 421–25.

19. Deborah E. Lipstadt, *The Eichmann Trial* (New York: Schocken Books, 2011), ix–xi.

20. Ibid., x.

21. Lawrence L. Langer, "The Alarmed Vision: Social Suffering and Holocaust Atrocity," in *Social Suffering*, ed. Arthur Kleinman, Veena Das, and Margaret M. Lock (Berkeley: University of California Press, 1997), 55.

22. Jean-Claude Favez, *The Red Cross and the Holocaust*, ed. and trans. John Fletcher and Beryl Fletcher (Cambridge: Cambridge University Press, 1999), 91.

23. See Stephen Hopgood, *Keepers of the Flame: Understanding Amnesty International* (Ithaca, NY: Cornell University Press, 2006), 205–7.

24. In USHMM focus groups, researchers found many people had "a deeply ingrained cultural image of the Holocaust [as] piles of bodies": Linenthal, *Preserving Memory*, 193. How graphic to make USHMM exhibits (and risk deterring people who found it unbearable) was a significant issue for the designers; see *Preserving Memory*, 192–98.

25. ICRC, "Humanitarian Action and Cinema."

26. Barbie Zelizer, *Remembering to Forget: Holocaust Memory through the Camera's Eye* (Chicago: University of Chicago Press, 1998).

27. See Primo Levi, *The Drowned and the Saved* (London: Abacus, 1988), and Giorgio Agamben, *Remnants of Auschwitz: The Witness and the Archive* (New York: Zone Books, 1999), 33–34. We know so much about Auschwitz because there were survivors, as compared with those, mostly Polish Jews, sent to extermination camps like Treblinka or shot and gassed in the "bloodlands"; see Timothy Snyder, *Bloodlands: Europe between Hitler and Stalin* (New York: Basic Books, 2010), viii.

28. Fassin and Rechtman, *Empire of Trauma*, xi, 10. See also Kerwin Lee Klein, "On the Emergence of *Memory* in Historical Discourse," *Representations*, no. 69 (Winter 2000): 139.

29. Fassin and Rechtman, *Empire of Trauma*, 28.

30. There is now an Institute for Dark Tourism Research in the UK; see http://www.dark-tourism.org.uk/about-us.

31. Jacobs, "Gender and Collective Memory," 219. She is referring to *Deviant Bodies*, ed. Jennifer Terry and Jacqueline Urla (Bloomington: Indiana University Press, 1995).

32. The other was into the private life of "direct and personal relations." See Max Weber, "Science as a Vocation," in *From Max Weber: Essays in Sociology*, ed. Hans Heinrich Gerth and C. Wright Mills (London: Kegan Paul, Trench, Trübner, 1947), 155.

33. He was commenting disparagingly on the miniseries *Holocaust*. The initial article was "Trivializing the Holocaust: Semi-fact and Semi-fiction," *New York Times*, April 16, 1978; these quotations are from Elie Wiesel, "Art and the Holocaust: Trivializing Memory," *New York Times*, June 11, 1989.

34. Peter Novick, *The Holocaust and Collective Memory: The American Experience* (London: Bloomsbury, 1999), 211.

35. Agamben, *Remnants of Auschwitz*, 32.

36. James E. Young, *The Texture of Memory: Holocaust Memorials and Meaning* (New Haven, CT: Yale University Press, 1993), 127–28.

37. This can lead to tension with survivors as the guardians of memory; Fassin and Rechtman, *Empire of Trauma*, 72.

38. Linenthal, *Preserving Memory*, 174.

39. Walter Benjamin, "The Work of Art in the Age of Mechanical Reproduction," in *Illuminations*, ed. Hannah Arendt, trans. Harry Zorn (London: Pimlico, 1999), 219.

40. Ibid., 214.

41. Ibid., 218.

42. Rachel Hughes, "The Abject Artefacts of Memory: Photographs from Cambodia's Genocide," *Media, Culture & Society* 25, no. 1 (2003): 34–41.

43. Roland Barthes, *Camera Lucida*, trans. Richard Howard (London: Vintage Books, 2000), 26–27.

44. Hughes, "Abject Artefacts of Memory," 38.

45. A man called Nhem En claimed to have been chief photographer at S-21 and started to give interviews when the photographs were at the MoMA, raising even more fraught issues about ownership, complicity, and culpability; ibid., 40.

46. Barthes, *Camera Lucida*, 26.

47. Tony Judt, *Postwar: A History of Europe since 1945* (London: Vintage Books, 2012), 811; Peter Novick, *The Holocaust in American Life* (Boston: Mariner Books, 2000), 209–14.

48. Although see, for example, iconic photos like Eddie Adams's *General Loan Executing a Vietcong Suspect* (1968) and Huynh Cong (Nick) Ut's *Children Fleeing a Napalm Strike* (1972) in *The Power of Photography: How Photography Changed Our Lives*, ed. Vicki Goldberg (New York: Abbeville Publishing Group, 1991), 227, 242.

49. Barthes, *Camera Lucida*, 55 (italics in original).

50. George Baker, "Photography's Expanded Field," *October*, no. 114 (2005): 125–26.

51. This archive is at the USC Shoah Foundation Institute at http://dornsife.usc.edu/vhi/. The archive now records personal testimony from survivors of other genocides, labeling this section of its website "Witnesses for Humanity." Spielberg's movie did not escape a great deal of criticism, including from Claude Lanzmann.

52. Lanzmann was an integral member of the intellectual group that surrounded Jean-Paul Sartre, whose 1945 speech "Existentialism Is a Humanism" is about life in the godless world.

53. See *"Shoah*—Official 25th Anniversary Trailer [HD]," YouTube video, 2:10, November 1985, posted by "VISO trailers," December 15, 2010, http://www.youtube.com/watch?v=wV6mJ6T1oU0.

54. Claude Lanzmann, "The Obscenity of Understanding: An Evening with Claude Lanzmann," in *Trauma: Explorations in Memory*, ed. Cathy Caruth (Baltimore: Johns Hopkins University Press, 1995), 206-7.

55. Fassin and Rechtman, *Empire of Trauma*, 97.

56. The Permanent International Court of Justice became the International Court of Justice (ICJ) or World Court in 1945.

57. In the words of the Peace Palace website: "What the Court lacked in authority as an international judicial institution in the early years, was more than compensated for by the formidable character, the artistic furnishings and exuberant symbolism of its housing." See Vredespaleis, "The Building," at http://www.vredespaleis.nl/index.php?pid=57&page=The_building.

58. Henry Russell Hitchcock and Philip Johnson, *The International Style* (New York: W. W. Norton, 1995).

59. Kenneth Frampton, *Le Corbusier* (London: Thames & Hudson, 2001), 81–87. The Le Corbusier Foundation is *still* angry about this, calling the disqualification an act "devoid of scruples": see Fondation Le Corbusier, "Palais de la Société des Nations, Geneva, Switzerland, 1927."

60. Ron Theodore Robin, *Enclaves of America: The Rhetoric of American Political Architecture Abroad, 1900–1965* (Princeton, NJ: Princeton University Press, 1992), 113–14.

61. Ibid., 146.

62. Geoffrey Robertson, *Crimes against Humanity: The Struggle for Global Justice*, 3rd ed. (London: Penguin Books, 2006), 427.

63. Thomas R. Metcalf, *An Imperial Vision: Indian Architecture and Britain's Raj* (London: Faber and Faber, 2002), 1.

64. Ibid., 225.

65. Bronwyn Law-Viljoen, ed., *Light on a Hill: Building the Constitutional Court of South Africa* (Johannesburg: David Krut, 2006), 7 (my italics).

66. Ibid., 46.

67. Ibid., 32.

68. International Criminal Court, *Report on the Future Permanent Premises of the International Criminal Court*, ICC-ASP/5/16, Assembly of States Parties, Fifth Session, The Hague, November 23 to December 1, 2006 (my italics).

69. For a selection of designs, including the eventual first choice by Schmidt Hammer Lassen (which was initially placed second but promoted after disagreements about the winner's costs), see http://www.bustler.net/index.php/article/winning_designs_for_new_international_criminal_court_building_have_been_sel/.

70. Coalition for the International Criminal Court (CICC), "Architectural Design Competition for the Permanent Premises of the ICC," Statement to the Jury, October 30–31, 2008.

71. Ibid.

72. The project is due for completion in 2015. To see the design video go to http://www.youtube.com/watch?v=h9USZNF1M_Y.

73. *Light on a Hill*, 46, 51.

74. International Criminal Court, *Report on the Future Permanent Premises*.

75. See http://www.unesco.org/new/en/communication-and-information/flagship-project-activities/memory-of-the-world/homepage/.

76. The Museum of Modern Art in New York was holding an exhibition of photographs and designs from the Palais competition. An open letter calling for a proper UN competition published by the American magazine *Progressive Architecture* in February 1946 refers to the MoMA exhibition, saying: "The Competition Failed! The Building Failed! The League Failed!" The letter adds that Le Corbusier's "honest design was discarded for the pretentious Palace." In April 1946 the same magazine published an article titled "A Home for the U.N.O." in which it described the Palais winners as "stodgy classical designs expressing in no way the aim for a saner world." The final building, it says, "typified a world organization that hesitated, compromised and died." Le Corbusier's submission was the only one to meet the criteria and standard, it claimed. Some of the winning submissions (there were nine!) are reproduced in the article, and almost all are hideous examples of vast, monumental, and palatial classical architecture, all stone columns and ornamentation. Intriguingly, one of the ten-man UN board, Howard Robertson from Britain, had been brought into the Palais process as a peacemaker between warring factions. He wanted the UN site to have the feel of a secluded Oxford college, suggesting he was more old world than new: see Edith Iglauer, "The UN Builds Its Home," *Harper's Magazine*, December 1947, 568.

77. Iglauer, "UN Builds Its Home," 567. There is a more detailed story to tell here of the behind-the-scenes politics, which saw Le Corbusier marginalized by the phlegmatic American director of planning, Wallace K. Harrison. In the end Le Corbusier was not even invited to the cornerstone ceremony, much to his fury.

78. Hitchcock and Johnson, *International Style*. Johnson, perhaps the most influential commercial American architect of the twentieth century, says the book was already an account of the past, and whatever "International Style" was, it was fragmenting by 1932.

79. Ibid., 46, 251.

80. Ibid., 79.

81. Colin Rose and Robert Slutzky, "Transparency: Literal and Phenomenal," *Perspecta* 8 (1963): 53.

82. Hitchcock and Johnson, *International Style*, 251, 261, 104.

83. James C Scott, *Seeing Like a State: How Certain Schemes to Improve the Human Condition Have Failed* (New Haven, CT: Yale University Press, 1998), 93–94.

84. Ibid., 112.

85. Ibid., 116.

86. On the selection of the site, see Charlene Mires, *Capital of the World: The Race to Host the United Nations* (New York University Press, 2013).

87. Le Corbusier was later to have this quoted back at him as post-design politics saw him battle to secure what he and his supporters considered his rightful place as the visionary behind the UN's headquarters. He also objected, not without reason, to the far greater remuneration of the architects subsequently implementing the vision the design team produced. Receiving neither income nor glory was for someone as strong-willed as Le Corbusier unbearable. He drew a surprisingly strong letter out of the French foreign minister, Robert Schumann, to UN Secretary-General Trygve Lie complaining about his treatment, for which he in the main blamed Harrison. Schumann said that the French government attached "particular importance" to Le Corbusier being properly recognized as the author of the scheme. This material is loosely filed in the boxes of series S-0472 of the Permanent Headquarters Planning Committee Records at the United Nations Archive and Records Management Section (ARMS), New York. Supplementary material is from boxes S-0532 and in the Serge Wolff Collection (series S-0553).

88. Permanent Headquarters Committee Records (S-0472), ARMS.

89. Ibid.

90. Lewis Mumford, "Stop and Think," *Progressive Architecture–Pencil Points* 27, April 1946.

91. Ibid.

92. Gertrude Samuels, "What Kind of Capitol for the U.N.?" *New York Times Magazine*, April 20, 1947.

93. German émigré Gropius was excluded from the committee because he had been a naturalized American since 1944 (and Harrison was "the American" on the committee). The same fate presumably befell Mies van der Rohe (also naturalized in 1944). Architects from Axis countries were barred. This excluded Finnish architect Alvar Aalto and left Le Corbusier head and shoulders above the others.

94. Lewis Mumford, "The Sky Line: Magic with Mirrors I," *New Yorker*, September 15, 1951, 84–93, and "The Sky Line: Magic with Mirrors II," *New Yorker*, September 22, 1951, 99–106.

95. Bruce Brooks Pfeiffer and Robert Wojtowicz, eds., *Frank Lloyd Wright and Lewis Mumford: Thirty Years of Correspondence* (Princeton, NJ: Princeton Architectural Press, 2001), 201.

96. This phrase links nicely to arguments for the superiority of the Western classical music canon as the high point of world civilization (god talks to Mozart, Beethoven talks to god, etc.).

97. Roland Barthes, "The Death of the Author," *Aspen*, no. 5–6 (1967).

98. See François Debrix, *Re-envisioning Peacekeeping: The United Nations and the Mobilization of Ideology* (Minneapolis: University of Minnesota Press, 1999), 5; Adam Bartos and Christopher Hitchens, *International Territory: The United Nations, 1945–95* (New York: Verso, 1994). Debrix draws here on the work of Jean Baudrillard.

99. *Sleuk rith* are dried leaves used by Cambodian religious leaders and scholars to record history, disseminate knowledge, and preserve culture.

100. Youk Chhang, interview by the author, Phnom Penh, November 2011.

101. On memorial museums see Paul Williams, *Memorial Museums: The Global Rush to Commemorate Atrocities* (Oxford: Berg, 2007).

102. Jacques Sémelin, *Purify and Destroy: The Political Uses of Massacre and Genocide* (London: Hurst, 2007), chap. 6.

5. Human Rights and American Power

1. Aryeh Neier, *The International Human Rights Movement: A History* (Princeton, NJ: Princeton University Press, 2012); Kenneth Roth, "Seeking Allies Worldwide to Carry the Human Rights Banner," *Global Policy* 3, no. 4 (2012): 513–14. The term "human rights movement" was also used uncritically throughout a research workshop of senior human rights figures, largely from Amnesty International but including Kenneth Roth, and senior and sympathetic human rights scholars (e.g., Kathryn Sikkink) at the University of Michigan in October 2010: see Carrie Booth Walling and Susan Waltz, eds., *Human Rights: From Practice to Policy* (Ann Arbor: Gerald R. Ford School of Public Policy, University of Michigan, October 2010). Waltz is a board member of AIUSA.

2. Kenneth Roth, "Defending Economic, Social, and Cultural Rights: Practical Issues Faced by an International Human Rights Organization," *Human Rights Quarterly* 26 (2004).

3. Ibid., 72.

4. Booth Walling and Waltz, *Human Rights*, 73.

5. Thomas Hughes, at that time president of the Carnegie Endowment for International Peace, argued that "American political culture rejects the idea of contradictions as unspeakably un-American," a historical myth Carter's rhetoric tended to reinforce: see Thomas L. Hughes, "Carter and the Management of Contradictions," *Foreign Policy*, no. 31 (1978): 35–36.

6. Quoted in Stuart A. Scheingold, *The Politics of Rights*, 2nd ed. (Ann Arbor: University of Michigan Press, 2004), 56–57.

7. Ibid., 57.

8. See Kenneth Cmiel, "The Emergence of Human Rights Politics in the United States," *Journal of American History* 86, no. 3 (1999), and Ethel Brooks and Dorothy L. Hodgson, "'An Activist Temperament': An Interview with Charlotte Bunch," *Women's Studies Quarterly* 35, no. 3–4 (2007): 60–74. Also Julie Mertus, "The Rejection of Human Rights Framings: The Case of LGBT Advocacy in the US," *Human Rights Quarterly* 29, no. 4 (2007): 1036–64.

9. Louis Henkin, "The United States and the Crisis in Human Rights," *Virginia Journal of International Law* 14, no. 4 (1973–1974): 663–64.

10. The one area where human rights have domestic traction is the death penalty, but even then the arguments for abolition are usually made in consequentialist terms, e.g., the danger of executing someone innocent.

11. See Elizabeth Drew, "A Reporter at Large: Human Rights," *New Yorker*, July 18, 1977, 36–62, and Daniel Horowitz, *The Anxieties of Affluence: Critiques of American Consumer Culture, 1939–1979* (Amherst: University of Massachusetts Press, 2004), chaps. 7 and 8.

12. David Harvey, *A Brief History of Neoliberalism* (Oxford: Oxford University Press, 2005), 10–11.

13. Samuel Moyn, *The Last Utopia: Human Rights in History* (Cambridge, MA: Belknap Press of Harvard University Press, 2010), 3. See also Robin Blackburn, "Reclaiming Human Rights," *New Left Review* 69 (May–June 2011), and Aryeh Neier, *Taking Liberties: Four Decades in the Struggle for Rights* (New York: Public Affairs, 2003), 365. Neier is more balanced in his 2012 *The International Human Rights Movement: A History*, seeing the shift as the intensification and expansion of an already existing movement (p. 7). See also Cmiel, "Emergence of Human Rights Politics," for the same claim about the 1970s. Also, Beth A. Simmons, *Mobilizing for Human Rights: International Law in Domestic Politics* (New York: Cambridge University Press, 2009), 50, and on the influence of the Ford Foundation during these years, see Yves Dezalay and Bryant Garth, "From the Cold War to Kosovo: The Rise and Renewal of the Field of International Human Rights," *Annual Review of Law and Social Science* 2 (2006), 241–43 and Winifred Tate, *Counting the Dead: The Culture of Human Rights Activism in Colombia* (Berkeley: University of California Press, 2007), 327, n 7.

14. Unsurprisingly, Human Rights Watch staffers like the version of the story in which the 1970s take on more significance than 1961 (the date Amnesty International was formed); see Samuel Moyn, "Reflections on 'The Last Utopia': A Conversation with Samuel Moyn," *Journal of Human Rights Practice* 3, no. 2: 130–31. In the 1980s and 1990s, many senior HRW staffers would have had prior Amnesty International experience. If anything, this situation is now reversed.

15. This was the decade in which the United Nations covenants on human rights were finally ratified, but it took twenty more years and the Cold War's end before human rights became a major force within the UN.

16. Stephen B. Cohen, "Conditioning US Security Assistance on Human Rights Practices," *American Journal of International Law* 76 (1982): 247–49.

17. Ibid., 251.

18. Drew, "Reporter at Large," 37.

19. Cohen, "Conditioning US Security Assistance," 258, 262.

20. David Carleton and Michael Stohl, "The Foreign Policy of Human Rights: Rhetoric and Reality from Jimmy Carter to Ronald Reagan," *Human Rights Quarterly* 7, no. 2 (May 1985): 218.

21. Drew, "Reporter at Large," 46.

22. Ibid., 37–38.

23. Nicolas Guilhot, *The Democracy Makers: Human Rights and International Order* (New York: Columbia University Press, 2005). Also, Neier, *Taking Liberties*, 150–51, and Dezalay and Garth, "From the Cold War to Kosovo," 237–40.

24. Horowitz, *Anxieties of Affluence*, 38–43.

25. Ibid., chap. 8.

26. Drew, "Reporter at Large," 41.

27. On Latin America and its role in the modern human rights regime, see Kathryn Sikkink, *The Justice Cascade: How Human Rights Prosecutions Are Changing World Politics* (New York: W. W. Norton, 2011), chap. 5.

28. For a recent argument about the human rights market that sees the needs of victims as supply and the preferences of advocacy groups as demand, see Clifford Bob, "The Market for Human Rights," in *Advocacy Organizations and Collective Action,* ed. Aseem Prakash and Mary Kay Gugerty (Cambridge: Cambridge University Press, 2010).

29. Neier, *Taking Liberties*, 149–57.

30. Stephen Hopgood, *Keepers of the Flame: Understanding Amnesty International* (Ithaca, NY: Cornell University Press, 2006), 108–9.

31. Ibid., 11.

32. Ann Marie Clark, *Diplomacy of Conscience: Amnesty International and Changing Human Rights Norms* (Princeton, NJ: Princeton University Press, 2001).

33. Vice President Walter Mondale as interviewed by Drew, "Reporter at Large," 61.

34. Guilhot, *Democracy Makers*, 75, 78–83, and 177–82. In a later paper, Guilhot argues more clearly that there were two antagonistic American projects wrestling to claim the human rights discourse: the liberal focused on international law (e.g., Human Rights Watch) and the neoconservative, particularly under the Reagan administration, seeking regime change in favor of democracy. My argument is that underlying both were two common features that make them much closer allies structurally than this suggests: the primacy of neoliberal democracy and the use of American power as a force for progress in the world. See Nicolas Guilhot, "Limiting Sovereignty or Producing Governmentality? Two Human Rights Regimes in US Political Discourse," *Social Science Research Council*, 2007.

35. For a recent version of the alibi see Anne-Marie Slaughter, *The Idea That Is America: Keeping Faith with Our Values in a Dangerous World* (New York: Basic Books, 2007). Slaughter was director of policy planning at the State Department from 2009 to 2011 in the Obama administration.

36. See Robert L. Bernstein, "Rights Watchdog, Lost in the Mideast," *New York Times*, October 19, 2009, and Aryeh Neier, "Human Rights Watch Should *Not* Be Criticized for Doing Its Job," *Huff Post World*, November 2, 2009.

37. Adam Roberts, "Humanitarian War: Military Intervention and Human Rights," *International Affairs* 69, no. 3 (July 1993).

38. See Tony Smith, *A Pact with the Devil: Washington's Bid for World Supremacy and the Betrayal of American Promise* (New York: Routledge, 2007) and Thomas M Franck, "The Emerging Right to Democratic Governance," *American Journal of International Law* 86, no. 1 (January 1992).

39. See "Women and Islam: An Exchange with Kenneth Roth of Human Rights Watch," *New York Review of Books*, March 22, 2012, 45.

40. The letter also notes that the Muslim Brotherhood support deniers of the holocaust (not capitalized) and the Bangladeshi genocide (1971), thereby anchoring their critique of HRW in the very metanarrative by which it is legitimated.

41. Sidney Tarrow, *Power in Movement: Social Movements and Contentious Politics*, 2nd ed. (Cambridge: Cambridge University Press, 1999), 131–32.

42. Hopgood, *Keepers of the Flame*, 111–14.

43. For a recent survey (by an insider) of Human Rights Watch's evaluation work that confirms how rudimentary it remains see Ian Gorvin, "Producing the Evidence That Human Rights Advocacy Works: First Steps towards Systematized Evaluation at Human Rights Watch," *Journal of Human Rights Practice* 1, no. 3 (2009): 477–87.

44. Kenneth Roth's distinction between success and impact perpetuates the output model, "impact" meaning "success in applying pressure," not measurable change: see Booth Walling and Waltz, *Human Rights*, 32–33.

45. For two arguments of what is required to improve compliance, see Thomas Risse, Stephen C. Ropp, and Kathryn Sikkink, eds., *The Persistent Power of Human Rights: From Commitment to Compliance* (Cambridge: Cambridge University Press, 2013) and Emilie M. Hafner-Burton, *Making Human Rights a Reality* (Princeton, NJ: Princeton University Press, 2013).

46. See, for example, Emilie Hafner-Burton and James Ron, "Seeing Double: Human Rights Impact through Qualitative and Quantitative Eyes," *World Politics* 61, no. 2, (2009).

47. Human Rights Watch, "George Soros to Give $100 Million to Human Rights Watch," September 2010.

48. On the growth of the humanitarian field and attempts to regulate the use of child images see Denis V. F. Kennedy, "Codified Compassion: Politics and Principles in Humanitarian Governance" (unpublished PhD dissertation, University of Minnesota, August 2012), chaps. 2 and 6.

49. This email was sent to me personally as an Amnesty International UK subscriber.

50. Human Rights Watch, "Cluster Bombs: Nations Reject Weakening of Global Ban." November 2011.

51. See Human Rights Watch, "Protecting Civilians through the Convention on Cluster Munitions," November 22, 2010, http://www.hrw.org/reports/2010/11/22/meeting challenge.

52. On "slacktivism" see Evgeny Morozov, *The Net Delusion: How Not to Liberate the World* (London: Penguin, 2012), and Morozov, "From Slacktivism to Activism," *Foreign Policy*, September 5, 2009.

53. Malcolm Gladwell, "Small Change: Why the Revolution Will Not Be Tweeted," *New Yorker*, October 4, 2010.

54. Elizabeth Hoffman, Kevin McCabe, and Vernon L. Smith, "Social Distance and Other-Regarding Behavior in Dictator Games," *American Economic Review* 86, no. 3 (June 1996): 654, n 3.

55. For a longer historically contextualized account of these changes within Amnesty see Stephen Hopgood, "Amnesty International's Growth and Development since 1961," in *50 Years of Amnesty International: Reflections and Perspectives*, SIM Special, no. 36, ed. Wilco

de Jonge, Brianne McGonigle Leyh, Anja Mihr, and Lars van Troost (Utrecht: Netherlands Institute of Human Rights, 2011).

56. Avaaz was founded by ex-International Crisis Group staffer Ricken Patel.

57. Mary Slosson, "Anti-Kony Campaign in Turmoil after Filmmaker's Breakdown," Reuters, March 23, 2012. For an analysis see Mareike Schomorus, Tim Allen, and Koen Vlassenroot, "KONY 2012 and the Prospects for Change: Examining the Viral Campaign," *Foreign Affairs*, March 2012.

58. See Mareike Schomorus, Tim Allen, and Koen Vlassenroot, "Obama Takes on the LRA: Why Washington Sent Troops to Central Africa," *Foreign Affairs*, November 2011.

59. But see Michael Wilkerson, "Joseph Kony Is Not in Uganda (and Other Complicated Things)," *Foreign Policy*, March 2012.

60. See Jeffrey Gettleman, "In Vast Jungle, U.S. Troops Aid in Search for Kony," *New York Times*, April 29, 2012.

61. For a suggestive description of some of these issues see Lilie Chouliaraki, *The Spectatorship of Suffering* (London: Sage Publications, 2006).

62. Anneke Van Woudenberg, "How to Catch Joseph Kony," *Human Rights Watch*, March 2012.

63. Hopgood, *Keepers of the Flame*, 69–71, 55, 100; Michael Barnett, *Empire of Humanity: A History of Humanitarianism* (Ithaca, NY: Cornell University Press, 2011), 137.

64. Hopgood, *Keepers of the Flame*, 110–11.

65. Ibid., 83.

66. Barnett, *Empire of Humanity*, 143–47.

67. Fabrice Weissman, "Silence Heals . . . ," in *Humanitarian Negotiations Revealed: The MSF Experience*, ed. Claire Magone, Michaël Neuman, and Fabrice Weissman (London: Hurst/MSF, 2011), 178.

68. Médecins Sans Frontières, *Financial Report 2011*, 4.

69. Neier, *Taking Liberties*, 154.

70. Drew, "Reporter at Large," 40.

71. On the effects of this transformation from solidarity to lawyer-led NGOs as it was experienced in Latin America in the 1990s see Tate, *Counting the Dead*, chap. 3.

72. Hopgood, *Keepers of the Flame*, 137–39.

73. Ibid., 140.

74. See www.hrw.org/about.

75. Human Rights Watch, "George Soros to Give $100 Million."

76. Colum Lynch, "With $100 Million Soros Gift, Human Rights Watch Looks to Expand Global Reach," *Washington Post*, September 12, 2010.

77. See Hopgood, "Amnesty International's Growth and Development since 1961."

78. Amnesty International, "BRICS Human Rights Initiative," August 26, 2010, ref: OSG 2012 049.

79. See "Making Amnesty International a Truly Global Movement for Human Rights: Blueprint for an Integrated and Results-Driven IS, Closer to the Ground," Draft 5, August 2011, ORG 30/011/2011: 4.

80. Ibid., 6.

81. Booth Walling and Waltz, *Human Rights*, 78.

82. Ibid., 22. Picken also ran the Cambodia office for the UN high commissioner for human rights in the 1990s.

83. Suzanne Nossel, "Smart Power: Reclaiming Liberal Internationalism," *Foreign Affairs*, April–May 2004.

84. Suzanne Nossel, "Advancing Human Rights in the UN System," *Council on Foreign Relations* working paper (May 2012).

85. Ibid., 11.

86. Human Rights First, previously the Lawyers Committee for International Human Rights (founded 1978), is a New York and Washington-based international NGO whose website banner reads: "American ideals. Universal values."

87. On the competition between secular and religious humanitarians see Stephen Hopgood and Leslie Vinjamuri, "Faith in Markets," in *Sacred Aid*, ed. Michael Barnett and Janice Stein (New York: Oxford University Press, 2012).

88. See Hafner-Burton, *Making Human Rights a Reality* and Thomas Risse and Stephen C Ropp, "Introduction and overview," in *The Persistent Power of Human Rights*, Risse, Ropp, and Sikkink, eds.

89. Guglielmo Verdirame, "The Divided West: International Lawyers in Europe and America," *European Journal of International Law* 18, no. 3 (2007): 559. See also Jack L Goldsmith and Eric A. Posner, *The Limits to International Law* (Oxford: Oxford University Press, 2005). Verdirame is reviewing Slaughter's *A New World Order* (Princeton, NJ: Princeton University Press, 2005) and Philippe Sands, *Lawless World: America and the Making and Breaking of Global Rules* (London: Allen Lane, 2005).

90. Verdirame, "Divided West," 562.

91. Ibid., 562–63.

6. Human Rights Empire

1. R. I. Moore, *The Formation of the Persecuting Society*, 2nd ed. (Oxford: Blackwell, 2007), 103.

2. James C. Scott, *Seeing Like a State: How Certain Schemes to Improve the Human Condition Have Failed* (New Haven, CT: Yale University Press, 1998), 96; Frédéric Mégret, "The Politics of International Criminal Justice," *European Journal of International Law* 13, no. 5 (2002): 1265.

3. See, for example, Jack Snyder and Leslie Vinjamuri, "Trials and Errors: Principle and Pragmatism in Strategies of International Justice," *International Security* 28, no. 3 (2003); Phil Clark, *The Gacaca Courts, Post-Genocide Justice and Reconciliation in Rwanda* (Cambridge: Cambridge University Press, 2010); Daniel Philpott, *Just and Unjust Peace: An Ethic of Political Reconciliation* (Oxford: Oxford University Press, 2012).

4. For the view that human rights rejuvenated, rather than colonized, the laws of war, see Helen M. Kinsella, *The Image before the Weapon: A Critical History of the Distinction between Combatant and Civilian* (Ithaca, NY: Cornell University Press, 2011): 136-37.

5. G. I. A. D. Draper, "Humanitarian Law and Human Rights," *Acta Juridica* (1979): 194–95. For a critique of this position see Theodor Meron, "On the Inadequate Reach of Humanitarian and Human Rights Law and the Need for a New Instrument," *American Journal of International Law* 77, no. 3 (1983): 602. On Tehran see Samuel Moyn, *The Last Utopia: Human Rights in History* (Cambridge, MA: Belknap Press of Harvard University Press, 2010), 126–27.

6. Draper, "Humanitarian Law and Human Rights," 203–5. He does accept that they emerge from the same root, the *idea of humanity* (205). See also René Provost, *International Human Rights and Humanitarian Law* (Cambridge: Cambridge University Press, 2002).

7. Kinsella, *The Image before the Weapon*.

8. Carrie Booth Walling and Susan Waltz, eds., *Human Rights: From Practice to Policy* (Ann Arbor: Gerald R. Ford School of Public Policy, University of Michigan, October 2010), 16–17.

9. Theodor Meron, "The Humanization of Humanitarian Law," *American Journal of International Law* 94, no. 2 (April 2000): 239–40.

10. Kinsella, *The Image before the Weapon*, 111.

11. Draper, "Humanitarian Law and Human Rights," 198.

12. Meron, "On the Inadequate Reach of Humanitarian and Human Rights Law," 603–6.

13. Meron, "Humanization of Humanitarian Law," 239.

14. Ibid., 246, 253.

15. Guglielmo Verdirame, "The Divided West: International Lawyers in Europe and America," *European Journal of International Law* 18, no. 3 (2007): 573.

16. Andreas L. Paulus, "The International Legal System as a Constitution," in *Ruling the World: Constitutionalism, International Law, and Global Governance*, ed. Jeffrey L. Dunoff and Joel P. Trachtman (Cambridge: Cambridge University Press, 2009), 74.

17. Frédéric Mégret, "Epilogue to an Endless Debate: The International Criminal Court's Third Party Jurisdiction and the Looming Revolution of International Law," *European Journal of International Law* 12, no. 2 (2001): 255.

18. Provost, *International Human Rights and Humanitarian Law*, 105–6.

19. Margaret McAuliffe deGuzman, "The Road from Rome: The Developing Law of Crimes against Humanity," *Human Rights Quarterly* 22, no. 2 (2000): 338 (my italics). See also Provost, *International Human Rights and Humanitarian Law*, 108.

20. Quoted in deGuzman, "Road from Rome," 339. Also Lawrence Douglas, *The Memory of Judgment: Making Law and History in the Trials of the Holocaust* (New Haven, CT: Yale University Press, 2001), 41.

21. DeGuzman, "Road from Rome," 339.

22. Mégret, "Politics of International Criminal Justice," 1276–77.

23. David Scheffer, *All the Missing Souls: A Personal History of the War Crimes Tribunals* (Princeton, NJ: Princeton University Press, 2012), 33. The situation was, he says, "dire," and no one, least of all himself, questioned Cassese's motives.

24. Allison Danner and Erik Voeten, "Who Is Running the International Criminal Justice System?" in *Who Governs the Globe?* ed. Deborah D. Avant, Martha Finnemore, and Susan K. Sell (Cambridge: Cambridge University Press, 2010), 39–40.

25. He was released in 2008 after serving eight years of a twenty-five-year sentence.

26. Jose E. Alvarez, "Nuremberg Revisited: The *Tadic* Case," *European Journal of International Law* 7, no. 2 (1996).

27. M. Cherif Bassiouni, "From Versailles to Rwanda in Seventy-Five Years: The Need to Establish a Permanent International Criminal Court," *Harvard Human Rights Journal* 10 (1997): 12–13.

28. Benjamin N. Schiff, *Building the International Criminal Court* (Cambridge: Cambridge University Press, 2008), 37–38.

29. According to Schiff, Bassiouni was blocked from becoming the first ICTY prosecutor by the British; Schiff, *Building the International Criminal Court*, 49.

30. Susan Waltz, "Prosecuting Dictators: International Law and the Pinochet Case," *World Policy Journal* 18, no. 1 (2001): 108–10. The internal politics of the ICTY remained highly fraught. See, for example, Geoffrey Nice, "Del Ponte's Deal," *London Review of Books* 32, no. 24 (2010).

31. Tim Kelsall, *Culture under Cross-Examination: International Justice and the Special Court for Sierra Leone* (Cambridge: Cambridge University Press, 2009), 36.

32. Judith N. Shklar, *Legalism: Law, Morals, and Political Trials* (Cambridge, MA: Harvard University Press, 1964), 143–51.

33. What Christopher Booker calls "overcoming the monster," *The Seven Basic Plots: Why We Tell Stories* (London: Continuum, 2004), 219. Also Mégret, "Politics of International Criminal Justice," 1283.

34. Aryeh Neier, *Taking Liberties: Four Decades in the Struggle for Rights* (New York: Public Affairs, 2003), 363.

35. CICC, "DRC Militia Leader Ntaganda in ICC Custody," http://us2.campaign-archive2.com/?u=8758bcde31bc78a5c32ceee50&id=c2f16a676a&e=63992dcba6.

36. Geoffrey Robertson, *Crimes against Humanity: The Struggle for Global Justice*, 3rd ed. (London: Penguin Books, 2006), 410–18.

37. Geoffrey Robertson, "Why It's Absurd to Claim that Justice Has Been Done," *Independent*, May 3, 2011.

38. Ibid.

39. Lynn Hunt, *Inventing Human Rights: A History* (New York: W. W. Norton, 2007), 94.

40. Lior Barshack, "The Totemic Authority of the Court," *Law and Critique* 11, no. 3 (2000): 305 (italics in original).

41. Martti Koskenniemi, "Between Impunity and Show Trials," *Max Planck Yearbook of United Nations Law* 6 (2002): 1–35.

42. Ibid., 11.

43. Ibid.

44. Ibid., 32.

45. Kofi Annan, "Advocating for an International Criminal Court," *Fordham International Law Journal* 21, no. 2 (1997): 366.

46. Annan has been reluctant to apologize for his decision, while head of UN peacekeeping, to stop Roméo Dallaire from seizing a Hutu arms cache in Rwanda in January 1994 and for not passing Dallaire's so-called "genocide memo" to the Security Council. In his recent memoirs, Annan makes a robust case for the decision not to take action based on Dallaire's cable: see Kofi Annan and Nader Mousavizadeh, *Interventions: A Life in War and Peace* (London: Penguin, 2012), 45–59; also "*Frontline* interview with Roméo Dallaire," April 2004; Michael N. Barnett, *Eyewitness to a Genocide: The United Nations and Rwanda* (Ithaca, NY: Cornell University Press, 2003), 77–88; and Jason A. Edwards, "The Mission of Healing: Kofi Annan's Failed Apology," *Atlantic Journal of Communication* 16, no. 2 (2008).

47. See, for example, Schiff, *Building the International Criminal Court*, William Schabas, *The International Criminal Court: A Commentary on the Rome Statute* (Oxford: Oxford University Press, 2010), and Joshua W. Busby, *Moral Movements and Foreign Policy* (Cambridge: Cambridge University Press, 2010), chap. 6. The complex literature on the ICC centers on peace versus justice, aggressive war, jurisdiction and complementarity, legitimacy, statute of limitations, powers of the prosecutor, impact and deterrence effect, and case selection.

48. For a detailed account from within the American delegation to Rome see Scheffer, *All the Missing Souls*, part 2.

49. Novelist and journalist Rebecca West famously called the Nuremberg courtroom a "citadel of boredom"; see *A Train of Powder* (Lanham, MD: Ivan R. Dee, 2000).

50. For a devastating and extremely well-informed account of Ocampo's time as chief prosecutor, see Julie Flint and Alex de Waal, "Case Closed: A Prosecutor without Borders," *World Affairs*, Spring 2009. See also Giles Whittell, "The World's Prosecutor," *Times Magazine* (London), May 2, 2012, 26. In this interview Ocampo again publicizes *Kony 2012*.

51. Flint and de Waal, "Case Closed."

52. Barry Stevens, dir., *Prosecutor*, White Pine Pictures (Toronto), 2010. The ICC is not, of course, a UN court, even though the Security Council can refer cases to it.

53. Flint and de Waal, "Case Closed."

54. See Alpha Sesay and Jeffrey Pierce, "Prosecutors and Victims' Representatives Make Closing Statements in Lubanga Trial," lubangatrial.org, August 25, 2011.

55. Flint and de Waal, "Case Closed."

56. See International Criminal Court, "Press Release: ICC Trial Chambers II Acquits Mathieu Ngudjolo Chui," December 18, 2012.

57. James Verini, "The Kenyatta Affair," *Foreign Policy*, March 20, 2013; Steve Coll, "When a Criminal Leads a Country," *The New Yorker*, March 7, 2013; Marlise Simons, "Court Is Asked to Drop Charges against Kenya's President-Elect," *New York Times*, March 18, 2013.

58. Simons, "Court Is Asked to Drop Charges."

59. Danilo Zolo, *Invoking Humanity: War, Law and Global Order* (London: Continuum, 2002), 39–41. This title echoes Carl Schmitt. Zolo's claim that the intervention in Kosovo was "a war against law" underestimates how such symbolic encounters can be used to found constitutional law in the longer term.

60. For the Kosovo Report, chaired by Goldstone, see Independent International Commission on Kosovo, *The Kosovo Report* (Oxford: Oxford University Press, 2000).

61. Zolo, *Invoking Humanity*, 74–75.

62. Kinsella, *The Image before the Weapon*, 137.

63. "Commemoration Day," *Economist*, July 14–22, 2012, 32. This article suggests Srebrenica may come to play for Bosnia the role Auschwitz has played for Israel in terms of political identity.

64. Eric A. Posner, *The Perils of Global Legalism* (Chicago: University of Chicago Press, 2009), 37.

65. Ibid., 181.

66. Jack L. Goldsmith and Eric A. Posner, *The Limits of International Law* (Oxford: Oxford University Press 2005), 184.

67. Anne Orford, *International Authority and the Responsibility to Protect* (Cambridge: Cambridge University Press, 2011), 10.

68. See Martha Finnemore and Kathryn Sikkink, "International Norm Dynamics and Political Change," *International Organization* 52, no. 4 (1998).

69. This is a very different kind of spiral model, one designed to enhance the power of Human Rights, than that in Thomas Risse, Stephen C. Ropp, and Kathryn Sikkink, eds., *The Persistent Power of Human Rights: From Commitment to Compliance* (Cambridge: Cambridge University Press, 2013).

70. See Eve Massingham, "Military Intervention for Humanitarian Purposes: Does the Responsibility to Protect Doctrine Advance the Legality of the Use of Force for Humanitarian Ends?" *International Review of the Red Cross* 91, no. 886 (2009), and Thomas G. Weiss, "The Sunset of Humanitarian Intervention? The Responsibility to Protect in a Unipolar Era," *Security Dialogue* 35, no. 2 (2004).

71. International Commission on Intervention and State Sovereignty, *The Responsibility to Protect* (Ottawa: IDRC, December 2001), xii–xiii.

72. Ibid., 54–55.

73. "Cyclone Nargis and the Responsibility to Protect: Myanmar/Burma Briefing No. 2," Asia-Pacific Centre for the Responsibility to Protect, May 16, 2008, http://www.r2 pasiapacific.org/documents/Burma_Brief2.pdf. See also Robert D. Kaplan, "Aid at the Point of a Gun," *New York Times*, May 14, 2008.

74. United Nations Security Council, "Responsibility to Protect: Timely and Decisive Response," July 25, 2012.

75. All references to Resolution 1970 as at "Full Text of UN Resolution Imposing Sanctions on Libya," *International Business Times*, February 27, 2011.

76. Thomas G. Weiss and Ramesh Thakur, *Global Governance and the UN: An Unfinished Journey* (Bloomington: Indiana University Press, 2010), 310, 338.

77. Gareth Evans, "No-Fly Zone Will Help Stop Gaddafi's Carnage," *Financial Times*, February 27, 2011.

78. United Nations Security Council, "Security Council Approves 'No-Fly Zone' over Libya, Authorising 'All Necessary Measures' to Protect Civilians, by Vote of 10 in Favour with 5 Abstentions," March 17, 2011.

79. Kevin Jon Heller, "The International Commission of Inquiry on Libya: A Critical Analysis," in Jens Meierhenrich, ed., *International Commissions: The Role of Commissions of Inquiry in the Investigation of International Crimes* (forthcoming), 50. Of the three-man commission, two members were M. Cherif Bassiouni and first ICC president Philippe Kirsch.

80. Heller, "International Commission of Inquiry on Libya," 50.

81. See David Rieff, "R2P, R.I.P.," *New York Times*, November 7, 2011, but also Alex Bellamy and Tim Dunne, "Syria: R2P on Trial," *Interpreter*, June 5, 2012. Also Adrian Johnson and Saqeb Mueen, eds., *Short War, Long Shadow: The Political and Military Legacies of the 2011 Libya Campaign* (London: Royal United Services Institute, 2012).

82. International Coalition for the Responsibility to Protect, "White House Mentions RtoP in May National Security Strategy, Human Rights Watch Letter to Secretary Clinton on Sri Lanka Investigation, Featured Reports, News Articles, and Upcoming Events," June 4, 2010.

83. Eric Schmitt and David E. Sanger, "Hints of Syrian Chemical Push Set Off Global Effort to Stop It," *New York Times*, January 7, 2013.

84. Bellamy and Dunne, "Syria: R2P on Trial."

85. Gareth Evans, "The Responsibility to Protect after Libya and Syria," Annual Castan Centre for Human Rights Law Conference (Melbourne, 2012), http://www.law.monash.edu.au/castancentre/conference/2012/evans-paper.pdf.

86. Confirming the view in the outcome document of 2005's UN World Summit rather than the ICISS's more expansionist reading. See also Ban Ki-moon's 2012 report on "timely and decisive response": Security Council, "Responsibility to Protect."

87. Amnesty International, *"I Wanted to Die": Syria's Torture Survivors Speak Out*, March 2012.

7. Of Gods and Nations

1. United Nations Office of the High Commissioner for Human Rights (OHCHR), *Democratic Republic of the Congo, 1993–2003: Report of the Mapping Exercise Documenting the Most Serious Violations of Human Rights and International Humanitarian Law Committed within the Territory of the Democratic Republic of the Congo between March 1993 and June 2003—Unofficial Translation from French Original*, August 2010, and "DR Congo: UN Report Exposes Grave Crimes," *Human Rights Watch*, October 1, 2010.

2. Alexander Cooley, "Principles in the Pipeline: Managing Transatlantic Values and Interests in Central Asia, *International Affairs* 84, no. 6 (2008): 1176.

3. Ibid., 1184–85. See also Alexander Cooley, *Great Games, Local Rules: The New Great Power Contest in Central Asia* (New York: Oxford University Press, 2012).

4. United Nations General Assembly, *Human Rights in Palestine and Other Occupied Arab Territories: Report of the United Nations Fact-Finding Mission on the Gaza Conflict*, September 25, 2009.

5. United Nations Human Rights Council (HRC), *Report of the Committee of Independent Experts in International Humanitarian and Human Rights Law Established pursuant to Council Resolution 13/9*, March 18, 2011.

6. Richard Goldstone, "Reconsidering the Goldstone Report on Israel and War Crimes," *Washington Post*, April 2, 2011.

7. "Israel Urges UN to Retract Goldstone Report," *Al-Jazeera*, April 3, 2011.

8. Eyal Weizman, "Short Cuts," *London Review of Books* 34, no. 23 (December 2012): 28.

9. "UN Security Council: Address Inconsistency in ICC Referrals," *Human Rights Watch*, October 16, 2012.

10. David P. Fidler, Sung Won Kim, and Sumit Ganguly, "Eastphalia Rising? Asian Influence and the Fate of Human Security," *World Policy Journal*, Summer 2009.

11. Balakrishnan Rajagopal, *International Law from Below: Development, Social Movements, and Third World Resistance* (Cambridge: Cambridge University Press, 2003), 213.

12. For an extended discussion see Doh Chull Shin, *Confucianism and Democratization in East Asia* (New York: Cambridge University Press, 2012).

13. Ibid., 57.

14. Fidler, Kim, and Ganguly, "Eastphalia Rising?" 53.

15. "Civil Society Denounces Adoption of Flawed ASEAN Human Rights Declaration," *Human Rights Watch*, November 19, 2012.

16. See Doris Buss and Didi Herman, *Globalizing Family Values: The Christian Right in International Politics* (Minneapolis: University of Minnesota Press, 2003), xvii; see also Jennifer S. Butler, *Born Again: The Christian Right Globalized* (London: Pluto Press, 2006). For Islam see *CEDAW and Muslim Family Laws: In Search of Common Ground*, Musawah (Sisters in Islam), Malaysia, 2011. Also Olivier Roy, *Holy Ignorance: When Religion and Culture Part Ways* (London: Hurst, 2010); Scott M. Thomas, "A Globalized God," *Foreign Affairs* 89, no.

6 (November–December 2010); and Scott M. Thomas, *The Global Resurgence of Religion and the Transformation of International Relations* (London: Palgrave Macmillan, 2005).

17. Clifford Bob, *The Global Right Wing and the Clash of World Politics* (New York: Cambridge University Press, 2012), chap. 3.

18. Doh Chull Shin, *Confucianism and Democratization*, 181.

19. Butler, *Born Again*, 91; but see Buss and Herman, *Globalizing Family Values*, xvii and 116–17.

20. Buss and Herman, *Globalizing Family Values*, 10, 38, and 42–43.

21. Butler, *Born Again*, 78–81.

22. See Stephen Hopgood, *Keepers of the Flame: Understanding Amnesty International* (Ithaca, NY: Cornell University Press, 2006), 116–21, and Julie Mertus, "Applying the Gatekeeper Model of Human Rights Activism: The US-Based Movement for LGBT Rights," in *The International Struggle for New Human Rights*, ed. Clifford Bob (Philadelphia: University of Pennsylvania Press, 2009).

23. As the work of women's rights activist Dorothy Thomas at Human Rights Watch in the 1990s demonstrates; see Mertus, "Applying the Gatekeeper Model," 64.

24. This phrase has been institutionalized in the so-called "Yogyakarta Principles"; see Yogyakarta Principles, "The Yogyakarta Principles—an Overview" (downloadable from numerous online sources); see also Michael O'Flaherty and John Fisher, "Sexual Orientation, Gender Identity and International Human Rights Law: Contextualising the Yogyakarta Principles," *Human Rights Law Review* 8, no. 2 (2008).

25. See *Freedom in the World 2011: The Authoritarian Challenges to Democracy*, Freedom House (Washington, DC: Freedom House 2011).

26. Economist Intelligence Unit, *Democracy Index 2011: Democracy under Stress, a Report from the Economist Intelligence Unit* (London: Economist Intelligence Unit, 2011).

27. Cambodian Ministry of Foreign Affairs and International Cooperation, "Cambodia Candidate Country for the United Nations Security Council 2013–2014." In the end South Korea won the seat.

28. United Nations, *Report of the Secretary-General's Panel of Experts on Accountability in Sri Lanka*, March 31, 2011.

29. OHCHR, "Message of the High Commissioner for Human Rights Navi Pillay at the Human Rights Council Special Session on the Human Rights Situation in Sri Lanka," May 26, 2009.

30. United Nations Human Rights Council, "Human Rights Council Adopts Resolution on Assistance to Sri Lanka in the Promotion and Protection of Human Rights," May 27, 2009.

31. All European members of the HRC voted against, Ukraine abstaining and Russia voting for. Both India and China voted in favor.

32. Sergei DeSilva Ranasinghe, "Sri Lanka—the New Great Game," Future Directions International Strategic Analysis Paper, March 24, 2010, 3.

33. David Lewis, "The Failure of a Liberal Peace: Sri Lanka's Counter-Insurgency in Global Perspective," *Conflict, Security & Development* 10, no. 5 (2010): 658.

34. David Miliband and Bernard Kouchner, "The Silence of Sri Lanka," *New York Times*, June 20, 2011.

35. Teresita C. Schaffer, "Sri Lanka's Day of Reckoning," *Hindu*, March 22, 2012.

36. Nick Cumming-Bruce, "In Resolution, U.N. Council Presses Sri Lanka on Civilian Deaths," *New York Times*, March 22, 2012.

37. Lewis claims that by November 2007 nearly 50 percent of the Sinhalese population supported the military option; see "Failure of a Liberal Peace," 655.

38. Simon Harris, "Humanitarianism in Sri Lanka: Lessons Learned?" Feinstein International Center Briefing Paper, June 2010, 8.

39. Fabrice Weissman, "Sri Lanka: Amid All-Out War," in *Humanitarian Negotiations Revealed: The MSF Experience*, ed. Claire Magone, Michaël Neuman, and Fabrice Weissman (London: Hurst/MSF, 2011), 32–33.

40. Harris, "Humanitarianism in Sri Lanka," 6.

41. Lewis, "Failure of a Liberal Peace," 658.

42. Ibid., 659. See also Richard Gowan, "Who Is Winning on Human Rights at the UN?" *European Council on Foreign Relations*, September 2012; and Richard Gowan and Franziska Brantner, "The EU and Human Rights at the UN: 2011 Review," *European Council on Foreign Relations*, September 2011. http://www.ecfr.eu/page/-/ECFR39_UN_UPDATE_2011_MEMO_AW.pdf.

43. "Resolution 'Balanced,' Manmohan Tells Rajapaksa," *Hindu*, March 24, 2012.

44. Amnesty International, "Sri Lanka: UN Resolution Shows Government Failure to Investigate Past and Present Rights Abuses," March 21, 2013.

45. "Sri Lanka: Address Rights Rollback at Review," *Human Rights Watch*, October 30, 2012.

46. United Nations, *Report of the Secretary-General's Internal Review Panel on United Nations' Action in Sri Lanka*, November 2012, 27.

47. Ibid., 30–31.

48. See Stephen Heder, "A Review of the Negotiations Leading to the Establishment of the Personal Jurisdiction of the Extraordinary Chambers in the Courts of Cambodia," August 1, 2011, 4–5. This is by far the most comprehensive account of this period.

49. Ibid., 5.

50. Ibid., 15–16. See also George Chigas, "The Politics of Defining Justice after the Cambodian Genocide," *Journal of Genocide Research* 2, no. 2 (2000): 252; Katheryn M. Klein, "Bringing the Khmer Rouge to Justice: The Challenges and Risks Facing the Joint Tribunal in Cambodia," *Northwestern Journal of Human Rights* 4, no. 3 (2006): 554; "Cambodia: Khmer Rouge Trial Is Justice Delayed," *Human Rights Watch*, June 24, 2011.

51. Seeta Scully, "Judging the Successes and Failures of the Extraordinary Chambers of the Courts of Cambodia," *Asian-Pacific Law and Policy Journal* 13, no. 1 (2011): 316.

52. Ralph Zacklin, assistant secretary-general for legal affairs at the UN, called the ICTY and ICTR "too costly, too inefficient and too ineffective," costing up to 10 percent of the annual UN regular budget by 2004: "The Failings of Ad Hoc International Tribunals," *Journal of International Criminal Justice* 2, no. 2 (2004): 543, 545.

53. Klein, "Bringing the Khmer Rouge to Justice," 551. Also Heder, "Review of the Negotiations," 39–40. For an account of the complex negotiations see the chronology available on the *Cambodia Tribunal Monitor* website at http://www.cambodiatribunal.org/sites/default/files/documents/CTM%20Composite%20Chronology%20-%201994-2011%20%28Nov%29.pdf.

54. "Serious Flaws: Why the UN General Assembly Should Require Changes to the Draft Khmer Rouge Tribunal Agreement," *Human Rights Watch*, April 30, 2003.

55. See Stephen Heder and Brian D. Tittemore, *Seven Candidates for Prosecution: Accountability for the Crimes of the Khmer Rouge* (Phnom Penh: Documentation Center of Cambodia, 2004).

56. Douglas Gillison, "Extra-Ordinary Justice," Investigative Fund, February 27, 2012.

57. See Mike Eckel, "Cambodia's Kangaroo Court," *Foreign Policy*, July 20, 2011.

58. "Recent Developments in the Extraordinary Chambers in the Courts of Cambodia," Open Society Justice Initiative, February 2012, p. 8.

59. "Recent Developments in the Extraordinary Chambers in the Courts of Cambodia," Open Society Justice Initiative, June 2011 update.

60. See Douglas Ellison, "Justice Denied," *Foreign Policy*, November 2011. This was not the end of the story; see "Press Release from the International Reserve Co-Investigating Judge," Extraordinary Chambers in the Courts of Cambodia.

61. See Mark Ellis, "The ECCC—a Failure of Credibility," *International Bar Association* 19 (February 2012): 19.

62. Ibid., 18.

63. Scully, "Judging the Successes and Failures," 349. She argues that international human rights instruments are not prescriptive (i.e., not a metanarrative), p. 304.

64. For current thinking on religion in theories of world politics, see Jack Snyder, ed., *Religion and International Relations Theory* (New York: Columbia University Press, 2011).

65. The figures in this paragraph are all taken from *Global Christianity: A Report on the Size and Distribution of the World's Christian Population*, Pew Forum on Religion and Public Life, December 2011, p. 9.

66. *The Future of the Global Muslim Population: Projections for 2010–2030*, Pew Forum on Religion and Public Life, January 17, 2011.

67. Eric P. Kaufmann, *Shall the Religious Inherit the Earth? Demography and Politics in the Twenty-First Century* (London: Profile Books, 2012).

68. Eric P. Kaufmann, Anne Goujon, and Vegard Skirbekk, "The End of Secularization in Europe? A Socio-Demographic Perspective," *Sociology of Religion*, 2011.

69. Musawah, *CEDAW and Muslim Family Laws*.

70. Ibid., 23.

71. For a contrary view, see Elizabeth Shakman Hurd, *The Politics of Secularism in International Relations* (Princeton, NJ: Princeton University Press, 2008).

72. See, for example, S. N. Eisenstadt, ed., *Multiple Modernities* (New Brunswick, NJ: Transaction Publishers, 2005); Michael Warner, Jonathan Van Antwerpen, and Craig J. Calhoun, eds., *Varieties of Secularism in a Secular Age* (Cambridge, MA: Harvard University Press, 2010); Peter J Katzenstein, ed., *Civilizations in World Politics: Plural and Pluralist Perspectives* (London: Routledge, 2010).

73. See Council of Europe Parliamentary Assembly, "Resolution 1464 (2005), Women and Religion in Europe," October 4, 2005.

74. Gilles Kepel, *The Revenge of God: The Resurgence of Islam, Christianity, and Judaism in the Modern World* (Cambridge: Polity, 1994).

75. UN Fourth World Conference on Women, "Platform for Action" (1995): paragraph 95. "Couples" is clearly a negotiating compromise. The paragraph also talks about "the responsible exercise of those rights."

76. See "Rio+20 Outcome Document Undermined by Human Rights Opponents," Amnesty International, June 22, 2012.

77. Muslim Brotherhood, "Statement Denouncing UN Women Declaration for Violating Sharia Principles," *IkhwanWeb*, March 14, 2013. IkhwanWeb is the Muslim Brotherhood's English language website. See also Rowan Harvey, "UN Conference on Women: Some Rights Won but More Battles Ahead," *The Guardian*, March 20, 2013. This post was in the *Guardian*'s "Poverty Matters Blog" which is supported by the Gates Foundation.

78. See Musawah, *CEDAW and Muslim Family Laws*, for an excellent account of objections.

79. See "What's in It for Us: The United States and CEDAW," CEDAW Task Force of the Leadership Conference on Civil and Human Rights.

80. See Michele Brandt and Jeffrey A. Kaplan, "The Tensions between Women's Rights and Religious Rights: Reservations to CEDAW by Egypt, Bangladesh and Tunisia," *Journal of Law and Religion* 12, no. 1 (1995–1996).

81. See Barbara Crossette, "Reproductive Health and the Millennium Development Goals: The 2005 World Summit," and "The Millennium Development Goals and Reproductive Health: Moving beyond the UN," William and Flora Hewlett Foundation, December 26, 2005.

82. Michelle Bachelet, "Focusing on Women's Participation and Leadership: In Pursuit of Equality," UN Women, July 2012. Bachelet resigned in March 2013 to return to Chile and a possible campaign to be president again.

83. Permanent Observer Mission of the Holy See to the United Nations, "Position Paper III Preparatory Committee Meeting of the United Nations Conference on Sustainable Development," June 13–15, 2012.

84. Ibid.

85. For a trenchant critique of the Vatican's position from within Catholicism see Catholics for Choice, "The Vatican at Rio—What's at Stake?" (2012).

86. Buss and Herman, *Globalizing Family Values*, 112.

87. This language of "tradition" was prominent in the verdict on the three female punk rockers from Pussy Riot who were sentenced to two years in prison in August 2012 after an impromptu performance in Moscow's Cathedral of Christ the Savior in February 2012. The women were prosecuted for "hooliganism" and "religious hatred" for singing their song "Mother of God, Put Putin Away."

88. See United Nations General Assembly, "Preliminary Study on Promoting Human Rights and Fundamental Freedoms through a Better Understanding of Traditional Values of Humankind," June 1, 2012, and "UNHRC's Advisory Committee Debates 'Traditional Values,'" *UN Watch*, http://blog.unwatch.org/index.php/2012/08/07/unhrcs-advisory-committee-debates-traditional-values/.

89. See, for example, the response of the women's rights group Women Living under Muslim Laws, at "UN: 'Traditional Values' Resolution Adopted at Twelfth Session of HRC," October 12, 2009.

90. For the report see United Nations General Assembly, "Preliminary Study"; for a discussion see United Nations Office of the High Commissioner for Human Rights, "Human Rights Council Advisory Committee Discusses Traditional Values and Human Rights," August 6, 2012, and *UN Watch*, "UNHRC's Advisory Committee Debates."

91. International Service for Human Rights, "Council Adopts Resolutions on Traditional Values without Considering Expert Input," September, 2012.

92. International Service for Human Rights, "Human Rights Council Must Take an Unequivocal Stand against Traditional Values," March 18, 2013.

93. Ibid.

94. Amanda M. Klasing, "The Future Women Want: Why Reproductive Rights Matters at Rio+20," *Human Rights Watch*, June 2012.

95. Sonia Harris-Short, "International Human Rights Law: Imperialist, Inept and Ineffective? Cultural Relativism and the UN Convention on the Rights of the Child, *Human Rights Quarterly* 25, no. 1 (2003): 177.

96. See, for example, Sally Engle Merry, *Human Rights and Gender Violence: Translating International Law into Local Justice* (Chicago: University of Chicago Press, 2005); Mark Goodale and Sally Engle Merry, eds., *The Practice of Human Rights: Tracking Law between the Global and the Local* (Cambridge: Cambridge University Press, 2007).

97. See Thomas, *Global Resurgence of Religion*, 221.

98. Naz K. Modirzadeh, "Taking Islamic Law Seriously: INGOs and the Battle for Muslim Hearts and Minds," *Harvard Human Rights Journal* 19 (2006): 193.

99. Madeline Baer and Alison Brysk, "New Rights for Private Wrongs: Female Genital Mutilation and Global Framing Dialogues," in Bob, *International Struggle for New Human*, 107. See also Margaret E. Keck and Kathryn Sikkink, *Activists beyond Borders: Advocacy Networks in International Politics* (Ithaca, NY: Cornell University Press, 1998).

100. See Nicholas Sambanis, "Has 'Europe' Failed?" *New York Times*, August 26, 2012.

101. See Timothy Garton Ash, "The Crisis of Europe," *Foreign Affairs*, September–October 2012. This picture is discussed by many authors, including Marianne Hirsch, "Projected Memory: Holocaust Photographs in Personal and Public Fantasy," in *Acts of Memory: Cultural Recall in the Present*, ed. Mieke Bal, Jonathan V. Crewe, and Leo Spitzer (Hanover, NH: University Press of New England, 1999), 10–11. It is also prominently on display in the information center under the Memorial to the Murdered Jews of Europe in Berlin.

102. Ash, "Crisis of Europe."

103. Timothy Garton Ash, "Can Europe Survive the Rise of the Rest?" *New York Times*, September 1, 2012, and also Richard McGregor, *The Party: The Secret World of China's Communist Rulers* (London: Allen Lane, 2010).

104. United States Department of Defense, *Sustaining U.S. Global Leadership: Priorities for 21st Century Defense*, January 2012.

105. David Scheffer, *All the Missing Souls: A Personal History of the War Crimes Tribunals* (Princeton, NJ: Princeton University Press, 2012). For the following paragraphs see chaps. 7–9.

106. Ibid., 237–38.

107. Ibid., 223.

108. Ibid., 247.

109. John R. Bolton, *Surrender Is Not an Option: Defending America at the United Nations and Abroad* (New York: Threshold Editions, 2007), 85; also Scheffer, *All the Missing Souls*, 243.

110. "U.S.: 'Hague Invasion Act' Becomes Law," *Human Rights Watch*, August 4, 2002.

111. Natalie Hevener Kaufman, *Human Rights Treaties and the Senate: A History of Opposition* (Chapel Hill: University of North Carolina Press, 1990), 38.

112. John Fonte, *Sovereignty or Submission: Will Americans Rule Themselves or Be Ruled by Others?* (New York: Encounter Books, 2011).

113. G. John Ikenberry and Anne-Marie Slaughter, "A World of Liberty under Law," *Global Asia* 2, no. 1 (Spring 2007).

114. G. John Ikenberry, "The End of the Neoconservative Moment," *Survival* 46, no. 1 (2004): 8. See also Nicolas Guilhot, "Limiting Sovereignty or Producing Governmentality? Two Human Rights Regimes in US Political Discourse," Social Science Research Council, 2007.

115. Andrew Moravcsik, "The Paradox of U.S. Human Rights Policy," in *American Exceptionalism and Human Rights*, ed. Michael Ignatieff (Princeton, NJ: Princeton University Press, 2005), 150.

8. The Neo-Westphalian World

1. Bryan Ward-Perkins, *The Fall of Rome* (Oxford: Oxford University Press, 2005), 183, as quoted in Slavoj Žižek, *Living in the End Times* (London: Verso, 2011), 89.

2. Hedley Bull coined the term "neo-medievalism" in 1977, suggesting that human rights might erode the power of sovereign states; see *The Anarchical Society: A Study of Order in World Politics* (London: Macmillan, 1977), 254–55. Jan Zielonka compares the concepts of a "neo-medieval empire" and a "Westphalian (or neo-Westphalian) super state" in the context of European Union enlargement. The neo-Westphalia I have in mind goes in the opposite direction to his: less homogeneity, less integration, more competition, and no universal norms; see Jan Zielonka, "Enlargement and the Finality of European Integration," Harvard Jean Monnet Working Paper, symposium in response to Joschka Fischer, 2000, and *Europe as Empire: The Nature of the Enlarged European Union* (Oxford: Oxford University Press, 2007). See also Andrew Hurrell, *On Global Order* (Oxford: Oxford University Press, 2007).

3. For an argument and examples that present a counter view to mine, using the lens of "civilizations" (including "American civilization" as an alternative to American "exceptionalism") and the idea of an emerging and more syncretic "civilization of modernity," of which human rights would be a pivotal part, see Peter J Katzenstein, ed., *Civilizations in World Politics: Plural and Pluralist Perspectives* (London: Routledge, 2010).

4. See Stephen D. Krasner, *Sovereignty: Organized Hypocrisy* (Princeton, NJ: Princeton University Press, 1999).

5. Mark Ellis, "The Decline of Universal Jurisdiction over International Crimes: Is It Irreversible?" (lecture, SOAS, London, February 22, 2012), http://www.unawestminster.org.uk/pdf/grot12_mark_ellis_lecture.pdf.

6. United Nations, *Report of the Secretary-General's Internal Review Panel on United Nations' Action in Sri Lanka*, November 2012, 26.

7. See "Protection of Civilians in Conflict—the ICRC Perspective," ICRC Resource Centre, May 9, 2007, http://www.icrc.org/eng/resources/documents/statement/children-statement-140507.htm.

8. See Marie-Pierre Allié, "Introduction: Acting at Any Price?" in Claire Magone, Michaël Neuman, and Fabrice Weissman, eds., *Humanitarian Negotiations Revealed: The MSF Experience* (London: Hurst/MSF, 2011), and Fabrice Weissman, " 'Not in Our Name': Why Médecins Sans Frontières Does Not Support the Responsibility to Protect," *Criminal*

Justice Ethics 29, no. 2 (2010). But see also Damien McElroy, "MSF Withdraws Staff over Libya Torture Cases," *Telegraph,* January 26, 2012.

9. Helen Young, "Diminishing Returns: The Challenges Facing Humanitarian Action in Darfur," in *The Golden Fleece: Manipulation and Independence in Humanitarian Action,* ed. Antonio Donini (Sterling, VA: Kumarian Press, 2012), 101.

10. Shannon Kindornay, James Ron, and R. Charli Carpenter, "Rights-Based Approaches to Development: Implications for NGOs," *Human Rights Quarterly* 34, no. 2 (2012).

11. See Philip K. Verleger Jr., "The Coming U.S. Boom and How Shale Gas Will Fuel It," *Financial Times,* April 23, 2012.

12. On the decline or otherwise of American power see Christopher Layne, "The Waning of U.S. Hegemony—Myth or Reality? A Review Essay," *International Security* 34, no. 1 (2009). See also Charles A. Kupchan, *No One's World: The West, the Rising Rest and the Coming Global Turn* (Oxford: Oxford University Press, 2012); Robert J. Lieber, *Power and Willpower in the American Future: Why the United States Is Not Destined to Decline* (New York: Cambridge University Press, 2012); Robert Kagan, "Not Fade Away: The Myth of American Decline," *National Review,* January 2012; Robert D. Kaplan, *Monsoon: The Indian Ocean and the Future of American Power* (New York: Random House, 2010); Fareed Zakaria, *The Post-American World* (New York: W. W. Norton, 2009).

13. G. John Ikenberry, "Liberal Internationalism 3.0: America and the Dilemmas of Liberal World Order," *Perspectives on Politics* 7, no. 1 (2009): 80.

14. G. John Ikenberry and Anne-Marie Slaughter (co-directors), "Forging a World of Liberty under Law: U.S. National Security in the Twenty-First Century," Princeton Project on National Security (2006).

15. Ikenberry, "Liberal Internationalism 3.0."

16. Ibid., 83.

17. Carl Schmitt, *Political Theology,* trans. George Schwab (Chicago: University of Chicago Press, 1985), 5.

18. Paul Eckert, "Clinton Declares 'America's Pacific Century,'" Reuters, November 10, 2011.

19. See, for example, Beth A. Simmons, *Mobilizing for Human Rights: International Law in Domestic Politics* (Cambridge: Cambridge University Press, 2009). Simmons shows how getting states to assent to human rights treaties empowers national and transnational activists in three specific ways: rewriting the domestic political agenda, facilitating legal challenges to the state (based around its new treaty commitments), and political mobilization (this being particularly acute when it comes to making new political alliances, for example, to leverage influence).

20. See Will Cohen, "Justice Goes Prime Time in Sierra Leone," Open Society Foundations, August 16, 2012.

21. R. Charli Carpenter, "Orphaned Again? Children Born of Wartime Rape as a Non-Issue for the Human Rights Movement," in *The International Struggle for New Human Rights,* ed. Clifford Bob (Philadelphia: University of Pennsylvania Press, 2009).

22. Mancur Olson argued the disproportionate role of middle-class advocates in organized action was to do with their possession of surplus time and money: see *The Logic of Collective Action: Public Goods and the Theory of Groups* (Cambridge, MA: Harvard University Press, 1971). See also Barrington Moore, *Social Origins of Dictatorship and Democracy: Lord and Peasant in the Making of the Modern World* (Boston: Beacon Press, 1966).

23. See Joseph Kahn and Daniel J. Wakin, "Western Classical Music, Made and Loved in China," *New York Times,* April 2, 2007. On cultural capital see Pierre Bourdieu, *Distinction: A Social Critique of the Judgment of Taste,* trans. Richard Nice (Cambridge, MA: Harvard University Press, 1984).

24. But see Kellee S. Tsai, *Capitalism without Democracy: The Private Sector in Contemporary China* (Ithaca, NY: Cornell University Press, 2007).

25. Richard Gowan and Franziska Brantner, *A Global Force for Human Rights? An Audit of European Power at the UN,* European Council on Foreign Relations (2008), 1, 37.

26. Ibid., 38–39.

27. Tracy McVeigh, "Melinda Gates Hits Out at 'War on Women' on Eve of Summit," *Observer*, July 7, 2012.

28. See David Cole, "Obama and Terror: The Hovering Questions," *New York Review of Books*, July 12–August 15, 2012, 32–34.

29. Ikenberry and Slaughter, "Forging a World of Liberty under Law," 6.

30. Gowan and Brantner, *Global Force for Human Rights?* 38.

31. Ibid., 3.

32. Jürgen Habermas, *The Divided West*, trans. Ciaran Cronin (Cambridge: Polity Press, 2006). See also George Weigel, *The Cube and the Cathedral: Europe, America, and Politics without God* (New York: Basic Books, 2006).

33. Boraine cofounded the International Center for Transitional Justice in New York in 2001.

34. Lawrence Weschler, *A Miracle, A Universe: Settling Accounts with Torturers* (University of Chicago Press, 1998): 243–45. The full conference report and papers are in Alice H Henkin, ed., *State Crimes: Punishment or Pardon* (Colorado: Aspen Institute, 1989). On Zalaquett see Margaret E Keck and Kathryn Sikkink, *Activists beyond Borders: Advocacy Networks in International Politics* (Ithaca, NY: Cornell University Press, 1998): 90–91; on Méndez, see Aryeh Neier, *Taking Liberties: Four Decades in the Struggle for Rights* (New York: Public Affairs, 2003), 194–95.

35. Tony Vaux, *The Selfish Altruist: Relief Work in Famine and War* (London: Earthscan Publications, 2001), 7. Today, avoiding contact with the locals can be just as much of a concern; Mark Duffield, "Risk-Management and the Fortified Aid Compound: Everyday Life in Post-Interventionary Society," *Journal of Intervention and Statebuilding* 4, no. 4 (2010).

36. Stephen Hopgood, *Keepers of the Flame: Understanding Amnesty International* (Ithaca, NY: Cornell University Press, 2006).

37. Allen D. Hertzke, *Freeing God's Children: The Unlikely Alliance for Global Human Rights* (Oxford: Rowman and Littlefield, 2004), 22.

38. *Fight to Save the World: Sergio*, HBO / Passion Pictures, 2009, dir. Greg Barker; Samantha Power, *Chasing the Flame: Sergio Vieira de Mello and the Fight to Save the World* (New York: Penguin Books, 2008). Power was an executive producer on the movie.

39. "UN Secretary-General Remarks at Funeral of Sergio Vieira de Mello," *Heroes* (blog), August 23, 2003, http://www.universalrights.net/heroes/display.php3?id=67.

40. Ibid.

41. Ibid.

42. Ibid.

43. "UN Iraq Envoy Laid to Rest," BBC News, August 28, 2003.

44. Ibid.

45. "Russian Memorial to Slain UN Iraq Envoy Unveiled in Geneva," UNHCR, June 29, 2007.

46. "Background: World Humanitarian Day," United Nations.

47. Sergio Vieira de Mello Foundation web page, http://www.sergiovdmfoundation.org/en/activities_whd.html.

48. "UN Iraq Envoy Laid to Rest."

49. De Mello was strongly secular, as the documentary *Sergio* makes clear. One of the American military paramedics helping him was an evangelical who recalls an extraordinary argument with de Mello, pinned and dying under the debris, about whether they should pray for his life.

bibliography

Books and Articles

Agamben, Giorgio. *Remnants of Auschwitz: The Witness and the Archive*. New York: Zone Books, 1999.

Albright, Madeleine, and William Cohen, co-chairs. *Preventing Genocide: A Blueprint for U.S. Policymakers*. United States Holocaust Memorial Museum: American Academy of Diplomacy and the United States Institute of Peace, 2008. http://www.ushmm.org/genocide/taskforce/.

Alexander, Jeffrey C. "On the Social Construction of Moral Universals: The 'Holocaust' from War Crime to Trauma Drama." *European Journal of Social Theory* 5, no. 1 (2002): 5–85.

Allié, Marie-Pierre. "Introduction: Acting at Any Price?" In *Humanitarian Negotiations Revealed: The MSF Experience*, edited by Claire Magone, Michaël Neuman, and Fabrice Weissman, 1–11. London: Hurst/MSF, 2011.

Alvarez, Jose E. "Nuremberg Revisited: The *Tadic* Case." *European Journal of International Law* 7, no. 2 (1996): 245–64.

Alves, J. A. Lindgren. "The Declaration of Human Rights in Postmodernity." *Human Rights Quarterly* 22, no. 2 (2000): 478–500.

Annan, Kofi. "Advocating for an International Criminal Court." *Fordham International Law Journal* 21, no. 2 (1997). http://ir.lawnet.fordham.edu/cgi/viewcontent.cgi?article=2237&context=ilj.

Annan, Kofi, with Nader Mousavizadeh. *Interventions: A Life in War and Peace*. London: Penguin, 2012.

Arendt, Hannah. *Eichmann in Jerusalem: A Report on the Banality of Evil*. London: Penguin Books, 2006.

Armstrong, J. D. "The International Committee of the Red Cross and Political Prisoners." *International Organization* 39, no. 4 (1985): 615–42.

Ash, Timothy Garton. "The Crisis of Europe," *Foreign Affairs*, September/October 2012. http://www.foreignaffairs.com/articles/138010/timothy-garton-ash/the-crisis-of-europe.

Ashworth, John. "The Relationship between Capitalism and Humanitarianism." *American Historical Review* 92, no. 4 (1987): 813–28.

Baer, Madeline, and Alison Brysk. "New Rights for Private Wrongs: Female Genital Mutilation and Global Framing Dialogues." In *The International Struggle for New Human Rights*, edited by Clifford Bob, 93–107. Philadelphia: University of Pennsylvania Press, 2009.

Baker, George. "Photography's Expanded Field." *October*, no. 114 (2005): 120–40.

Bal, Mieke, Jonathan V. Crewe, and Leo Spitzer. *Acts of Memory: Cultural Recall in the Present*. Hanover, NH: University Press of New England, 1999.

Barnett, Michael. *Empire of Humanity: A History of Humanitarianism*. Ithaca, NY: Cornell University Press, 2011.

_____. *Eyewitness to a Genocide: The United Nations and Rwanda*. Ithaca, NY: Cornell University Press, 2003.

Barshack, Lior. "The Totemic Authority of the Court." *Law and Critique* 11, no. 3 (2000): 301–28.

Barthes, Roland. *Camera Lucida: Reflections on Photography*. Translated by Richard Howard. London: Vintage Books, 2000.

_____. "The Death of the Author." *Aspen*, no. 5–6 (1967). http://www.ubu.com/aspen/aspen5and6/threeEssays.html.

Bartos, Adam, and Christopher Hitchens. *International Territory: The United Nations, 1945–95*. New York: Verso, 1994.

Bass, Gary Jonathan. *Stay the Hand of Vengeance: The Politics of War Crimes Tribunals*. Princeton, NJ: Princeton University Press, 2000.

Bassiouni, M. Cherif. "Crimes against Humanity." In *Crimes of War 2.0: What the Public Should Know*, edited by Roy Gutman, David Rieff, and Anthony Dworkin, 135–36. New York: W. W. Norton, 2007.

_____. "From Versailles to Rwanda in Seventy-Five Years: The Need to Establish a Permanent International Criminal Court." *Harvard Human Rights Journal* 10 (1997): 11–62.

Baughan, Emily. " 'Every Citizen of Empire Implored to Save the Children!' Empire, Internationalism, and the Save the Children Fund in Inter-war Britain." *Institute of Historical Research* (2012).

Bauman, Zygmunt. *Modernity and the Holocaust*. Cambridge: Polity Press, 2000.

Benjamin, Walter. "The Work of Art in the Age of Mechanical Reproduction." Translated by Harry Zorn. In *Illuminations: Essays and Reflections*, edited by Hannah Arendt, 211–44. New York: Pimlico, 1999.

Bertschinger, Claire, and Fanny Blake. *Moving Mountains*. London: Doubleday, 2005.

Blackburn, Robin. *The American Crucible: Slavery, Emancipation and Human Rights*. London: Verso, 2011.

_____. "Reclaiming Human Rights." *New Left Review* 68 (May–June 2011): 126–38.

Bob, Clifford. *The Global Right Wing and the Clash of World Politics*. New York: Cambridge University Press, 2012.

_____. "The Market for Human Rights." In *Advocacy Organizations and Collective Action*, edited by Aseem Prakash and Mary Kay Gugerty, 133–54. Cambridge: Cambridge University Press, 2010.

Boissier, Pierre. *History of the International Committee of the Red Cross: From Solferino to Tsushima*. Geneva: Henry Dunant Institute, 1985.

Boltanski, Luc. *Distant Suffering: Morality, Media, and Politics*. Cambridge: Cambridge University Press, 1999.

Bolton, John R. *Surrender Is Not an Option: Defending America at the United Nations and Abroad*. New York: Threshold Editions, 2007.

Booker, Christopher. *The Seven Basic Plots: Why We Tell Stories*. London: Continuum, 2004.

Booth Walling, Carrie, and Susan Waltz, eds. *Human Rights: From Practice to Policy*. Ann Arbor: Gerald R. Ford School of Public Policy, University of Michigan, October 2010. http://deepblue.lib.umich.edu/handle/2027.42/89426.

Borgwardt, Elizabeth. " 'Constitutionalizing' Human Rights: The Rise and Rise of the Nuremberg Principles." In *The Human Rights Revolution: An International History*, edited by Akira Iriye, Petra Goedde, and William I. Hitchcock, 73–92. New York: Oxford University Press, 2012.

_____. *A New Deal for the World: America's Vision for Human Rights.* Cambridge, MA: Belknap Press of Harvard University Press, 2005.

Bortolotti, Dan. *Hope in Hell: Inside the World of Doctors without Borders.* Buffalo, NY: Firefly Books, 2004.

Bourdieu, Pierre. *Distinction: A Social Critique of the Judgment of Taste.* Translated by Richard Nice. Cambridge, MA: Harvard University Press, 1984.

_____. *Language and Symbolic Power.* Cambridge: Cambridge University Press, 1991.

Bouvier, Antoine. "Special Aspects of the Use of the Red Cross or Red Crescent Emblem." *International Review of the Red Cross* 29, no. 272 (1989): 438–58.

Brandt, Michele, and Jeffrey A. Kaplan. "The Tension between Women's Rights and Religious Rights: Reservations to CEDAW by Egypt, Bangladesh and Tunisia." *Journal of Law and Religion* 12, no. 1 (1995): 105–42.

Browning, Christopher R. *The Origins of the Final Solution: The Evolution of Nazi Jewish Policy, 1939–1942.* London: Arrow Books, 2005.

Brysk, Alison. *Global Good Samaritans: Human Rights as Foreign Policy.* Oxford: Oxford University Press, 2009.

Bugnion, François. "Dialogue with the Past: The ICRC and the Nazi Death Camps." ICRC Resource Centre. November 5, 2002. http://www.icrc.org/eng/resources/documents/misc/6ayg86.htm.

_____. "From Solferino to the Birth of Contemporary International Humanitarian Law." International Committee of the Red Cross. April 2009. http://www.icrc.org/eng/assets/files/other/solferino-bugnion-icrc.pdf.

_____. *The International Committee of the Red Cross and the Protection of War Victims.* Oxford: Macmillan/ICRC, 2003.

_____. "The Red Cross and Red Crescent Emblems." *International Review of the Red Cross* 29, no. 272 (1989): 408–19.

Bull, Hedley. *The Anarchical Society: A Study of Order in World Politics.* London: Macmillan, 1977.

Burnett, John S. *Where Soldiers Fear to Tread: A Relief Worker's Tale of Survival.* New York: Bantam Books, 2005.

Busby, Joshua W. *Moral Movements and Foreign Policy.* Cambridge: Cambridge University Press, 2010.

Buss, Doris, and Didi Herman. *Globalizing Family Values: The Christian Right in International Politics.* Minneapolis: University of Minnesota Press, 2003.

Butler, Jennifer S. *Born Again: The Christian Right Globalized.* London: Pluto Press, 2006.

Cain, Kenneth, Heidi Postlewait, and Andrew Thomson. *Emergency Sex and Other Desperate Measures.* London: Ebury Press, 2006.

Carleton, David, and Michael Stohl. "The Foreign Policy of Human Rights: Rhetoric and Reality from Jimmy Carter to Ronald Reagan." *Human Rights Quarterly* 7, no. 2 (1985): 205–29.

Carpenter, R. Charli. "Orphaned Again? Children Born of Wartime Rape as a Non-Issue for the Human Rights Movement." In *The International Struggle for New Human Rights*, edited by Clifford Bob, 14–29. Philadelphia: University of Pennsylvania Press, 2009.

Cassese, Antonio. *International Law.* 2nd ed. Oxford: Oxford University Press, 2005.

Chigas, George. "The Politics of Defining Justice after the Cambodian Genocide." *Journal of Genocide Research* 2, no. 2 (2000): 245–65.

Chouliaraki, Lilie. *The Spectatorship of Suffering.* London: Sage Publications, 2006.

Clark, Ann Marie. *Diplomacy of Conscience: Amnesty International and Changing Human Rights Norms.* Princeton, NJ: Princeton University Press, 2001.

Clark, Phil. *The Gacaca Courts, Post-Genocide Justice and Reconciliation in Rwanda.* Cambridge: Cambridge University Press, 2010.

Cmiel, Kenneth. "The Emergence of Human Rights Politics in the United States." *Journal of American History* 86, no. 3 (1999): 1231–50.

Cohen, G. Daniel. "The Holocaust and the 'Human Rights Revolution.'" In *The Human Rights Revolution: An International History*, edited by Akira Iriye, Petra Goedde, and William I. Hitchcock, 53–72. New York: Oxford University Press, 2012.

Cohen, Stephen B. "Conditioning US Security Assistance on Human Rights Practices." *American Journal of International Law* 76 (1982): 246–79.

Cole, David. "Obama and Terror: The Hovering Questions." *New York Review of Books*, July 12–August 15, 2012, 32–34.

Cooley, Alexander. *Great Games, Local Rules: The New Great Power Contest in Central Asia.* New York: Oxford University Press, 2012.

———. "Principles in the Pipeline: Managing Transatlantic Values and Interests in Central Asia." *International Affairs* 84, no. 6 (2008): 1173–88.

Cooper, John. *Raphael Lemkin and the Struggle for the Genocide Convention.* London: Palgrave Macmillan, 2008.

Crossette, Barbara. "Reproductive Health and the Millennium Development Goals: The 2005 World Summit" and "The Millennium Development Goals and Reproductive Health: Moving beyond the UN." William and Flora Hewlett Foundation, December 26, 2005. http://www.hewlett.org/library/search?order=name&sort=asc&page=12.

Crowdy, Rachel E. "The Humanitarian Activities of the League of Nations." *Journal of the Royal Institute of International Affairs* 6, no. 3 (1927): 153–69.

Dallaire, Roméo. *Shake Hands with the Devil: The Failure of Humanity in Rwanda.* London: Arrow Books, 2004.

Danner, Allison, and Erik Voeten. "Who Is Running the International Criminal Justice System?" In *Who Governs the Globe?* edited by Deborah D. Avant, Martha Finnemore, and Susan K. Sell, 35–71. Cambridge: Cambridge University Press, 2010.

Daudin, Guillaume, Matthias Morys, and Kevin H. O'Rourke. "Globalization, 1870–1914." Department of Economics Discussion Papers, no. 395. Oxford: University of Oxford, 2008.

Davey, Eleanor. "From tiers-mondisme to sans-frontiérisme: Revolutionary Idealism in France from the Algerian War to Ethiopian Famine." Unpublished manuscript: Queen Mary, University of London, November 2011.

Davies, Katherine. "Continuity, Change and Contest: Meanings of 'Humanitarian' from the 'Religion of Humanity' to the Kosovo War." Humanitarian Policy Group. August 2012.

Davis, David Brion. *The Problem of Slavery in the Age of Revolution, 1770–1823.* New York: Oxford University Press, 1999.

———. *Slavery and Human Progress.* New York: Oxford University Press, 1984.

Debrix, François. *Re-envisioning Peacekeeping: The United Nations and the Mobilization of Ideology.* Minneapolis: University of Minnesota Press, 1999.

deGuzman, Margaret McAuliffe. "The Road from Rome: The Developing Law of Crimes against Humanity." *Human Rights Quarterly* 22, no. 2 (2000): 335–403.

de Jonge, Wilco, Brianne McGonigle Leyh, Anja Mihr, and Lars van Troost, eds. *50 Years of Amnesty International: Reflections and Perspectives.* SIM Special, no. 36. Utrecht: Netherlands Institute of Human Rights, 2011.

Dezalay, Yves, and Bryant Garth. "From the Cold War to Kosovo: The Rise and Renewal of the Field of International Human Rights." *Annual Review of Law and Social Science* 2 (2006): 231–55.

Dikötter, Frank. *Mao's Great Famine.* London: Bloomsbury, 2012.

Douglas, Lawrence. *The Memory of Judgment: Making Law and History in the Trials of the Holocaust.* New Haven, CT: Yale University Press, 2001.

Douzinas, Costas. *The End of Human Rights: Critical Legal Thought at the Turn of the Century.* Oxford: Hart Publishing, 2000.

Draper, G. I. A. D. "Humanitarian Law and Human Rights." *Acta Juridica* (1979): 193–206.

Drew, Elizabeth. "A Reporter at Large: Human Rights." *New Yorker*, July 18, 1977, 36–62.

Drumbl, Mark. *Reimagining Child Soldiers in International Law and Policy*. Oxford: Oxford University Press, 2012.

Duffield, Mark. "Risk-Management and the Fortified Aid Compound: Everyday Life in Post-Interventionary Society." *Journal of Intervention and Statebuilding* 4, no. 4 (2010): 454–72.

Dunant, Henry. *A Memory of Solferino*. Geneva: Henry Dunant Institute, 1985. http://www.icrc.org/eng/resources/documents/publication/p0361.htm.

Durand, André. *From Sarajevo to Hiroshima: History of the International Committee of the Red Cross*. Geneva: Henry Dunant Institute, 1984.

Durkheim, Émile. *The Division of Labor in Society*. New York: Free Press, 1984.

_____. *The Elementary Forms of Religious Life*. Translated by Carol Cosman. Oxford: Oxford University Press, 2001.

_____. *Sociology and Philosophy*. Translated by D. F. Pocock. London: Routledge, 2010.

Eckel, Mike. "Cambodia's Kangaroo Court." *Foreign Policy*, July 20, 2011. http://www.foreignpolicy.com/articles/2011/07/20/cambodias_kangaroo_court?page=0,3.

Economist. "Commemoration Day." July 14–22, 2012.

Edwards, Jason A. "The Mission of Healing: Kofi Annan's Failed Apology." *Atlantic Journal of Communication* 16, no. 2 (2008): 88–104.

Egeland, Jan. *A Billion Lives: An Eyewitness Report from the Frontlines of Humanity*. New York: Simon & Schuster, 2008.

Egerton, George W. "Collective Security as Political Myth: Liberal Internationalism and the League of Nations in Politics and History." *International History Review* 5, no. 4 (1983): 496–524.

Eisenstadt, S. N., ed. *Multiple Modernities*. New Brunswick, NJ: Transaction Publishers, 2005.

Ellis, Charles Howard. *The Origin, Structure and Working of the League of Nations*. Clark, NJ: Lawbook Exchange, 2003.

Ellis, Mark. "The ECCC—a Failure of Credibility." *International Bar Association* 19 (February 2012): 1–28.

Ellison, Douglas. "Justice Denied." *Foreign Policy*, November 2011.

Elon, Amos. "The Excommunication of Hannah Arendt." Introduction to *Eichmann in Jerusalem: A Report on the Banality of Evil*, by Hannah Arendt. London: Penguin Books, 2006.

Evans, Gareth J. *The Responsibility to Protect: Ending Mass Atrocity Crimes Once and for All*. Washington, DC: Brookings Institution Press, 2008.

Fassin, Didier. *Humanitarian Reason: A Moral History of the Present*. Berkeley: University of California Press, 2012.

Fassin, Didier, and Richard Rechtman. *The Empire of Trauma: An Inquiry into the Condition of Victimhood*. Princeton, NJ: Princeton University Press, 2009.

Favez, Jean-Claude. *The Red Cross and the Holocaust*. Translated and edited by John Fletcher and Beryl Fletcher. Cambridge: Cambridge University Press, 1999.

Fidler, David P., Sung Won Kim, and Sumit Ganguly. "Eastphalia Rising? Asian Influence and the Fate of Human Security." *World Policy Journal* (Summer 2009): 53–64.

Finkelstein, Norman G. *The Holocaust Industry: Reflections on the Exploitation of Jewish Suffering*. 2nd ed. London: Verso, 2003.

Finnemore, Martha, and Kathryn Sikkink. "International Norm Dynamics and Political Change." *International Organization* 52, no. 4 (1998): 887–917.

Flint, Julie, and Alex de Waal. "Case Closed: A Prosecutor without Borders." *World Affairs*, Spring 2009. http://www.worldaffairsjournal.org/article/case-closed-prosecutor-without-borders.

Fonte, John. *Sovereignty or Submission: Will Americans Rule Themselves or Be Ruled by Others?* New York: Encounter Books, 2011.

Ford, Stuart. "How Leadership in International Criminal Law Is Shifting from the U.S. to Europe and Asia: An Analysis of Spending on and Contributions to International Criminal Courts." *Saint Louis University Law Journal* 55 (2010): 953–1000.

Forsythe, David P. *Humanitarian Politics: The International Committee of the Red Cross.* Baltimore: Johns Hopkins University Press, 1977.

_____. "Human Rights and the International Committee of the Red Cross." *Human Rights Quarterly* 12, no. 2 (1990): 265–89.

Forsythe, David P., and Barbara Ann J. Rieffer-Flanagan. *The International Committee of the Red Cross: A Neutral Humanitarian Actor.* London: Routledge, 2007.

Foucault, Michel. *Discipline and Punish: The Birth of the Prison.* London: Penguin, 1991.

_____. "On Popular Justice: A Discussion with Maoists." In *Power/Knowledge: Selected Interviews and Other Writings, 1972–1977,* edited by Colin Gordon, 1–36. New York: Vintage Books, 1980.

Frampton, Kenneth. *Le Corbusier.* London: Thames & Hudson, 2001.

Franck, Thomas M. "The Emerging Right to Democratic Governance." *American Journal of International Law* 86, no. 1 (January 1992): 46–91.

Fukuyama, Francis. *The End of History and the Last Man.* New York: Free Press, 1992.

Gardbaum, Stephen. "Human Rights and International Constitutionalism." In *Ruling the World: Constitutionalism, International Law, and Global Governance,* edited by Jeffrey L. Dunoff and Joel P. Trachtman, 233–57. Cambridge: Cambridge University Press, 2009.

Gladwell, Malcolm. "Small Change: Why the Revolution Will Not Be Tweeted." *New Yorker,* October 4, 2010. http://www.newyorker.com/reporting/2010/10/04/101004fa_fact_gladwell?currentPage=all%7C.

Glover, Jonathan. *Humanity: A Moral History of the Twentieth Century.* London: Pimlico, 2001.

Goldberg, Vicki. *The Power of Photography: How Photographs Changed Our Lives.* New York: Abbeville Press, 1991.

Goldsmith, Jack L., and Eric A. Posner. *The Limits of International Law.* Oxford: Oxford University Press, 2005.

Goldstone, Richard L. "From the Holocaust: Some Legal and Moral Implications." In *Is the Holocaust Unique? Perspectives on Comparative Genocide,* edited by Alan S. Rosenbaum, 47–53. Boulder, CO: Westview Press, 2009.

Goodale, Mark. *Surrendering to Utopia: An Anthropology of Human Rights.* Palo Alto, CA: Stanford University Press, 2009.

Goodale, Mark, and Sally Engle Merry, eds. *The Practice of Human Rights: Tracking Law between the Global and the Local.* Cambridge: Cambridge University Press, 2007.

Gorvin, Ian. "Producing the Evidence That Human Rights Advocacy Works: First Steps towards Systematized Evaluation at Human Rights Watch." *Journal of Human Rights Practice* 1, no. 3 (2009): 477–87.

Gowan, Richard, and Franziska Brantner. "The EU and Human Rights at the UN: 2011 Review." *European Council on Foreign Relations,* September 2011. http://www.ecfr.eu/page/-/ECFR39_UN_UPDATE_2011_MEMO_AW.pdf.

_____. "A Global Force for Human Rights? An Audit of European Power at the UN." *European Council on Foreign Relations,* 2008.

Guilhot, Nicolas. *The Democracy Makers: Human Rights and International Order.* New York: Columbia University Press, 2005.

Gutman, Roy. *A Witness to Genocide.* New York: Macmillan, 1993.

_____. "Limiting Sovereignty or Producing Governmentality: Two Human Rights Regimes in US Political Discourse." *Social Science Research Council,* 2007.

Guttenplan, D. D. *The Holocaust on Trial.* New York: W. W. Norton, 2002.

Habermas, Jürgen. *The Divided West.* Translated by Ciaran Cronin. Cambridge: Polity Press, 2006.

_____. *The Structural Transformation of the Public Sphere.* Cambridge, MA: MIT Press, 1989.

_____. *The Theory of Communicative Action.* Vol. 2, *A Critique of Functionalist Reason.* Cambridge: Polity Press, 1995.

Hafner-Burton, Emilie M. *Making Human Rights a Reality*. Princeton, NJ: Princeton University Press, 2013.

Hafner-Burton, Emilie, and James Ron. "Seeing Double: Human Rights Impact through Qualitative and Quantitative Eyes." *World Politics* 61, no. 2 (2009): 360–401.

Hall, Christopher Keith. "The First Proposal for a Permanent International Criminal Court." *International Review of the Red Cross* 38, no. 322 (1998): 57–74.

Harris, Simon. "Humanitarianism in Sri Lanka: Lessons Learned?" Feinstein International Center Briefing Paper, 1–12. June 2010.

Harris-Short, Sonia. "International Human Rights Law: Imperialist, Inept and Ineffective? Cultural Relativism and the UN Convention on the Rights of the Child." *Human Rights Quarterly* 25, no. 1 (2003): 130–81.

Hart, H. L. A. *The Concept of Law*. Oxford: Clarendon Press, 1961.

Harvey, David. *A Brief History of Neoliberalism*. Oxford: Oxford University Press, 2005.

Haskell, Thomas L. "Capitalism and the Origins of the Humanitarian Sensibility, Part 1." *American Historical Review* 90, no. 2 (1985): 339–61.

_____. "Capitalism and the Origins of the Humanitarian Sensibility, Part 2." *American Historical Review* 90, no. 3 (1985): 547–66.

Heder, Stephen, and Brian D. Tittermore. *Seven Candidates for Prosecution: Accountability for the Crimes of the Khmer Rouge*. Phnom Penh: Documentation Center for Cambodia, 2004.

Heller, Kevin Jon. "The International Commission of Inquiry on Libya: A Critical Analysis." In *International Commissions: The Role of Commissions of Inquiry in the Investigation of International Crimes*, edited by Jens Meierhenrich, 1–51. Forthcoming.

Henckaerts, Jean-Marie. "Study on Customary International Humanitarian Law: A Contribution to the Understanding and Respect for the Rule of Law in Armed Conflict." *International Review of the Red Cross* 87, no. 857 (2005).

Henkin, Alice H., ed. *State Crimes: Punishment or Pardon*. Aspen, CO: Aspen Institute, 1989.

Henkin, Louis. "The United States and the Crisis in Human Rights." *Virginia Journal of International Law* 14, no. 4 (1973–1974): 653–71.

Hertzke, Allen D. *Freeing God's Children: The Unlikely Alliance for Global Human Rights*. Oxford: Rowman and Littlefield, 2004.

Hilberg, Raul. *The Destruction of the European Jews*. 3rd ed. New Haven, CT: Yale University Press, 2003.

Hirsch, Marianne. "Projected Memory: Holocaust Photographs in Personal and Public Fantasy." In *Acts of Memory: Cultural Recall in the Present*, edited by Mieke Bal, Jonathan Crewe, and Leo Spitzer, 3–23. Hanover, NH: University Press of New England, 1999.

Hitchcock, Henry Russell, and Philip Johnson. *The International Style*. New York: W. W. Norton, 1995.

Hoffman, Elizabeth, Kevin McCabe, and L. Smith Vernon. "Social Distance and Other-Regarding Behavior in Dictator Games." *American Economic Review* 86, no. 3 (1996): 653–60.

Hoffmann, Stefan-Ludwig. "Genealogies of Human Rights." In *Human Rights in the Twentieth Century*, edited by Stefan-Ludwig Hoffmann, 1–26. New York: Cambridge University Press, 2011.

_____. *Human Rights in the Twentieth Century*. New York: Cambridge University Press, 2011.

Hopgood, Stephen. "Amnesty International's Growth and Development since 1961." In *50 Years of Amnesty International: Reflections and Perspectives*. SIM Special, no. 36, edited by Wilco de Jonge, Brianne McGonigle Leyh, Anja Mihr, and Lars van Troost, 75–100. Utrecht: Netherlands Institute of Human Rights, 2011.

_____. *Keepers of the Flame: Understanding Amnesty International*. Ithaca, NY: Cornell University Press, 2006.

_____. "Moral Authority, Modernity and the Politics of the Sacred." *European Journal of International Relations* 15, no. 2 (2009): 229–55.

Hopgood, Stephen, and Leslie Vinjamuri. "Faith in Markets." In *Sacred Aid: Faith and Humanitarianism*, edited by Michael Barnett and Janice Gross Stein, 37–64. New York: Oxford University Press, 2012.

Horowitz, Daniel. *The Anxieties of Affluence: Critiques of American Consumer Culture, 1939– 1979*. Amherst: University of Massachusetts Press, 2004.

Hughes, Rachel. "The Abject Artefacts of Memory: Photographs from Cambodia's Genocide." *Media, Culture & Society* 25, no. 1 (2003): 23–44.

Hughes, Thomas L. "Carter and the Management of Contradictions." *Foreign Policy*, no. 31 (1978): 34–55.

Hunt, Lynn. *Inventing Human Rights: A History*. New York: W. W. Norton, 2007.

Hurd, Elizabeth Shakman. *The Politics of Secularism in International Relations*. Princeton, NJ: Princeton University Press, 2008.

Hurrell, Andrew. *On Global Order*. Oxford: Oxford University Press, 2007.

Hutchinson, John F. *Champions of Charity: War and the Rise of the Red Cross*. Boulder, CO: Westview Press, 1996.

Iglauer, Edith. "The UN Builds Its Home." *Harper's Magazine*, December 1947.

Ignatieff, Michael, ed. *American Exceptionalism and Human Rights*. Princeton, NJ: Princeton University Press, 2005.

Ikenberry, G. John. "The End of the Neo-Conservative Moment." *Survival* 46, no. 1 (2004): 7–22.

———. "Liberal Internationalism 3.0: America and the Dilemmas of Liberal World Order." *Perspectives on Politics* 7, no. 1 (2009): 71–87.

Ikenberry, G. John, and Anne-Marie Slaughter. "Forging a World of Liberty under Law: U.S. National Security in the 21st Century." Princeton Project on National Security. September 2006. http://www.princeton.edu/~ppns/report/FinalReport.pdf.

———. "A World of Liberty under Law." *Global Asia* 2, no. 1 (Spring 2007). http://globalasia.org/pdf/issue2/World_of_Liberty_Under_Law.pdf.

Iriye, Akira, Petra Goedde, and William I. Hitchcock. *The Human Rights Revolution: An International History*. New York: Oxford University Press, 2012.

Jacob, Margaret C. *Strangers Nowhere in the World*. Philadelphia: University of Pennsylvania Press, 2006.

Jacobs, Janet. "Gender and Collective Memory: Women and Representation at Auschwitz." *Memory Studies* 1, no. 2 (2008): 211–25.

Jisheng, Yang. *Tombstone: The Untold Story of Mao's Great Famine*. New York: Allen Lane, 2012.

Johnson, Adrian, and Saqeb Mueen, eds. *Short War, Long Shadow: The Political and Military Legacies of the 2011 Libya Campaign*. London: Royal United Services Institute, 2012.

Judt, Tony. *Postwar: A History of Europe since 1945*. London: Vintage Books, 2012.

Kagan, Robert. "Not Fade Away: The Myth of American Decline." *National Review*, January 2012. http://www.tnr.com/article/politics/magazine/99521/america-world-power-declinism#.

Kaplan, Robert D. *Monsoon: The Indian Ocean and the Future of American Power*. New York: Random House, 2010.

Katzenstein, Peter J. ed. *Civilizations in World Politics: Plural and Pluralist Perspectives*. London: Routledge, 2010.

Kaufman, Natalie Hevener. *Human Rights Treaties and the Senate: A History of Opposition*. Chapel Hill: University of North Carolina Press, 1990.

Kaufmann, Eric P. *Shall the Religious Inherit the Earth? Demography and Politics in the Twenty-First Century*. London: Profile Books, 2012.

Kaufmann, Eric P., Anne Goujon, and Vegard Skirbekk. "The End of Secularization in Europe? A Socio-Demographic Perspective." *Sociology of Religion* (2011): 1–23.

Keck, Margaret E., and Kathryn Sikkink. *Activists beyond Borders: Advocacy Networks in International Politics*. Ithaca, NY: Cornell University Press, 1998.

Kelsall, Tim. *Culture under Cross-Examination: International Justice and the Special Court for Sierra Leone*. Cambridge: Cambridge University Press, 2009.

Kennedy, David. *Of War and Law*. Princeton, NJ: Princeton University Press, 2006.

Kennedy, Denis V.F. "Codified Compassion: Politics and Principles in Humanitarian Governance." Unpublished PhD dissertation, University of Minnesota, August 2012.

Kepel, Gilles. *The Revenge of God: The Resurgence of Islam, Christianity, and Judaism in the Modern World*. Cambridge: Polity, 1994.

Kindornay, Shannon, James Ron, and R. Charli Carpenter. "Rights-Based Approaches to Development: Implications for NGOs." *Human Rights Quarterly* 34, no. 2 (2012): 472–506.

Kinsella, Helen M. *The Image before the Weapon: A Critical History of the Distinction between Combatant and Civilian*. Ithaca, NY: Cornell University Press, 2011.

Klein, Katheryn M. "Bringing the Khmer Rouge to Justice: The Challenges and Risks Facing the Joint Tribunal in Cambodia." *Northwestern Journal of Human Rights* 4, no. 3 (2006): 549–66.

Klein, Kerwin Lee. "On the Emergence of Memory in Historical Discourse." *Representations* 69 (Winter 2000): 127–50.

Koskenniemi, Martti. "Between Impunity and Show Trials." *Max Planck Yearbook of United Nations Law* 6 (2002): 1–35.

_____. *The Gentle Civilizer of Nations: The Rise and Fall of International Law, 1870–1960*. Cambridge: Cambridge University Press, 2001.

Krasner, Stephen D. *Sovereignty: Organized Hypocrisy*. Princeton, NJ: Princeton University Press, 1999.

Krüger, Christine G. "German Suffering in the Franco-Prussian War, 1870–1871." *German History* 29, no. 3 (2011): 404–22.

Kunz, Josef L. "The Chaotic Status of the Laws of War and the Urgent Necessity for Their Revision." *American Journal of International Law* 45, no. 1 (1951): 37–61.

Kupchan, Charles A. *No One's World: The West, the Rising Rest, and the Coming Global Turn*. Oxford: Oxford University Press, 2012.

Laber, Jeri. *The Courage of Strangers: Coming of Age in the Human Rights Movement*. New York: PublicAffairs, 2002.

Laclau, Ernesto, and Chantal Mouffe. *Hegemony and Socialist Strategy: Towards a Radical Democratic Politics*. 2nd ed. London: Verso, 2001.

Langer, Lawrence L. "The Alarmed Vision: Social Suffering and Holocaust Atrocity." In *Social Suffering*, edited by Arthur Kleinman, Veena Das, and Margaret M. Lock, 47–66. Berkeley: University of California Press, 1997.

Lanzmann, Claude. "The Obscenity of Understanding: An Evening with Claude Lanzmann." In *Trauma: Explorations in Memory*, edited by Cathy Caruth, 200–20. Baltimore: Johns Hopkins University Press, 1995.

Laplante, Lisa J. "Outlawing Amnesty: The Return of Criminal Justice in Transitional Justice Schemes." *Virginia Journal of International Law* 49, no. 4 (2009): 915–84.

Laquer, Thomas W. "Bodies, Details, and the Humanitarian Narrative." In *The New Cultural History*, edited by Lynn Hunt, 176–204. Berkeley: University of California Press, 1989.

Law-Viljoen, Bronwyn. *Light on a Hill: Building the Constitutional Court of South Africa*. Johannesburg: David Krut, 2006.

Layne, Christopher. "The Waning of U.S. Hegemony—Myth or Reality? A Review Essay." *International Security* 34, no. 1 (Summer 2009): 147–72.

Levi, Primo. *The Drowned and the Saved*. London: Abacus, 1988.

Levy, Daniel, and Natan Sznaider. *The Holocaust and Memory in the Global Age*. Philadelphia: Temple University Press, 2006.

Lewis, David. "The Failure of a Liberal Peace: Sri Lanka's Counter-Insurgency in Global Perspective." *Conflict, Security & Development* 10, no. 5 (2010): 647–71.

Lieber, Robert J. *Power and Willpower in the American Future: Why the United States Is Not Destined to Decline*. New York: Cambridge University Press, 2012.

Linenthal, Edward T. "The Boundaries of Memory: The United States Holocaust Memorial Museum." *American Quarterly* 46, no. 3 (1994): 406–33.

_____. *Preserving Memory: The Struggle to Create America's Holocaust Museum.* New York: Columbia University Press, 2001.

Lipstadt, Deborah E. *The Eichmann Trial.* New York: Schocken Books, 2011.

Lowe, Kimberly A. "Humanitarianism and National Sovereignty: Red Cross Intervention on Behalf of Political Prisoners in Soviet Russia, 1921–1923." *Journal of Contemporary History* (forthcoming).

Luban, David. "Carl Schmitt and the Critique of Lawfare." Georgetown Public Law and Legal Theory Research Paper, no. 11–33 (2011): 1–13.

Lyotard, Jean-François. *The Postmodern Condition: A Report on Knowledge.* Manchester: Manchester University Press, 1984.

Mahood, Linda. "Eglantyne Jebb: Remembering, Representing and Writing a Rebel Daughter." *Women's History Review* 17, no. 1 (2007): 1–20.

Malanima, Paulo, and Oliver Volckart. "Urbanisation, 1700–1870." Centre for Economic Policy Research, 2010. http://www.cepr.org/meets/wkcn/1/1679/papers/Malanima-Volckart-Chapter.pdf.

Mamdani, Mahmood. "The Politics of Naming: Genocide, Civil War, Insurgency." *London Review of Books* 29, no. 5 (2007).

Marx, Karl. *Selected Writings.* Edited by Lawrence H. Simon. London: Hackett, 1994.

Marx, Karl, and Friedrich Engels. *The Communist Manifesto.* Penguin Classics. Edited, with an introduction and notes, by Gareth Stedman Jones. London: Penguin, 2002.

Massingham, Eve. "Military Intervention for Humanitarian Purposes: Does the Responsibility to Protect Doctrine Advance the Legality of the Use of Force for Humanitarian Ends?" *International Review of the Red Cross* 91, no. 886 (2009): 803–31.

Mazower, Mark. *No Enchanted Palace: The End of Empire and the Ideological Origins of the United Nations.* Princeton, NJ: Princeton University Press, 2009.

McGregor, Richard. *The Party: The Secret World of China's Communist Rulers.* London: Allen Lane, 2010.

Mégret, Frédéric. "Epilogue to an Endless Debate: The International Criminal Court's Third Party Jurisdiction and the Looming Revolution of International Law." *European Journal of International Law* 12, no. 2 (2001): 247–68.

_____. "The Politics of International Criminal Justice." *European Journal of International Law* 13, no. 5 (2002): 1261–84.

Meron, Theodor. "The Humanization of Humanitarian Law." *American Journal of International Law* 94, no. 2 (2000): 239–78.

_____ *The Humanization of International Law.* Leiden: Martinus Nijhoff, 2006.

_____. "On the Inadequate Reach of Humanitarian and Human Rights Law and the Need for a New Instrument." *American Journal of International Law* 77, no. 3 (1983): 589–606.

Merry, Sally Engle. *Human Rights and Gender Violence: Translating International Law into Local Justice.* Chicago: University of Chicago Press, 2005.

Mertus, Julie. "Applying the Gatekeeper Model of Human Rights Activism: The US-Based Movement for LGBT Rights." In *The International Struggle for New Human Rights,* edited by Clifford Bob, 52–67. Philadelphia: University of Pennsylvania Press, 2009.

Metcalf, Thomas R. *An Imperial Vision: Indian Architecture and Britain's Raj.* London: Faber and Faber, 2002.

Mires, Charlene. *Capital of the World: The Race to Host the United Nations.* New York: New York University Press, 2013.

Modirzadeh, Naz K. "Taking Islamic Law Seriously: INGOs and the Battle for Muslim Hearts and Minds." *Harvard Human Rights Journal* 19 (2006): 191–233.

Moore, Barrington. *Social Origins of Dictatorship and Democracy: Lord and Peasant in the Making of the Modern World.* Boston: Beacon Press, 1966.

Moore, R. I. *The Formation of a Persecuting Society.* 2nd ed. Oxford: Blackwell, 2007.

Moorehead, Caroline. *Dunant's Dream: War, Switzerland and the History of the Red Cross.* London: HarperCollins, 1998.

Moravcsik, Andrew. "The Paradox of U.S. Human Rights Policy." In *American Exceptionalism and Human Rights*, edited by Michael Ignatieff, 147–97. Princeton, NJ: Princeton University Press, 2005.

Morozov, Evgeny. "From Slacktivism to Activism." *Foreign Policy*, September 5, 2009. http://neteffect.foreignpolicy.com/posts/2009/09/05/from_slacktivism_to_activism.

_____. *The Net Delusion: How Not to Liberate the World.* London: Penguin Books, 2012.

Morsink, Johannes. "World War Two and the Universal Declaration." *Human Rights Quarterly* 15, no. 2 (1993): 357–405.

Moyn, Samuel. "Empathy in History, Empathizing with Humanity." *History and Theory* 45 (2006): 397–415.

_____. *The Last Utopia: Human Rights in History.* Cambridge, MA: Belknap Press of Harvard University Press, 2010.

Mumford, Lewis. "The Sky Line: Magic with Mirrors I." *New Yorker,* September 15, 1951, 84–93.

_____. "The Sky Line: Magic with Mirrors II." *New Yorker,* September 22, 1951, 99–106.

_____. "Stop and Think." *Progressive Architecture–Pencil Points* 27 (April 1946).

Musawah (Sisters in Islam). "CEDAW and Muslim Family Laws: In Search of Common Ground." Malaysia, 2011. http://www.musawah.org/sites/default/files/CEDAW%20%26%20Muslim%20Family%20Laws.pdf.

Mutua, Makau. *Human Rights: A Political and Cultural Critique.* Philadelphia: University of Pennsylvania Press, 2002.

Nadelmann, Ethan A. "Global Prohibition Regimes: The Evolution of Norms in International Society." *International Organization* 44, no. 4 (1990): 479–526.

Neier, Aryeh. *The International Human Rights Movement: A History.* Princeton, NJ: Princeton University Press, 2012.

_____. *Taking Liberties: Four Decades in the Struggle for Rights.* New York: Public Affairs, 2003.

New York Review of Books. "Women and Islam: An Exchange with Kenneth Roth of Human Rights Watch," March 22, 2012.

Nice, Geoffrey. "Del Ponte's Deal." *London Review of Books* 32, no. 24 (2010): 25–26.

Nietzsche, Friedrich. *The Gay Science.* Translated by Josefine Nauckhoff. Cambridge: Cambridge University Press, 2001.

Normand, Roger, and Sarah Zaidi. *Human Rights at the UN.* Bloomington: Indiana University Press, 2008.

Nossel, Suzanne. "Advancing Human Rights in the UN System." *Council on Foreign Relations* working paper, May 2012.

_____. "Smart Power: Reclaiming Liberal Internationalism." *Foreign Affairs*, April/May 2004: 131–42.

Novick, Peter. *The Holocaust and Collective Memory: The American Experience.* London: Bloomsbury, 1999.

_____. *The Holocaust in American Life.* Boston: Houghton Mifflin, 1999.

Nussbaum, Martha C. "Patriotism and Cosmopolitanism." In *For Love of Country? A New Democracy Forum on the Limits of Patriotism*, edited by Martha C. Nussbaum and Joshua Cohen, 3–20. Boston: Beacon Press, 2002.

Oberleitner, Gerd. *Global Human Rights Institutions.* Cambridge: Polity Press, 2007.

O'Connell, Mary Ellen. *The Power and Purpose of International Law: Insights from the Theory and Practice of Enforcement.* Oxford: Oxford University Press, 2008.

O'Flaherty, Michael, and John Fisher. "Sexual Orientation, Gender Identity and International Human Rights Law: Contextualising the Yogyakarta Principles." *Human Rights Law Review* 8, no. 2 (2008): 207–48.

Olson, Mancur. *The Logic of Collective Action: Public Goods and the Theory of Groups.* Cambridge, MA: Harvard University Press, 1971.

Orbinski, James. *An Imperfect Offering: Dispatches from the Medical Frontline.* London: Rider Books, 2008.

Orentlicher, Diane F. "That Someone Guilty Be Punished: The Impact of the ICTY in Bosnia." Open Society Justice Initiative and International Center for Transitional Justice, 2010. http://www.opensocietyfoundations.org/publications/someone-guilty-be-punished-impact-icty-bosnia.

Orford, Anne. *International Authority and the Responsibility to Protect*. Cambridge: Cambridge University Press, 2011.

Patterson, Orlando. *Slavery and Social Death: A Comparative Study*. Cambridge, MA: Harvard University Press, 1985.

Paulus, Andreas L. "The International Legal System as a Constitution." In *Ruling the World: Constitutionalism, International Law, and Global Governance*, edited by Jeffrey L. Dunoff and Joel P. Trachtman, 69–109. Cambridge: Cambridge University Press, 2009.

Peterson, V. Spike, and Laura Parisi. "Are Women Human? It's Not an Academic Question." In *Human Rights Fifty Years On: A Reappraisal*, edited by Tony Evans, 132–60. Manchester: Manchester University Press, 1998.

Pfeiffer, Bruce Brooks, and Robert Wojtowicz, eds. *Frank Lloyd Wright and Lewis Mumford: Thirty Years of Correspondence*. Princeton, NJ: Princeton Architectural Press, 2001.

Philpott, Daniel. *Just and Unjust Peace: An Ethic of Political Reconciliation*. Oxford: Oxford University Press, 2012.

Popper, Karl. *The Open Society and Its Enemies*. 4th ed. 2 vols. London: Routledge & Kegan Paul, 1962.

Posner, Eric A. *The Perils of Global Legalism*. Chicago: University of Chicago Press, 2009.

Power, Samantha. *Chasing the Flame: Sergio Vieira de Mello and the Fight to Save the World*. New York: Penguin Books, 2008.

——. *A Problem from Hell: America and the Age of Genocide*. New York: Harper Perennial, 2002.

Provost, René. *International Human Rights and Humanitarian Law*. Cambridge: Cambridge University Press, 2002.

Pustogarov, Vladimir. "Fyodor Fyodorovich Martens (1845–1909)—a Humanist of Modern Times." *International Review of the Red Cross* 36, no. 312 (1996): 300–14.

Rabinbach, Anson. "From Explosion to Erosion: Holocaust Memorialization in America since Bitburg." *History and Memory* 9, no. 1/2 (1997): 226–55.

Rajagopal, Balakrishnan. *International Law from Below: Development, Social Movements, and Third World Resistance*. Cambridge: Cambridge University Press, 2003.

Ranasinghe, Sergei DeSilva. "Sri Lanka—the New Great Game." Future Directions International Strategic Analysis Paper, March 2010.

Risse, Thomas, Stephen C. Ropp, and Kathryn Sikkink, eds. *The Persistent Power of Human Rights: From Commitment to Compliance*. Cambridge: Cambridge University Press, 2013.

Robbins, Bruce. *Feeling Global: Internationalism in Distress*. New York: NYU Press, 1999.

Roberts, Adam. "Humanitarian War: Military Intervention and Human Rights." *International Affairs* 69, no. 3 (July 1993): 429–49.

Robertson, Geoffrey. *Crimes against Humanity: The Struggle for Global Justice*. 3rd ed. London: Penguin Books, 2006.

Robin, Ron Theodore. *Enclaves of America: The Rhetoric of American Political Architecture Abroad, 1900–1965*. Princeton, NJ: Princeton University Press, 1992.

Rolle, Baptiste, and Edith Lafontaine. "The Emblem That Cried Wolf: ICRC Study on the Use of the Emblems." *International Review of the Red Cross* 91, no. 876 (2009): 759–78.

Rose, Colin, and Robert Slutzky. "Transparency: Literal and Phenomenal." *Perspecta* 8 (1963): 45–54.

Roth, Kenneth. "Defending Economic, Social, and Cultural Rights: Practical Issues Faced by an International Human Rights Organization." *Human Rights Quarterly* 26 (2004): 63–73.

——. "Seeking Allies Worldwide to Carry the Human Rights Banner." *Global Policy* 3, no. 4 (2012): 513–14.

Roy, Olivier. *Holy Ignorance: When Religion and Culture Part Ways*. London: Hurst, 2010.

Sandoz, Yves. Foreword in *Customary International Humanitarian Law*. Vol. 1, *Rules*, edited by Jean-Marie Henckaerts and Louise Doswald-Beck. Cambridge: Cambridge University Press, 2005.

Sands, Philippe. *Lawless World: America and the Making and Breaking of Global Rules*. London: Allen Lane, 2005.

_____. *Torture Team: Rumsfeld's Memo and the Betrayal of American Values*. London: Palgrave Macmillan, 2008.

Schabas, William. *The International Criminal Court: A Commentary on the Rome Statute*. Oxford: Oxford University Press, 2010.

Scheffer, David. *All the Missing Souls: A Personal History of the War Crimes Tribunals*. Princeton, NJ: Princeton University Press, 2012.

Scheingold, Stuart A. *The Politics of Rights: Lawyers, Public Policy, and Political Change*. 2nd ed. Ann Arbor: University of Michigan Press, 2004.

Schiff, Benjamin N. *Building the International Criminal Court*. Cambridge: Cambridge University Press, 2008.

Schlag, Pierre. "Law as the Continuation of God by Other Means." *California Law Review* 85, no. 2 (1997): 427–40.

Schmitt, Carl. *The Nomos of the Earth*. New York: Telos Press, 2003.

_____. *Political Romanticism*. Translated by Guy Oakes. New Brunswick, NJ: Transaction Publishers, 2011.

_____. *Political Theology*. Translated by George Schwab. Chicago: University of Chicago Press, 1985.

Schomorus, Mareike, Tim Allen, and Koen Vlassenroot. "Kony 2012 and the Prospects for Change: Examining the Viral Campaign." *Foreign Affairs*, March 2012. http://www.foreignaffairs.com/articles/137327/mareike-schomerus-tim-allen-and-koen-vlassenroot/kony-2012-and-the-prospects-for-change.

_____. "Obama Takes on the LRA: Why Washington Sent Troops to Central Africa." *Foreign Affairs*, November 2011. http://www.foreignaffairs.com/articles/136673/mareike-schomerus-tim-allen-and-koen-vlassenroot/obama-takes-on-the-lra.

Scott, James C. *Seeing Like a State: How Certain Schemes to Improve the Human Condition Have Failed*. New Haven, CT: Yale University Press, 1998.

Scott, James C. *Two Cheers for Anarchism*. Princeton, NJ: Princeton University Press, 2012.

Scully, Seeta. "Judging the Successes and Failures of the Extraordinary Chambers of the Courts of Cambodia." *Asian-Pacific Law and Policy Journal* 13, no. 1 (2011): 300–353.

Sémelin, Jacques. *Purify and Destroy: The Political Uses of Massacre and Genocide*. London: Hurst, 2007.

Shawcross, William. *Deliver Us from Evil: Warlords and Peacekeepers in a World of Endless Conflict*. London: Bloomsbury, 2000.

Shin, Dol Chull. *Confucianism and Democratization in East Asia*. New York: Cambridge University Press, 2012.

Shklar, Judith N. *Legalism: Law, Morals, and Political Trials*. Cambridge, MA: Harvard University Press, 1964.

Sikkink, Kathryn. *The Justice Cascade: How Human Rights Prosecutions Are Changing World Politics*. New York: W. W. Norton, 2011.

Simmel, Georg. *The Philosophy of Money*. London: Routledge, 1978.

_____. "The Stranger." In *On Individuality and Social Forms: Selected Writings*, edited by Donald N. Levine. Chicago: University of Chicago Press, 1971.

Simmons, Beth A. *Mobilizing for Human Rights: International Law in Domestic Politics*. Cambridge: Cambridge University Press, 2009.

Slaughter, Anne-Marie. *The Idea That Is America: Keeping Faith with Our Values in a Dangerous World*. New York: Basic Books, 2007.

_____. *A New World Order*. Princeton, NJ: Princeton University Press, 2005.

Slaughter, Joseph R. *Human Rights, Inc*. New York: Fordham University Press, 2007.

Smith, Adam. *The Theory of Moral Sentiments*. Minneapolis, MN: Filiquarian Publishing, 2007.

Smith, Tony. *A Pact with the Devil: Washington's Bid for World Supremacy and the Betrayal of American Promise*. New York: Routledge, 2007.

Snyder, Jack, ed. *Religion and International Relations Theory*. New York: Columbia University Press, 2011.

Snyder, Jack, and Leslie Vinjamuri. "Trials and Errors: Principle and Pragmatism in Strategies of International Justice." *International Security* 28, no. 3 (2003): 5–44.

Snyder, Timothy. *Bloodlands: Europe between Hitler and Stalin*. New York: Basic Books, 2010.

Sommaruga, Cornelio. "Foreword: Mirror of Humanity, Experience and Conscience." In *The International Committee of the Red Cross and the Protection of War Victims*, edited by François Bugnion. Oxford: Macmillan/ICRC, 2003.

_____. "Gustave Moynier, Builder of the Red Cross." *International Review of the Red Cross* 29, no. 272 (1989): 484–87.

Steinweis, Alan E. "The Auschwitz Analogy: Holocaust Memory and American Debates over Intervention in Bosnia and Kosovo in the 1990s." *Holocaust and Genocide Studies* 19, no. 2 (2005): 276–89.

Stoddard, Abby, Adele Harmer, and Victoria DiDomenico. "Providing Aid in Insecure Environments: 2009 Update." In Humanitarian Policy Group Brief 34, April 2009. http://www.odi.org.uk/resources/docs/269.pdf.

Stone, Dan, ed. *The Historiography of Genocide*. London: Palgrave Macmillan, 2008.

_____. "Raphael Lemkin on the Holocaust." *Journal of Genocide Research* 7, no. 4 (2005): 539–50.

Strachey, Lytton. *Eminent Victorians*. London: Penguin, 1986.

Straus, Scott. "Darfur and the Genocide Debate." *Foreign Affairs*, January/February 2005, 123–33.

_____. "Identifying Genocide and Related Forms of Mass Atrocity." USHMM Working Paper, October 7, 2001. http://www.ushmm.org/genocide/pdf/indentifying-genocide.pdf.

_____. "Second-Generation Comparative Research on Genocide." *World Politics* 59, no. 3 (2007): 476–501.

Taithe, Bertrand. "Pyrrhic Victories? French Catholic Missionaries, Modern Expertise, and Secularizing Technologies." In *Sacred Aid: Faith and Humanitarianism*, edited by Michael Barnett and Janice Gross Stein, 166–87. New York: Oxford University Press, 2012.

_____. "The Red Cross Flag in the Franco-Prussian War: Civilians, Humanitarians and War in the 'Modern Age.'" In *War, Medicine and Modernity*, edited by Roger Cooter, Mark Harrison, and Steve Sturdy, 22–47. Stroud, UK: Sutton Publishing, 1998: 22–47

Tarrow, Sidney. *Power in Movement: Social Movements and Contentious Politics*. 2nd ed. Cambridge: Cambridge University Press, 1998.

Tate, Winifred. *Counting the Dead: The Culture and Politics of Human Rights Activism in Colombia*. Berkeley: University of California Press, 2007.

Taylor, Telford. *The Anatomy of the Nuremberg Trials: A Personal Memoir*. London: Bloomsbury, 1993.

Teitel, Ruti G. *Humanity's Law*. New York: Oxford University Press, 2011.

Terry, Jennifer, and Jacqueline Urla, eds. *Deviant Bodies*. Bloomington: Indiana University Press, 1995.

Thomas, Scott M. "A Globalized God." *Foreign Affairs*, November/December 2010, 93–101.

_____. *The Global Resurgence of Religion and the Transformation of International Relations*. London: Palgrave Macmillan, 2005.

Tsai, Kellee S. *Capitalism without Democracy: The Private Sector in Contemporary China*. Ithaca, NY: Cornell University Press, 2007.

Tusa, Ann, and John Tusa. *The Nuremberg Trial*. London: BBC, 1995.

Van Woudenberg, Anneke. "How to Catch Joseph Kony." *Human Rights Watch*, March 2012. http://www.hrw.org/news/2012/03/09/how-catch-joseph-kony.

Vaux, Tony. *The Selfish Altruist: Relief Work in Famine and War*. London: Earthscan, 2001.

Verdirame, Guglielmo. "'The Divided West': International Lawyers in Europe and America." *European Journal of International Law* 18, no. 3 (2007): 553–80.

Vinjamuri, Leslie. "Deterrence, Democracy, and the Pursuit of International Justice." *Ethics & International Affairs* 24, no. 2 (2010): 191–211.

Vitalis, Robert. "The Graceful and Generous Liberal Gesture: Making Racism Invisible in American International Relations." *Millennium: Journal of International Studies* 29, no. 2 (2000): 331–56.

Waltz, Susan. "Prosecuting Dictators: International Law and the Pinochet Case." *World Policy Journal* 18, no. 1 (2001): 101–12.

Ward-Perkins, Bryan. *The Fall of Rome*. Oxford: Oxford University Press, 2005.

Warner, Michael, Jonathan Van Antwerpen, and Craig J. Calhoun. *Varieties of Secularism in a Secular Age*. Cambridge, MA: Harvard University Press, 2010.

Watenpaugh, Keith David. "The League of Nations Rescue of Armenian Genocide Survivors and the Making of Modern Humanitarianism, 1920–1927." *American Historical Review* 115, no. 5 (2010): 1315–39.

Weber, Max. "Science as a Vocation." In *From Max Weber: Essays in Sociology*, edited by Hans Heinrich Gerth and C. Wright Mills, 129–56. London: Kegan Paul, Trench, Trübner, 1947.

Weigel, George. *The Cube and the Cathedral: Europe, America, and Politics without God*. New York: Basic Books, 2006.

Weiss, Thomas G. "The Sunset of Humanitarian Intervention? The Responsibility to Protect in a Unipolar Era." *Security Dialogue* 35, no. 2 (2004): 135–53.

Weiss, Thomas G., and Ramesh Thakur. *Global Governance and the UN: An Unfinished Journey*. Bloomington: Indiana University Press, 2010.

Weissman, Fabrice. "'Not in Our Name': Why Médecins Sans Frontières Does Not Support the Responsibility to Protect." *Criminal Justice Ethics* 29, no. 2 (2010): 194–207.

_____. "Silence Heals . . . ." In *Humanitarian Negotiations Revealed: The MSF Experience*, edited by Claire Magone, Michaël Neuman, and Fabrice Weissman, 177–98. London: Hurst/MSF, 2011.

_____. "Sri Lanka: Amid All-Out War." In *Humanitarian Negotiations Revealed: The MSF Experience*, edited by Claire Magone, Michaël Neuman, and Fabrice Weissman, 15–34. London: Hurst/MSF, 2011.

Weschler, Lawrence. *A Miracle, a Universe: Settling Accounts with Torturers*. Chicago: University of Chicago Press, 1998.

West, Rebecca. *A Train of Powder*. Lanham, MD: Ivan R. Dee, 2000.

White, Peter T. "A Little Humanity amid the Horrors of War." *National Geographic*, November 1986, 646–79.

Wilkerson, Michael. "Joseph Kony Is Not in Uganda (and Other Complicated Things)." *Foreign Policy*, March 2012. http://blog.foreignpolicy.com/posts/2012/03/07/guest_post_joseph_kony_is_not_in_uganda_and_other_complicated_things.

Williams, Paul. *Memorial Museums: The Global Rush to Commemorate Atrocities*. Oxford: Berg, 2007.

Witte, John, Jr. *The Reformation of Rights*. Cambridge: Cambridge University Press, 2007.

Yablonka, Hannah. "Holocaust Survivors in Israel: Time for an Initial Taking of Stock." In *Holocaust Survivors: Resettlement, Memories, Identities*, edited by Dalia Ofer, Françoise Ouzan, and Judith Tydor Baumel-Schwartz, 185–207. New York: Berghahn Books, 2012.

Young, Helen. "Diminishing Returns: The Challenges Facing Humanitarian Action in Darfur." In *The Golden Fleece: Manipulation and Independence in Humanitarian Action*, edited by Antonio Donini, 89–108. Sterling, VA: Kumarian Press, 2012.

Young, James E. *The Texture of Memory: Holocaust Memorials and Meaning*. New Haven, CT: Yale University Press, 1993.

Zacklin, Ralph. "The Failings of Ad Hoc International Tribunals." *Journal of International Criminal Justice* 2, no. 2 (2004): 541–45.

Zakaria, Fareed. *The Post-American World*. New York: W. W. Norton, 2009.

Zelizer, Barbie. *Remembering to Forget: Holocaust Memory through the Camera's Eye*. Chicago: University of Chicago Press, 1998.

Zielonka, Jan. "Enlargement and the Finality of European Integration." Symposium in Response to Joschka Fischer: Harvard Jean Monnet Working Paper, 2000.

_____. *Europe as Empire: The Nature of the Enlarged European Union*. Oxford: Oxford University Press, 2007.

Žižek, Slavoj. *Living in the End Times*. London: Verso, 2011.

Zolo, Danilo. *Invoking Humanity: War, Law, and Global Order*. London: Continuum, 2002.

Newspapers and Reports

Al-Jazeera. "Israel Urges UN to Retract Goldstone Report." April 3, 2011. http://www.aljazeera.com/news/middleeast/2011/04/201142231017418.html.

Alvarez, Lizette. "At Memorial in Bosnia, Clinton Helps Mourn 7,000." *New York Times*, September 21, 2003. http://www.nytimes.com/2003/09/21/world/at-memorial-in-bosnia-clinton-helps-mourn-7000.html?pagewanted=all&src=pm.

Amnesty International. *"I Wanted to Die": Syria's Torture Survivors Speak Out*. March 2012. http://www.amnesty.org/en/library/asset/MDE24/016/2012/en/708c3f40–538e-46a9–9798-ebae27f56946/mde240162012en.pdf.

_____. "Making Amnesty International a Truly Global Movement for Human Rights: Blueprint for an Integrated and Results-Driven IS, Closer to the Ground, ORG 30/011/2011." Draft. August 5, 2011.

_____. "Rio+20 Outcome Document Undermined by Human Rights Opponents." June 22, 2012. http://www.amnesty.org/en/news/rio20-outcome-document-undermined-human-rights-opponents-2012-06-22.

_____. "Sri Lanka: UN Resolution Shows Government Failure to Investigate Past and Present Rights Abuses." March 21, 2013. http://www.amnesty.org/en/for-media/press-releases/sri-lanka-un-resolution-shows-government-failure-investigate-past-and-prese.

Ash, Timothy Garton. "Can Europe Survive the Rise of the Rest?" *New York Times*, September 1 2012. http://www.nytimes.com/2012/09/02/opinion/sunday/can-europe-survive-the-rise-of-the-rest.html?hp.

Auschwitz Institute. "Auschwitz Institute Praises U.S. Creation of Atrocities Prevention Board." April 23, 2012. http://www.auschwitzinstitute.org/auschwitz_institute_praises_creation_of_atrocities_prevention_board.html.

Bachelet, Michelle. "Focusing on Women's Participation and Leadership: In Pursuit of Equality." UN Women, July 2012. http://www.unwomen.org/2012/07/focusing-on-womens-political-participation-and-leadership-in-pursuit-of-equality.

Bathala, Sandeep. "Pop at Rio + 20: Reproductive Rights Missing from Outcome Document – Assessing the Disappointment." June 22, 2012. *NewSecurityBeat*. http://www.newsecuritybeat.org/2012/06/pop-at-rio20-reproductive-rights-missing-from-outcome-document-assessing-the-disappointment/.

BBC News. "Betancourt Rescuer Wore Red Cross." July 17, 2008. http://news.bbc.co.uk/1/hi/7510423.stm.

_____. "Clinton Unveils Bosnia Memorial." September 20, 2003. http://news.bbc.co.uk/1/hi/world/europe/3124642.stm.

_____. "UN Iraq Envoy Laid to Rest." August 28, 2003. http://news.bbc.co.uk/1/hi/world/europe/3187167.stm.

Bellamy, Alex, and Tim Dunne. "Syria: R2P on Trial." *Interpreter*, June 5, 2012. http://www.lowyinterpreter.org/post/2012/06/05/Syria-R2P-on-trial.aspx.

Bernstein, Robert L. "Rights Watchdog, Lost in the Mideast." *New York Times*, October 19, 2009. http://www.nytimes.com/2009/10/20/opinion/20bernstein.html?_r=2&ref=todayspaper.

Cambodian Ministry of Foreign Affairs and International Cooperation. "Cambodia Candidate Country for the United Nations Security Council 2013–2014." http://www.cambodianembassy.org.uk/downloads/Cambodia%20UN%20Brochure%20BLUE.pdf.

Catholics for Choice. "The Vatican at Rio—What's at Stake?" 2012. http://www.catholicsforchoice.org/hidden/documents/CFC_BrRpt_Rio20.pdf.

CEDAW Task Force of the Leadership Conference on Civil and Human Rights. "What's in It for Us: The United States and CEDAW." http://www.cedaw2010.org/index.php/whats-in-it-for-us.

Coalition for the International Criminal Court (CICC). "Architectural Design Competition for the Permanent Premises of the ICC." Statement to the Jury, October 30–31, 2008. http://www.iccnow.org/documents/CICC_Statement_to_Premises_Architectural_Competition_Jury.pdf. The CICC is quoting Mies van der Rohe.

Cohen, Will. "Justice Goes Prime Time in Sierra Leone." Open Society Foundations. August 16, 2012. http://www.soros.org/voices/justice-goes-prime-time-sierra-leone.

Coll, Steve. "When a Criminal Leads a Country." *The New Yorker*, March 7, 2013. http://www.newyorker.com/online/blogs/comment/2013/03/when-a-criminal-leads-a-country.html#ixzz2Mrt7ZncI.

Council of Europe Parliamentary Assembly. "Resolution 1464 (2005), Women and Religion in Europe." October 4, 2005. http://www.assembly.coe.int/Mainf.asp?link=/Documents/AdoptedText/ta05/ERES1464.htm.

Cumming-Bruce, Nick. "In Resolution, U.N. Council Presses Sri Lanka on Civilian Deaths." *New York Times*, March 22, 2012. http://www.nytimes.com/2012/03/23/world/asia/rights-body-passes-measure-on-sri-lanka.html.

Dallaire, Roméo. "Interview with Roméo Dallaire." *Frontline*, April 2004. http://www.pbs.org/wgbh/pages/frontline/shows/ghosts/interviews/dallaire.html.

Eckert, Paul. "Clinton Declares 'America's Pacific Century.' " Reuters, November 10, 2011. http://www.reuters.com/article/2011/11/11/us-apec-usa-clinton-idUSTRE7AA0GJ20111111.

Economist Intelligence Unit. *Democracy Index 2011: Democracy under Stress, a Report from the Economist Intelligence Unit.* London, Economist Intelligence Unit, 2011. http://www.sida.se/Global/About%20Sida/Så%20arbetar%20vi/EIU_Democracy_Index_Dec2011.pdf.

Elders, The. "Rio+20 Is Not the Response We Need to Safeguard People and the Planet." June 21, 2012. http://theelders.org/article/rio20-not-response-we-need-safeguard-people-and-planet.

Evans, Gareth. "No-Fly Zone Will Help Stop Gaddafi's Carnage." *Financial Times*, February 27, 2011. http://www.ft.com/cms/s/0/8ac9d1dc-4279-11e0-8b34-00144feabdc0.html.

Extraordinary Chambers in the Courts of Cambodia. "Press Release from the International Reserve Co-Investigating Judge." http://www.eccc.gov.kh/en/articles/press-release-international-reserve-co-investigating-judge.

Fondation Le Corbusier. "Palais de la Société des Nations, Geneva, Switzerland, 1927." http://www.fondationlecorbusier.fr.

Freedom House. *Freedom in the World 2011: The Authoritarian Challenges to Democracy.* Washington, DC: Freedom House 2011. http://www.freedomhouse.org/report/freedom-world/freedom-world-2011.

Gates Foundation. Cambodia Tribunal Monitor website. "Chronology." http://www.cambodiatribunal.org/sites/default/files/documents/CTM%20Composite%20Chronology%20-%201994-2011%20%28Nov%29.pdf.

_____. "Polio Eradication—a Must-Win Battle in the Global War on Disease." February 2011. http://www.gatesfoundation.org/polio/Documents/polio-white-paper.pdf.

Gettleman, Jeffrey. "In Vast Jungle, U.S. Troops Aid in Search for Kony," *New York Times*, April 29, 2012. http://www.nytimes.com/2012/04/30/world/africa/kony-tracked-by-us-forces-in-central-africa.html?pagewanted=all.

Gillison, Douglas. "Extra-Ordinary Justice." The Investigative Fund, February 27, 2012. http://www.genocidewatch.org/images/Cambodia_12_2_27_Extraordinary_injustice.pdf.

Goldsmith, Jack L. "Mea Culpa: Lawfare." *Lawfare: Hard National Security Choices* (blog), September 8, 2011. http://www.lawfareblog.com/2011/09/mea-culpa-lawfare/.

Goldstone, Richard. "Reconsidering the Goldstone Report on Israel and War Crimes." *Washington Post*, April 2, 2011. http://www.washingtonpost.com/opinions/reconsidering-the-goldstone-report-on-israel-and-war-crimes/2011/04/01/AFg111JC_story.html.

Gowan, Richard. "Who Is Winning on Human Rights at the UN?" European Council on Foreign Relations, September 2012. http://ecfr.eu/content/entry/commentary_who_is_winning_on_human_rights_at_the_un.

Harvey, Rowan. "UN Conference on Women: Some Rights Won but More Battles Ahead." *The Guardian*, March 20, 2013. http://www.guardian.co.uk/global-development/poverty-matters/2013/mar/20/un-conference-women-rights-won.

Heder, Stephen. "A Review of the Negotiations Leading to the Establishment of the Personal Jurisdiction of the Extraordinary Chambers in the Courts of Cambodia." August 1, 2011, 4–5. http://www.cambodiatribunal.org.

Heroes (blog). "UN Secretary-General Remarks at Funeral of Sergio Vieira de Mello." August 23, 2003. http://www.universalrights.net/heroes/display.php3?id=67.

Hindu. "Resolution 'Balanced,' Manmohan Tells Rajapaksa." March 24, 2012. http://www.thehindu.com/news/national/article3220236.ece.

Human Rights Watch. "Cambodia: Khmer Rouge Trial Is Justice Delayed." June 24, 2011. http://www.hrw.org/news/2011/06/24/cambodia-khmer-rouge-trial-justice-delayed.

——. "Civil Society Denounces Adoption of Flawed ASEAN Human Rights Declaration." November 19, 2012. http://www.hrw.org/news/2012/11/19/civil-society-denounces-adoption-flawed-asean-human-rights-declaration.

——. "Cluster Bombs: Nations Reject Weakening of Global Ban." November 2011. http://www.hrw.org/news/2011/11/25/cluster-bombs-nations-reject-weakening-global-ban.

——. "DR Congo: UN Report Exposes Grave Crimes." October 1, 2010. http://www.hrw.org/news/2010/10/01/dr-congo-un-report-exposes-grave-crimes.

——. "George Soros to Give $100 Million to Human Rights Watch." September 2010. http://www.hrw.org/en/news/2010/09/07/global-challenge.

——. "ICC: Congolese Rebel Leader Acquitted in Court's Second Case." December 18, 2012. http://www.hrw.org/news/2012/12/18/icc-congolese-rebel-leader-acquitted-courts-second-case.

——. "Meeting the Challenge." November 2010. http://www.hrw.org/reports/2010/11/22/meeting-challenge.

——. "Serious Flaws: Why the UN General Assembly Should Require Changes to the Draft Khmer Rouge Tribunal Agreement." April 30 2003. http://www.hrw.org/reports/2003/04/30/serious-flaws-why-un-general-assembly-should-require-changes-draft-khmer-rouge-tr.

——. "Sri Lanka: Address Rights Rollback at Review." October 30, 2012. http://www.hrw.org/news/2012/10/29/sri-lanka-address-rights-rollback-review.

——. "UN Security Council: Address Inconsistency in ICC Referrals." October 16, 2012. http://www.hrw.org/news/2012/10/16/un-security-council-address-inconsistency-icc-referrals-0.

——. "U.S.: 'Hague Invasion Act' Becomes Law." August 4, 2002. http://www.hrw.org/en/news/2002/08/03/us-hague-invasion-act-becomes-law.

Independent International Commission on Kosovo. *The Kosovo Report.* Oxford: Oxford University Press, 2000. http://reliefweb.int/report/albania/kosovo-report.

International Business Times. "Full Text of UN Resolution Imposing Sanctions on Libya." February 27, 2011. http://www.ibtimes.com/articles/116663/20110227/un-resolution-libya-sanctions-original-text-un-resolution-1970–2011.htm#ixzz1GU72N76p.

International Coalition for the Responsibility to Protect. "BRICS Human Rights Initiative." August 26, 2010, ref: OSG 2012 049.

_____. "White House Mentions RtoP in May National Security Strategy, Human Rights Watch Letter to Secretary Clinton on Sri Lanka Investigation, Featured Reports, News Articles, and Upcoming Events." June 4, 2010. http://www.responsibilitytoprotect.org.

International Commission on Intervention and State Sovereignty. *The Responsibility to Protect*. Ottawa: IDRC, December 2001.

International Committee of the Red Cross. *International Red Cross and Red Crescent Museum Catalogue*. Geneva: ICRC, 2000.

_____. *International Review of the Red Cross*. April 1963, third year, no. 25. http://www.loc.gov/rr/frd/Military_Law/pdf/RC_Apr-1963.pdf.

_____. "A Memory of Solferino." ICRC Resource Centre (last updated December 12, 2012). http://www.icrc.org/eng/resources/documents/publication/p0361.htm.

International Council on Human Rights Policy. "When Legal Worlds Overlap: Human Rights, State and Non-State Law." 2009. http://www.ichrp.org/files/reports/50/135_report_en.pdf.

International Criminal Court. "Press Release: ICC Trial Chambers II Acquits Mathieu Ngudjolo Chui." December 18, 2012. http://www.icc-cpi.int/en_menus/icc/press%20and%20media/press%20releases/news%20and%20highlights/Pages/pr865.aspx.

_____. *Report on the Future Permanent Premises of the International Criminal Court*. ICC-ASP/5/16. Assembly of States Parties, Fifth Session, The Hague, November 23–December 1, 2006.

International Service for Human Rights. "Council Adopts Resolutions on Traditional Values without Considering Expert Input." September, 2012. http://www.ishr.ch/council/376-council/1365-council-adopts-resolution-on-traditional-values-without-considering-expert-input.

_____. "Human Rights Council Must Take an Unequivocal Stand against Traditional Values." March 18, 2013. http://www.ishr.ch/council/376-council/1478-human-rights-council-must-take-an-unequivocal-stand-against-traditional-values.

Kahn, Joseph, and Daniel J. Wakin. "Western Classical Music, Made and Loved in China." *New York Times*, April 2, 2007. http://www.nytimes.com/2007/04/02/world/asia/02iht china.html?pagewanted=all.

Kaplan, Robert D. "Aid at the Point of a Gun." *New York Times*, May 14, 2008. http://www.nytimes.com/2008/05/14/opinion/14kaplan.html?_r=0.

Klasing, Amanda M. "The Future Women Want: Why Reproductive Rights Matters at Rio+20." Human Rights Watch, June 2012. http://www.huffingtonpost.com/amanda klasing/the-future-women-want-why_b_1607312.html.

Lynch, Colum. "With $100 Million Soros Gift, Human Rights Watch Looks to Expand Global Reach." *Washington Post*, September 12, 2010. http://www.washingtonpost.com/wp-dyn/content/article/2010/09/11/AR2010091105057.html.

McElroy, Damien. "MSF Withdraws Staff over Libya Torture Cases." *Telegraph*, January 26, 2012. http://www.telegraph.co.uk/news/worldnews/africaandindianocean/libya/9042501/MSF-withdraws-staff-over-Libya-torture-cases.html.

McVeigh, Tracy. "Melinda Gates Hits Out at 'War on Women' on Eve of Summit." *Observer*, July 7, 2012. http://www.guardian.co.uk/world/2012/jul/07/melinda-gates-family-planning-summit.

Médecins Sans Frontières. *Financial Report 2011*. http://www.msf.org/msf/articles/2012/06/msf-financial-report-2011.cfm.

Miliband, David, and Bernard Kouchner. "The Silence of Sri Lanka." *New York Times*, June 20, 2011. http://www.nytimes.com/2011/06/21/opinion/21iht-edmiliband21.html.

Muslim Brotherhood. "Statement Denouncing UN Women Declaration for Violating Sharia Principles." *IkhwanWeb*, March 14, 2013. http://www.ikhwanweb.com/article.php?id=30731.

Neier, Aryeh. "Human Rights Watch Should *Not* Be Criticized for Doing Its Job." *Huff Post World*, November 2, 2009. http://www.huffingtonpost.com/aryeh-neier/human-rights-watch-should_b_342680.html.

Open Society Justice Initiative. "Recent Developments in the Extraordinary Chambers in the Courts of Cambodia." June 2011 update. http://www.opensocietyfoundations.org/sites/default/files/cambodia-eccc-20110614.pdf.

_____. "Recent Developments in the Extraordinary Chambers in the Courts of Cambodia." February 2012. http://www.soros.org/sites/default/files/cambodia-eccc-20120223.pdf.

Otero, Maria. "Remarks at a Briefing to the Diplomatic Community on the Atrocities Prevention Board." U.S. Department of State, April 23, 2012. http://www.state.gov/j/189208.htm.

Permanent Observer Mission of the Holy See to the United Nations. "Position Paper III Preparatory Committee Meeting of the United Nations Conference on Sustainable Development." June 13–15, 2012. http://www.holyseemission.org/statements/statement.aspx?id=383.

Pew Forum on Religion and Public Life. *The Future of the Global Muslim Population: Projections for 2010–2030*. January 17, 2011. http://www.pewforum.org/The-Future-of-the-Global-Muslim-Population.aspx.

_____. *Global Christianity: A Report on the Size and Distribution of the World's Christian Population*. December 2011. http://www.pewforum.org/uploadedFiles/Topics/Religious_Affiliation/Christian/Christianity-fullreport-web.pdf.

Rieff, David. "R2P, R.I.P." *New York Times*, November 7, 2011. http://www.nytimes.com/2011/11/08/opinion/r2p-rip.html?pagewanted=all&_r=0.

Robertson, Geoffrey. "Why It's Absurd to Claim That Justice Has Been Done." *Independent*, May 3, 2011. http://www.independent.co.uk/opinion/commentators/geoffrey-robertson-why-its-absurd-to-claim-that-justice-has-been-done-2278041.html.

Sambanis, Nicholas. "Has 'Europe' Failed?" *New York Times*, August 26, 2012. http://www.nytimes.com/2012/08/27/opinion/has-europe-failed.html.

Samuels, Gertrude. "What Kind of Capitol for the U.N.?" *New York Times Magazine*, April 20, 1947.

Savage, Charlie. "Secret U.S. Memo Made Legal Case to Kill a Citizen." *New York Times*, October 8, 2011. http://www.nytimes.com/2011/10/09/world/middleeast/secret-us-memo-made-legal-case-to-kill-a-citizen.html?_r=1&pagewanted=all.

Save Darfur. "The Genocide in Darfur—Briefing Paper." June 2008. http://www.savedarfur.org/pages/background/.

_____. "What Has Happened to Darfur?" http://www.savedarfur.org/pages/primer.

Schaffer, Teresita C. "Sri Lanka's Day of Reckoning." *Hindu*, March 22, 2012. http://www.thehindu.com/opinion/lead/article3025593.ece.

Schmitt, Eric, and David E. Sanger. "Hints of Syrian Chemical Push Set Off Global Effort to Stop It." *New York Times*, January 7, 2013. http://www.nytimes.com/2013/01/08/world/middleeast.

Sesay, Alpha, and Jeffrey Pierce. "Prosecutors and Victims' Representatives Make Closing Statements in Lubanga Trial." http://www.lubangatrial.org/2011/08/25/prosecutors-and-victims-representatives-make-closing-statements-in-lubanga-trial/.

Simons, Marlise. "Court Is Asked to Drop Charges against Kenya's President-Elect." *New York Times*, March 18, 2013. http://www.nytimes.com/2013/03/19/world/europe/uhuru-kenyattas-lawyers-ask-hague-court-to-drop-charges.html.

Slack, Megan. "Join the Conversation: Honoring the Pledge of 'Never Again.'" *White House Blog*, April 20, 2012. http://www.whitehouse.gov/blog/2012/04/20/join-conversation-honoring-pledge-never-again.

Slosson, Mary. "Anti-Kony Campaign in Turmoil after Filmmaker's Breakdown." Reuters, March 23, 2012. http://www.reuters.com/article/2012/03/24/entertainment-us-usa-kony-future-idUSBRE82N01720120324.

Task Force for International Cooperation on Holocaust Education, Remembrance, and Research. "Declaration of the Stockholm International Forum on the Holocaust." January 28, 2000. http://www.holocausttaskforce.org/about-the-itf/stockholm-declaration.html.

United Nations. "Background: World Humanitarian Day." http://www.un.org/en/events/humanitarianday/background.shtml.

———. *Report of the International Commission of Inquiry on Darfur to the United Nations Secretary-General*. 2005. http://www.un.org/news/dh/sudan/com_inq_darfur.pdf.

———. *Report of the Secretary-General's Internal Review Panel on United Nations' Action in Sri Lanka*. November 2012, 27.

———. *Report of the Secretary-General's Panel of Experts on Accountability in Sri Lanka*. March 31, 2011. http://www.un.org/News/dh/infocus/Sri_Lanka/POE_Report_Full.pdf.

United Nations Fourth World Conference on Women. "Platform for Action," 1995, paragraph 95. http://www.un.org/womenwatch/daw/beijing/platform/health.htm.

United Nations General Assembly. *Human Rights in Palestine and Other Occupied Arab Territories: Report of the United Nations Fact-Finding Mission on the Gaza Conflict*. September 25, 2009. http://www2.ohchr.org/english/bodies/hrcouncil/docs/12session/A-HRC-12-48.pdf.

———. "Preliminary Study on Promoting Human Rights and Fundamental Freedoms through a Better Understanding of Traditional Values of Humankind." June 1, 2012. http://www.ohchr.org/Documents/HRBodies/HRCouncil/AdvisoryCom/Session9/A-HRC-AC-9-2_en.pdf.

———. "Resolution Adopted by the General Assembly on the Holocaust Remembrance (A/RES/60/7, 1 November 2005)." November 1, 2005. http://www.un.org/en/holocaustremembrance/docs/res607.shtml.

United Nations High Commissioner for Refugees. "Russian Memorial to Slain UN Iraq Envoy Unveiled in Geneva." June 29, 2007. http://www.unhcr.org/46852da94.html.

United Nations Human Rights Council. "Human Rights Council Adopts Resolution on Assistance to Sri Lanka in the Promotion and Protection of Human Rights." May 27, 2009. http://www.unhcr.ch/huricane/huricane.nsf/view01/B298103AA4EC07DDC1 2575C4002AA5EC?opendocument.

———. *Report of the Committee of Independent Experts in International Humanitarian and Human Rights Law Established Pursuant to Council Resolution 13/9*. March 18, 2011. http://www2.ohchr.org/english/bodies/hrcouncil/docs/16session/A.HRC.16.24_AUV.pdf.

United Nations Office of the High Commissioner for Human Rights. *Democratic Republic of the Congo, 1993–2003: Report of the Mapping Exercise Documenting the Most Serious Violations of Human Rights and International Humanitarian Law Committed within the Territory of the Democratic Republic of the Congo between March 1993 and June 2003—Unofficial Translation from French Original*. August 2010. http://www.ohchr.org/Documents/Countries/ZR/DRC_MAPPING_REPORT_FINAL_EN.pdf.

———. "Human Rights Council Advisory Committee Discusses Traditional Values and Human Rights." August 6, 2012. http://www.ohchr.org/EN/NewsEvents/Pages/DisplayNews.aspx?NewsID=12414&LangID.

———. "Message of the High Commissioner for Human Rights Navi Pillay at the Human Rights Council Special Session on the Human Rights Situation in Sri Lanka." May 26, 2009. http://www.unhcr.ch/huricane/huricane.nsf/view01/1BBA5307164D4708C125 75C20054FB10?opendocument.

United Nations Security Council. *An Agenda for Peace: Report of the Secretary-General pursuant to the Statement Adopted by the Summit Meeting of the Security Council on 31 January 1992*. June 17, 1992. http://www.un.org/Depts/dhl/landmark_sc/topical.htm.

_____. "Responsibility to Protect: Timely and Decisive Response." July 25, 2012. http://www.responsibilitytoprotect.org/UNSG%20Report_timely%20and%20decisive%20response.pdf.

_____. "Security Council Approves 'No-Fly Zone' over Libya, Authorising 'All Necessary Measures' to Protect Civilians, by Vote of 10 in Favour with 5 Abstentions." March 17, 2011. http://www.un.org/News/Press/docs/2011/sc10200.doc.htm.

United States Department of Defense. *Sustaining U.S. Global Leadership: Priorities for 21st Century Defense.* January 2012. http://www.defense.gov/news/Defense_Strategic_Guidance.pdf.

United States Holocaust Museum. "Vice-President Biden's Address in Honor of Tom Lantos." February 24, 2011. http://www.ushmm.org/genocide/analysis/details.php?content=2011-02-24.

United States White House Office of the Press Secretary. "Presidential Study Directive on Mass Atrocities." August 4, 2011. http://www.whitehouse.gov/the-press-office/2011/08/04/presidential-study-directive-suspension-entry-immigrants-and-nonimmigran.

UN Watch. "UNHRC's Advisory Committee Debates 'Traditional Values.'" August 7, 2012. http://blog.unwatch.org/index.php/2012/08/07/unhrcs-advisory-committee-debates-traditional-values/.

Verini, James. "The Kenyatta Affair." *Foreign Policy,* March 20, 2013. http://www.foreignpolicy.com/articles/2013/03/20/the_kenyatta_affair_kenya_election?page=0,2.

Verleger, Philip K., Jr. "The Coming U.S. Boom and How Shale Gas Will Fuel It." *Financial Times,* April 23, 2012. http://www.ft.com/cms/s/0/09fbb2ac-87b8-11e1-ade2-00144feab49a.html#axzz2HmxKLFqD.

Vredespaleis. "The Building." http://www.vredespaleis.nl/index.php?pid=57&page=The_building.

Went 2 the Bridge (blog). "Letter to Board of Directors, Amnesty International–USA." July 11, 2012. http://went2thebridge.blogspot.co.uk/2012/07/letter-to-board-of-directors-amnesty.html.

Wiesel, Elie. "Art and the Holocaust: Trivializing Memory." *New York Times,* June 11, 1989. http://www.nytimes.com/1989/06/11/movies/art-and-the-holocaust-trivializing-memory.html.

_____. "Trivializing the Holocaust: Semi-fact and Semi-fiction." *New York Times,* April 16, 1978.

Whittell, Giles. "The World's Prosecutor." *Times Magazine* (London), May 2, 2012, 24–29.

Women Living under Muslim Laws. "UN: 'Traditional Values' Resolution Adopted at Twelfth Session of HRC." October 12, 2009. http://www.wluml.org/node/5581.

Yogyakarta Principles. "The Yogyakarta Principles—an Overview." http://www.yogyakartaprinciples.org/backgrounder_en.pdf.

Films, Video, and Online Resources

Barker, Greg, dir. *Fight to Save the World: Sergio.* HBO / Passion Pictures. United States, 2009.

Coalition for the International Criminal Court website. http://www.coalitionfortheicc.org/.

ICC Watch website. http://www.iccwatch.org/iccfaq.html.

ICRC. *Humanitarian Action and Cinema: ICRC Films in the 1920s.* Two DVDs. ICRC, Memoriav, and Jean-Blaise Junod, 2005. http://www.icrc.org/eng/resources/documents/audiovisuals/video/cd13-icrc-historic-films-activities-1920.htm.

Institute for Dark Tourism Research website. http://www.dark-tourism.org.uk/about-us.
International Criminal Court design video. http://www.youtube.com/watch?v=h9USZ NF1M_Y.
Sergio Vieira de Mello Foundation webpage. http://www.sergiovdmfoundation.org/en/ activities_whd.html.
"Shoah—Official 25th Anniversary Trailer [HD]." YouTube video, 2:10, November 1985. Posted by "VISO trailers," December 15, 2010. http://www.youtube.com/watch?v= wV6mJ6T1oU0.
Stevens, Barry, dir. *Prosecutor*. White Pine Pictures. Toronto, 2010.
UNESCO website. http://www.unesco.org/new/en/communication-and-information/ flagship-project-activities/memory-of-the-world/homepage/.
University of Southern California, Shoah Foundation Institute website. http://dornsife. usc.edu/vhi/.

index

Page numbers followed by letter *f* refer to figures.

Martens, Fyodor, xiv, 41
Martens Clause, 16, 17, 49, 122
Marx, Karl, 9, 10, 32
materialism. *See* consumerism
Mazower, Mark, 43
Meas Muth, 151, 152
Médecins Sans Frontières (MSF), 21, 103,
    110–11; Holocaust memory and, 52–53;
    income of, 104–5; silence on human
    rights, 168; in Sri Lanka, 148
Mégret, Frédéric, 119, 189n14
memorial museums: in Cambodia,
    proposed design for, 93–94, 94*f*, 95*f*;
    witnessing of suffering through, 75–77.
    See also United States Holocaust Memo-
    rial Museum
memory politics, 49–50, 52, 58–59
Méndez, Juan E., 178
Meron, Theodor, 7, 122
metanarrative of humanism, 45–46, 142;
    categorical dimension of, 147; de Mello's
    commemoration and, 182; as façade,
    64, 144; Holocaust and, 46, 57–58, 59,
    67; memorial museums and, 76–77; vs.
    national policies, 148; questioning of, 48,
    62–67; retrofitting of, 53; trials used to
    dramatize, 126
middle class: and human rights advo-
    cacy, 97, 173, 221n22; and pressure on
    religious conservatives, 155. *See also*
    bourgeois class
Mies van der Rohe, Ludwig, 92, 206n93
Miliband, David, 147
Millennium Development Goals, 157, 174
Milošević, Slobodan, 126, 127, 128
Mises, Ludwig von, 97
Mladić, Ratko, 60, 155
Modirzadeh, Naz, 160
Mohammed, Khalid Sheikh, 13
Moore, R.I., 119
Moorhead, Caroline, 30
moral authority, humanist, 3, 45; court
    dramatization and, 129; eclipse of, 179,
    182; legitimation of, ix, 6, 68; liberal
    power and money and loss of, xiii, 182;
    politics and, 136, 137; questioning of,
    63–64, 159–60; secular religiosity and,
    xii–xiii, 2, 116; as social magic, 7, 12, 38;
    victims and survivors and, 96
Moravcsik, Andrew, 165
Moreno-Ocampo, Luis, 1, 55, 108, 130–33
Morsink, Johannes, 54
Moskowitz, Moses, 188n4
Moyn, Samuel, 54, 98
Moynier, Gustave, 30, 31*f*, 32, 35, 36, 39–40,
    43, 125
Mtintso, Thenjiwe, 83

multipolar world, 20, 141, 166–67, 169–70,
    175
Mumford, Lewis, 90–91, 92, 99
Muslim Brotherhood, 156, 157
Muslims, worldwide distribution of, 154
Muthaura, Francis, 134
Mutua, Makau, 62

Nansen, Fridtjof, 74, 179
nationalism. *See* sovereignty
NATO: Human Rights Regime and, 3;
    Kosovo intervention by, 5, 60, 134–35,
    136, 137; Libya intervention by, xii, 3, 5,
    57, 101, 138–39
natural law, 189n21; charge of crimes
    against humanity as, 5; disguised as
    customary and treaty law, 13; fusing
    with positive law, 7, 136; and human
    dignity, language of, 158; human rights
    law as, 121; at Tokyo tribunal (1946), 135
Neier, Aryeh, 50, 98, 111, 126, 178
neoliberalism: and global spread of
    human rights, 171; and humanitarian
    marketplace, 103, 104; and human rights
    in U.S., 97, 100. *See also* liberal democ-
    racy
neo-Westphalian world, xiii, xv, 20–22,
    166–67, 169–71, 176–77, 220n2
Netanyahu, Benjamin, 143
neutrality principle, 35–36, 39, 194n52
Ngudjolo Chui, Mathieu, 132
Niemeyer, Oscar, 89, 91
Nietzsche, Friedrich, x, 11, 32
Nightingale, Florence, 9, 32, 34, 179, 192n7,
    194n44
Nikolić, Tomislav, 135
Nobel Peace Prize, 34, 111, 114, 179
norms: double meaning of, 13. *See also*
    global norms
North Korea, 140
Nossel, Suzanne, 15, 115–16
Novick, Peter, 51
Ntaganda, Bosco, 127, 168
Nuon Chea, 150–51
Nuremberg trials, 17, 49, 53–54, 128, 135;
    images of, 50, 52*f*; and memory politics,
    49–50

Obama, Barack: Atrocities Prevention
    Board under, 56–57, 59; foreign policy
    priorities under, 18, 19; human rights
    under, 13, 135, 164; Nobel Peace Prize
    for, 179
Ocampo. *See* Moreno-Ocampo, Luis
Oosting, Dick, 110
open society, idea of, 6, 189n19
Open Society Justice Initiatives (OSJI), 152